A TRAILS BOOKS GUIDE

GREAT IOWA
WEEKEND ADVENTURES

MIKE WHYE

TRAILS BOOKS
Black Earth, Wisconsin

Library of Congress Control Number: 2001093464
ISBN: 1-931599-03-3

Editor: Stan Stoga
Book design: Jennifer Walde
Photos: Mike Whye
Cover design: John Huston
Cover photo: Mike Whye
Maps: Mapping Specialists

Printed in the United States of America.

06 05 04 03 02 01   6 5 4 3 2 1

Trails Books, a division of Trails Media Group, Inc.
P.O. Box 317 • Black Earth, WI 53515
(800) 236-8088 • e-mail: books@wistrails.com
www.trailsbooks.com

This book is dedicated to my wife, Dorie,
and children, Graham, Meredith, and Alex.

They taught me other ways to see when they traveled
with me and provided much support and understanding
during the other times when I've been on the road.

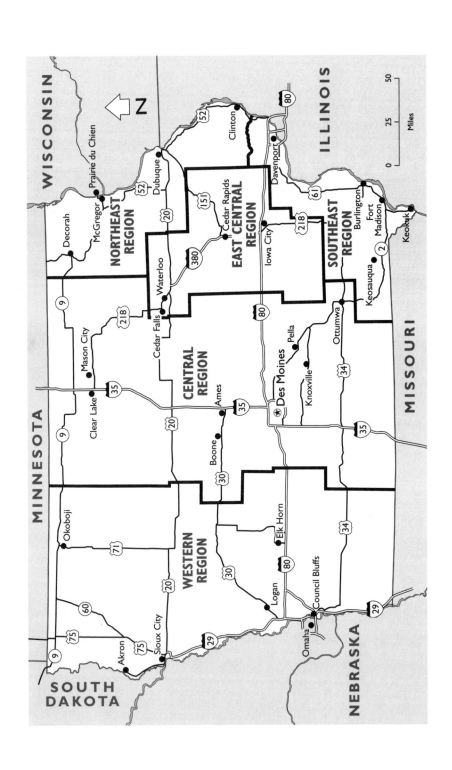

Contents

Introduction
The Many Ways of Seeing Iowa

I didn't grow up in Iowa, a circumstance that probably has given me a different perspective on the state than that of the people who were raised here. I grew up as a military brat, with a father who was transferred around the states a lot. We were basically long-term tourists, and we tried to make the most of wherever we stayed.

This adaptability served me well when I first moved to Iowa, during my two years at Iowa State University where I worked on a masters degree in journalism in the mid-1970s. From Ames I visited the state capitol in Des Moines and the covered bridges in Madison County—long before they became famous—tasted wine in the Amanas, and pondered about the people who created all those knolls at Effigy Mounds National Monument.

After a brief stay in Nebraska following my graduation, I moved to Rock Rapids, way up in the northwestern corner of Iowa. Again, I ranged far and near out of curiosity. On many an evening, I would visit the old amusement park at Okoboji, about an hour from where I lived, and rattle my bones on the wooden roller coaster. Then, on Saturday morning I'd arise, travel all the way across the state to camp at Pikes Peak State Park, and later gaze at the magnificent houses of Rock Glen in Mason City on my way back. And instead of taking the fast route—I-29—to travel up and down western Iowa, I began to take the back roads and discovered the wonders of the Loess Hills, one of the state's great natural treasures.

I hope this book convinces you to get out and discover Iowa's many other attractions, both the seldom-seen and the well-known This is a state where many travel discoveries are quieter, more hidden than those in some other states. Some folks think of Iowa as flat. Try roaming up, down, and around the hills in the state's northeast corner and you'll never again think of Iowa as topographically challenged. Or enjoy the surprise of finding the nation's tallest interurban railroad bridge near the center of this "flat" state as you ride across it on a train pulled by the last steam engine manufactured in China.

And there's a lot of history to be experienced here. Flanked by two of the nation's greatest rivers, the Mississippi and the Missouri, Iowa has long been associated with the big, palatial riverboats that plied their waters, and the boats are still steaming today. Towns that sprang up alongside these rivers are among the oldest in the state—Dubuque, Keokuk, McGregor, Sioux City, and more— and the past is easily seen in their well-preserved buildings.

Pioneer trails, too, have played quite a role in Iowa, from the Pioneer-Mormon, Oregon, and California Trails, to the Underground Railroad and the route used by Lewis and Clark on their way to and from the Pacific two centuries ago. Even prerecorded history is here, in the form of 400-million-year-old fossils that you can pick for yourself near Rockford and ancient burial sites such as those at Fish Farm Mounds near Lansing.

Besides history, there's plenty to do for all ages. Children can romp through the Iowa Children's Museum at Coralville, hold on as the Space Shot ride at Adventureland propels them into the air, accompany their families to watch tows pass through Lock and Dam 15 at the Quad Cities, and explore the Maquoketa Caves. Young singles can enjoy the rhythm of the fashionable Court Avenue District in Des Moines and get above it all with a hot-air balloon flight at Waukon. Others might enjoy fishing quietly in the trout stream at Backbone State Park, taking in live entertainment at one of several casinos around the state, or watching minor league baseball and a variety of collegiate sporting events.

In short, Iowa does have it all for everyone, and that's why this book was written—to show off these attractions. The book is organized into chapters that concentrate on places where visitors can stay for two to three days and take in a number of easy-to-reach attractions and events.

To help correlate with the *Iowa Travel Guide* that is printed annually by the state's Division of Tourism (and available free at Iowa Welcome Centers), the book's five sections are arranged from west to east across the state. Individual chapters within each region are organized from north to south. Each chapter begins with that area's attractions, followed by lists of places to stay, dine, and obtain more information. Because of space, it was not possible to include all of the state's attractions, lodging places, and restaurants; but the information about those that are listed is as accurate as possible up to the time of the printing of this book.

As for me, I had fun writing this book and hope you have as much fun using it to explore Iowa.

Mike Whye

For more information about Iowa, consider contacting the following agencies and groups.

Iowa Division of Tourism, 200 E. Grand Avenue, Des Moines, IA 50309, (800) 345-IOWA, (515) 242-4705; www.traveliowa.com

Iowa Department of Transportation, 800 Lincoln Way, Ames, IA 50010, (515) 239-1372.

Iowa Department of Natural Resources, Wallace State Office Building, Des Moines, IA 50319-0034, (515) 281-5145; www.state.ia.us/dnr

State Historical Society of Iowa, 600 E. Locust, Des Moines, IA 50319, (515) 281-6258; www.iowahistory.org

Iowa Lodging Association/Iowa Bed & Breakfast Guild, 9001 Hickman Road, Suite 220, Des Moines, IA 50322, (800) 743-IOWA, (515) 278-8700.

Iowa Bed and Breakfast Innkeepers Association, 1543 305th Avenue, Fort Atkinson, IA 52144, (800) 888-INNS.

Road Condition Hotline, (800) 288-1047, (515) 288-1047.

KEY FOR THE RATE INFORMATION ABOUT PLACES TO STAY IN EACH CHAPTER.

$ $49 and under
$$ $50–79
$$$ $80–99
$$$$ $100 and over

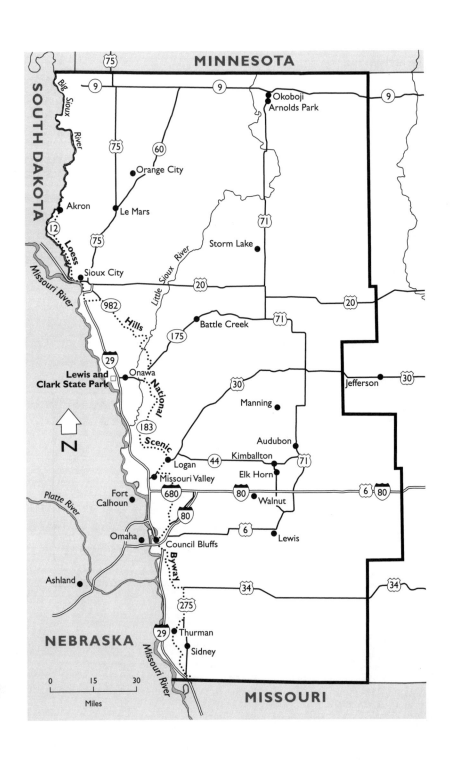

Section I

Western Iowa

Something for Everybody

Chapter 1

Okoboji:
Iowa's Water World

Every state has a playground that's more known to its residents than to outsiders. In Iowa that's Okoboji, home to three large lakes: Spirit Lake, East Lake Okoboji and West Lake Okoboji, the one around which much of the recreation is centered. However, Okoboji is what most Iowans call the entire area though some call the region Iowa's Great Lakes.

Attractions

Start your visit in the town of Arnolds Park with some old-fashioned fun by visiting the highlight of the entire area: **Arnolds Park Amusement Park**, Highway 71 and Lake Park Drive, (712) 332-2183; (800) 599-6995; admission. The oldest amusement park west of the Mississippi, Arnolds Park opened in 1889 and is still very much attuned to the entire family. Highlights include the 63-foot-tall Ferris wheel and the wooden roller coaster, which was built in 1927 but still generates screams on the downslopes and fast curves. Not to be overlooked are the arcade and 30 other attractions and rides, including many designed for children. New in 2001 is a water log ride with a 90-foot drop.

An adjunct to the amusement park is the **Roof Garden** (admission), where nationally known entertainers often perform on summer nights. A few more steps away is the dock of the *Queen II*, 37 Lake Street, (712) 332-2183; admission. A replica of an earlier excursion boat, the *Queen II* offers 75-minute narrated tours of West Lake Okoboji.

Near all of this is the Okoboji Spirit Center, home of the **Iowa Great Lakes Maritime Museum,** (712) 332-5264. The museum's main attraction is its collection of classic wooden runabouts ranging from an old gray Fitzgerald made in the 1890s to a 30-foot Canadian Ditchburn and polished beauties made by

West Lake Okoboji, with Arnolds Park in the background

the local Hafer Boatworks in the 1940s. However, the star of the museum, in the eyes of some people, is a 1939 barrelback Chris Craft Deluxe Runabout that is literally a wreck. No joke. It sank after colliding with another boat in 1946, was recovered in 1994, and is now displayed with her right side still stove in from the collision.

Other displays include sailboats, outboard motors, homemade water skis and surfboards, a boat shed, a collection of swimsuits, and items once used at the amusement park such as bumper cars, kiddie boats, warped mirrors, and posters.

In another part of the building, the **Iowa Welcome Center,** (712) 332-2209; free, offers a myriad of information about the region, and its gift shop carries numerous items, including shirts, pants, caps, and more emblazoned with the official Iowa Navy emblems.

If you have your swimsuit, you're in luck because the newly constructed Beach House is at the Arnolds Park public beach, which has not only places to change but a concession and patio area as well. If you're a scuba diving enthusiast, visit **Blue Water Divers** near the amusement park, (712) 332-6383, to rent the equipment needed to explore West Lake Okoboji, which at 136 feet in one spot, is Iowa's deepest natural lake.

Should you want other ways to enjoy the water, not far away are several places that rent skis, pontoon boats, pleasure boats, wakeboards, kneeboards, tubes of all sorts, and personal watercraft. Located just north and south of the bridge that spans the narrow waterway connecting the east and west parts of Lake Okoboji, these places are **Funtime Rentals**, Highway 71 south of the bridge, (712) 332-2540; **Oak Hill Marina**, Highway 71 south of the bridge, (712) 332-2701; **Mau Marina**, Highway 71 north of the bridge, (712) 332-

5626; and **Triggs Bay Resort**, 180 Linden Drive, two blocks east of Highway 71, (712) 332-2215.

To soar above it all, visit **Extreme Watersports** near the amusement park, (712) 332-5406, which provides quite a lift by strapping you into a parasail for a view on high as a boat tows you around West Lake Okoboji. And although no one rents wind surfboards, bring yours if you have one, because there are places where you can really kick up the white wake.

The **Okoboji Yacht Club**, on Millers Bay off Highway 86 on the west side of West Lake Okoboji, (712) 337-0121, hosts colorful sailing regattas on West Okoboji on Saturdays and Sundays.

Meanwhile, **Okoboji Expedition Company**, 1021 Highway 71 South, (712) 332-9001, rents bikes and rollerblades (as well as tents, packs, cross-country skis, snowboards, and other outdoor-related items) for visitors to use while rolling on more than 14 miles of paved trails that wander through the region.

A block west of the amusement park is a quieter part of the lakes and one of Iowa's smallest historic sites. Sitting where it was built, the **Abbie Gardner Cabin**, 34 Monument Drive, (712) 332-7248; free, recalls the strife between white settlers and Sioux Indians on the 1850s frontier when tensions erupted in what is called the Spirit Lake Massacre even though most of the action occurred around West Lake Okoboji. At the time of the massacre in March 1857, Abbie Gardner was 13 years old. One of four survivors held captive by the Sioux, she was released more than a month later in South Dakota.

West Lake Okoboji

We'll tour around West Lake Okoboji in a clockwise fashion and the first stop is on the south side at **Boji Bay Water Park**, Highway 71 and Highway 86, (712) 338-2473; admission. A large aquatic park that fills its pools with more than two million gallons of water, Boji Bay's mainstay is its huge wave pool. Also on hand are water slides, tube rides, a children's pool, beach, and volleyball courts.

Upon leaving Boji Bay, take Highway 86 to the west. As the highway turns to go north up the west side of West Lake Okoboji, you'll see **Treasure Village** on the left, 2033 Highway 86, (712) 337-3730; admission. A family-oriented entertainment center, Treasure Village offers 27 holes of miniature golf, a children's theater, antique flea markets, and Sunday evening gospel concerts.

At about the same point but to the right of the highway is **Emerson Bay State Park**, 3100 Emerson Street, (712) 337-3805 in summer; (712) 337-3211 in winter, and a bit north of there is **Gull Point State Park**, 1500 Harpen Street, (712) 377-3870 in summer; (712) 337-3211 in winter. Both have public beaches as well as boat ramps, campgrounds, and picnic areas under the cottonwoods. Changing facilities are limited.

Less than a mile north of Gull Point State Park are signs leading to **Village West,** a resort where you can rent a variety of watercraft ranging from tubes and skis to boats and personal watercraft at **Parks Marine Rentals,** 16010 Highway 86, (712) 337-3223.

At the far northwest corner of West Lake Okoboji is **Triboji Beach,** another bit of state-owned land with a beach open to the public.

Continue up to Highway 9 and then go east until you reach Highway 71 again, where you head south. About two miles south of that intersection you'll reach the **Lakes Art Center,** 2201 Highway 71, (712) 332-7013; free, which features the works of local and distant artists, as well as free foreign films and concerts. Very close by on the highway is the **Okoboji Summer Theater,** (712) 332-7773; admission. Run by students and faculty from Stephens College in Columbia, Missouri, the theater's musicals, dramas, and comedies have long been a hit with visitors on summer evenings. Plays are also staged by the Boji Bantam Children's Theater and the Lakes Area Community Theater.

Almost across the highway from the theater is the **Ranch Amusement Park,** Highway 71, (712) 332-2159, another family entertainment center. Featuring the Wet Rock Mine mini-golf course, the Ranch has the state's longest and curviest Go-Kart track, Water Buffalo Bumper Boats, an arcade, ice cream parlor, and more.

When you leave the park heading south on Highway 71, watch for Sanborn Avenue and take a turn on it to visit the **Higgins Museum,** (712) 332-5859; free. A rare museum about banking in the United States, the Higgins may have

Abbie Gardner Cabin, West Lake Okoboji

the finest collection of bank notes from 1863 to 1935, with an emphasis on those issued in Iowa, Nebraska, Minnesota, and South Dakota. It also has nearly 20,000 postcards of Iowa produced over many years.

Once back on Highway 71, you'll arrive once more at the bridge leading to Arnolds Park, where your journey began. If you want to travel around the lakes region without the hassle of finding parking spaces, contact **Rides**, a service of the Regional Transit Authority, (800) 358-5037. Its 9- to 31-passenger buses go up and down Highway 71 between Milford and Spirit Lake Mall from 11 a.m. to 3 a.m. seven days a week from Memorial Day to Labor Day. Each ride is $1.50. On-demand buses run from 9 a.m.-5 p.m. for other nearby areas off Highway 71 (such as the west shore of West Lake Okoboji); cost is $1.50-$2.

SIDE TRIPS

To the North

For another view of Okoboji and environs, visit Spirit Lake. Iowa's largest natural lake is called the quiet lake by locals who like fishing its shallow water (22 feet at most) instead of contending with all the activity on West Lake Okoboji. Among the fish in these waters—plus those of West and East Lake Okoboji—are bluegill, crappie, perch, catfish, bullhead, walleye, smallmouth and largemouth bass, northern, and muskie.

Spirit Lake offers three public beaches: **Miniwaukon Beach** in the town of Orleans on the lake's southeast side, **Crandall's Beach** on the northwest corner, and **Marble Beach State Recreation Area**, (712) 336-4437; (712) 337-3211, on Highway 276 on the lake's west side.

To the South

Less than an hour's drive to the south is Storm Lake, the name for both a body of water and the community that embraces the north side of that lake. Compared to the hustle and bustle of tourism in the Okoboji area, both Storm Lakes are much quieter to visit.

However, don't drive straight there on Highway 71. Instead, about 15 miles south of Spencer take Highway 10 to the west. Just past Peterson is County Highway M27; take a left there and go south.

In a short while you'll see something that's relatively new to Iowa—tall, elegant windmills generating electricity. At first there are just a few. Then dozens appear as you pass through miles and miles of them, all turning in unison like some hypnotic ballet. In all, 259 windmills on this wind farm provide power to more than 70,000 households.

Cross Highway 3 and at Highway 7 take a left (southeast) to Storm Lake. Continue into town until you reach Northwestern Avenue (the first stoplight you meet), where you turn to the right and follow the signs to reach the **Living Heritage Tree Farm**, (712) 732-3780, on the edge of the lake. One of the

Water action on West Lake Okoboji

nation's larger tree museums, this park has trees grown from cuttings taken from famous places across the nation such as George Washington's Mount Vernon. The park also has public docks and a band shell for evening concerts in the summertime.

Farther along the shore is **Chataugua Park**, (712) 732-8027, where you can park under the trees and hike on part of a 5-mile paved trail system or stretch out for an afternoon nap either near the lake or under the tall trees.

If you don't have a boat with you, you can rent paddleboats and canoes at **Lakeside Marina**, 96 Lake Shore Drive, (712) 732-7465, which also has a boat ramp and facilities for powerboats and sailboats. Some public beaches can be found on the lake, such as around the east shore; but they're small, tucked between private houses, and have no changing facilities.

When leaving the north shore to return to Okoboji, use Cayuga Street so you can visit the **Witter Gallery**, 609 Cayuga, (712) 732-3400, a few blocks east of the downtown retail area. Despite being in a small town, this public gallery has had some very nice exhibits over the years.

LODGING

Arnolds Park

Blue Lake Resort, 113 Monument Drive, (712) 332-2817, on Pillsbury Point on West Lake Okoboji. Near Arnolds Park Amusement Park and Gardner Cabin. Cottages and motel-style units with kitchenettes. Swimming, boating, fishing, and sunbathing on the dock. $$-$$$$.

Fillenwarth Beach, 87 Lakeshore Drive, (712) 332-5646. Longtime family-run resort with cottages, duplexes, motel-style rooms, and apartments. Cruises, paddleboats, water-skiing, indoor and outdoor pools, dock. $$-$$$$

Four Seasons Resort, Highway 71, (712) 332-2103; (800) 876-2103. Lakeside rooms, motel-style rooms, and apartments, some with patios. Beach, dock, restaurant, and lounge. $-$$$

Triggs Bay Resort, 180 Linden Drive, (712) 332-2215. On East Lake Okoboji south of the bridge and two blocks east of Highway 71, with a 250-foot beach. Apartment-style units with 1-3 bedrooms and a view of the lake. Docks, boat ramp, and rentals. $$-$$$

Pick's Lakeshore Resort, 108 Monument Drive, (712) 332-2688 (summer); (712) 786-2144 (winter). Family-run resort on West Lake Okoboji within walking distance of Abbie Gardner Cabin and Arnolds Park Amusement Park. Dock for sunbathing, boating, and fishing. $$-$$$$

Milford

Crescent Beach Lodge, 1620 Lakeshore Drive, (712) 337-3351; (800) 417-1117. On the west shore of West Lake Okoboji. Suites, condos, cottages, beach, island playground, paddleboats, canoes, fishing boats, restaurant. $-$$$$

Okoboji

AmericInn Motel & Suites, 1407 North Highway 71, (712) 332-9000; (800) 634-3444. Located at the Brooks Golf Club. Indoor pool, recreation area, fireplace, and whirlpool suites. $$-$$$$

Country Club Motel, 1107 Sanborn Avenue, (712) 332-5617; (800) 831-5615. Outdoor pool, kitchenettes, and rooms with whirlpool baths. Close to East Lake Okoboji, restaurants, and attractions. $-$$$$

Village East Resort and Conference Center, 1405 Highway 71, (712) 332-2161; (800) 727-4561. North of the bridge, near major attractions and 27-hole Brooks Golf Course. Outdoor and indoor pools, some Jacuzzi suites, restaurant. $$$$

Spencer

Iron Horse Motel & Suites, Highways 71/18, (712) 262-9123. On south side of town. Continental breakfast. $-$$

Super 8, 209 11th Street SW, (712) 262-8500; (800) 800-8000. Southwest side of town near intersection of Highway 71/18. Near restaurants. $-$$

Spirit Lake

Beaches Resort, 15109 215th Avenue, (712) 336-2230. Named as one of the 50 Best Family Resorts by *Midwest Living* magazine. On the northwest shore of West Lake Okoboji. Paddleboats, boat rides, docks. $$-$$$$

Moorland Country Inn, (507) 847-4707. B&B in the country a mile north of the north shore of Spirit Lake. Rooms in the English manor, carriage house, and gate house. $$-$$$

Oaks Motel, 1701 Chicago Avenue, (712) 336-2940. On the shore of East Lake Okoboji. Close to lakeside park and playground. Continental breakfast. $-$$$

Pioneer Beach, 14991 252nd Avenue, (712) 336-3785. On east shore of East Lake Okoboji north of downtown Spirit Lake. Housekeeping cabins, boat rentals. $$-$$$$

Ramada Limited, 2704 17th Street, (712) 336-3984; (800) 272-6232. Near intersection of Highways 71 and 9. Indoor pool, whirlpool suites, continental breakfast. $-$$$$

Sand Bar Beach Resort, 13302 270th Avenue, (712) 336-0538 (summer); (972) 596-8645 (winter). Housekeeping cabins on the northeast side of Spirit Lake. Motorboat, pontoon boat, and paddleboat rentals. $300/wk. for a two-person cabin; $800/wk. for a cabin sleeping nine.

Shamrock Inn, intersection of Highways 71 and 9, (712) 336-2668; (800) 324-2008. Outdoor pool, continental breakfast. Newly remodeled in 2000. $-$$$

Vergie's Southside Resort, 24168 140th Street, (712) 336-3491. Housekeeping cabins on the south shore of Spirit Lake. Beach, boat rentals. Cabins $375-650/wk.; house $1,200-1,400/wk.

DINING

Arnolds Park

Koffee Kup Kafe, Highway 71, (712) 332-7657. Homemade meals and desserts. Breakfast and lunch specials.

Maxwell's On the Lake, located next to the amusement park, (712) 332-7578. Nice view of West Lake Okoboji. Dock. Open May-September.

Mother Nature's, Highway 71, (712) 332-9469. Steaks and prime rib. Indoor or patio seating; live music.

Mrs. Lady's, Highway 71, (712) 332-7373. Mexican food.

Smokin' Jake's, 117 Broadway in Old Town, (712) 332-5152. Smoked meats and barbecue. Lunch, dinner, and late-night breakfast.

Yesterdays, 131 W. Broadway, (712) 332-2353. Seafood. Lunch and dinner. April-December.

Okoboji

Bud's Pub, Brooks Park Lane, (712) 332-7885. Southwestern selections. Overlooks Brooks Golf Club. April-December.

Getting Around

Okoboji

There some things to know about getting around Okoboji.

First, Highway 71 is the main route through the region and many attractions and resorts, or roads leading to resorts, are along this highway. The highway has an unnamed bridge that spans a waterway between West Lake Okoboji and East Lake Okoboji and many businesses refer to their location on Highway 71 as simply north or south of the bridge.

Second, you should know the names of the communities and lakes. Otherwise you're going to get very frustrated trying to figure out what's where. So here goes, alphabetically:

Arnolds Park is the community between East Lake Okoboji and West Lake Okoboji and immediately south of the bridge. First-time visitors might be confused because an amusement park, also called Arnolds Park, is in the community of Arnolds Park. When locals talk of Arnolds Park, they're talking about the community; when they speak of the amusement park, they say, "amusement park." Simple, huh?

East Lake Okoboji is the lake that's east of West Lake Okoboji and south of the lake called Spirit Lake. It's the longest natural lake in Iowa.

Iowa Great Lakes refers basically to West Lake Okoboji, East Lake Okoboji, and the lake of Spirit Lake.

Milford is a community on Highway 71 south of Arnolds Park.

Minnewashta is a small lake that is an appendage off the south end of East Lake Okoboji. Oddly, the northern part of Minnewashta is called Upper Gar Lake and its southern end is Lower Gar Lake.

Okoboji is not just the name many Iowans call the region but a specific community as well. The community straddles Highway 71 just north of the bridge, touching both East Lake Okoboji and West Lake Okoboji.

Orleans is a small community on the southern side of the lake of Spirit Lake but north of the community of Spirit Lake … got that?

Spirit Lake is not only the name of the northernmost of the big lakes in this region but also a community that is south of the lake (and, just to make things interesting, it's on the northwest shore East Lake Okoboji!). When the locals talk about Spirit Lake, they're referring to the community and when they talk about Big Spirit, they mean the lake. There is a Little Spirit Lake, if you must know, hence the locals' reason for "big" and "small" when referring to the lakes.

Wahpeton is a small community on the west side of West Lake Okoboji.

West Okoboji is a small community at the south end of West Lake Okoboji.

West Lake Okoboji is the westernmost and most popular of the three big lakes in the region.

Finally, Okoboji is pronounced by the locals as O-ko-bo-ja, not O-ko-bo-jee. Now: go out and talk like a local.

Lighthouse Bar and Grill, Highway 71, (712) 332-5995. Steak, seafood, sandwiches. Lunch and dinner. Inside seating or on the screened-in deck. Dock and bike trail nearby.

Minervas Village East, Highway 71, (712) 332-5296. Overlooking Brooks Golf Club. Breakfast, lunch, dinner, and Sunday breakfast buffet.

O'Farrell Sisters, 1109 Lakeshore Drive, (712) 332-7901. Homemade breakfasts and lunches. They don't bring out the homemade pies until 11 a.m. but if you want a piece of one of them as well as a place to sit, you had better be there shortly after 11—this place is that popular.

RJ's Restaurant, Okoboji Plaza, Highway 71, (712) 332-7926. Barbecued ribs, prime rib, steak, seafood, vegetarian, Mexican, Italian. Dock nearby.

Spirit Lake

Betsy's Diner, Village West Resort, (712) 337-3223. Fifties-style diner atmosphere and food.

Oscar's, Village West Resort, (712) 337-3223. The resort's top restaurant.

Wahpeton

Crescent Beach Resort, 1620 Lakeshore Drive, (712) 337-3351. Waterfront view from dining room on west shore of West Lake Okoboji. Piano music. Dock.

West Lake Okoboji

Taco House, Terrace Park Boulevard, which locals call Old Highway 71, no phone. Mexican food. A place that draws repeat visitors.

INFORMATION

Okoboji Tourism Committee, PO Box 215, Okoboji, IA 51355, (712) 332-2209; (800) 270-2574; www.vacationokoboji.com

Western Iowa Tourism Region, 103 3rd Street, Red Oak, IA 51566, (712) 623-4232; (888)-623-4232; www.traveliowa.org

Chapter 2

Loess Hills Scenic Byway: The Western Edge

This tour is going to be unlike the others in that it does not have a city as a destination. Instead, the focal point is a 220-mile route called the Loess Hills National Scenic Byway. Starting at the southern border, the Byway winds its way through the unique Loess Hills in western Iowa and ends north of Sioux City near the community of Westfield.

What are the Loess Hills? When the last round of glaciers advanced upon what is now Iowa several thousand years ago, they ground everything beneath them to powder. And when they started melting 10,000 to 20,000 years ago, their runoff carried a lot of that finely ground powder downstream. Each winter, the waterways would freeze and shrink, leaving that powder high and dry, able to be picked up by the prevailing northwesterlies. When the winds hit the eastern bank of one of those massive waterways—now called the Missouri River—they broke and the silt tumbled out of the air. Over the span of a few thousand years this wind-blown soil, called loess (and pronounced "luss"), formed dunes that were eventually covered with enough matter to form topsoil that helped stabilize them. Actually, the Loess Hills that flank the Missouri River don't just begin and end at Iowa's borders. Sometimes the winds that formed the hills blew to the west, forming another set of Loess Hills in Nebraska although they aren't as high as their Iowa counterparts. Also, the hills continue below Iowa's southern border, eventually meshing with other landforms near St. Joseph, Missouri.

You might hear some Iowans say that these are the only Loess Hills outside of China. Well, that's not exactly true. You see, there are plenty of hills made of loess in other places, such as those south of North Platte, Nebraska, but they're generally shorter than those in western Iowa. So if Iowans are going to claim their Loess Hills are unique, what they need to say is that nowhere else in the world are there similar hills of such height—up to nearly 260 feet—as those that are here and along the Yellow River in China.

When the explorers Lewis and Clark saw the Loess Hills in 1804, they described them as being "bald-pated hills" that were covered with prairie. Whatever trees tried to grow on the hills were swept away by prairie fires that renewed the prairie grasses. However, the arrival of European-Americans led to the creation of towns, cities, roads, and farmlands that have virtually eliminated the wildfires, allowing trees to overtake the prairie on many of the hills not utilized directly by humans.

There are a few oddities about the Loess Hills compared to other landforms. Since their southwest slopes are often leeward, they receive less snow and what falls evaporates quickly in the sunlight. The dryness maintains a prairie environment that remains in small and large patches despite the increasing number of trees. Of 20,000 acres of native prairie remaining in Iowa (out of 30 million acres of prairie that were in the state when it was designated in 1837), 15,000 of those acres are in the Loess Hills. These prairie remnants support a shrinking population of flora and fauna species not found again until some 300 miles to the west of here. In short, the Loess Hills are like a very isolated archipelago of prairie ecosystems surrounded by lush, green fields.

Another unique item about the Loess Hills is their composition. Cut through a hill at many other places in the world and you'll see various strata of materials deposited over countless years. Look at any of the road cuts in the Loess Hills and you'll more than likely see a wall of yellowish soil from top to bottom—pure loess. When the plants and trees atop a Loess Hill are removed with the topsoil, the underlying loess erodes easily. Thus, the Loess Hills are actually very fragile. Compared to other hills that are rocky just under the topsoil and can withstand heavy foot traffic, simple footpaths in the Loess Hills wear into the soil very fast and can turn into waterways and ruts in a short time. Because of their highly erosive nature, there is much concern about what to do with the Loess Hills, whether to continue to use them, preserve them from human disturbance, or strike a balance between those options. If you really want to learn about the Loess Hills, read *Fragile Giants* by Cornelia Mutel, which is available at many area bookstores.

The Byway

Finally, a few words about the Loess Hills National Scenic Byway. Electa Strub, the owner of the Apple Orchard Inn, a Byway B&B a few miles east of Missouri Valley, found herself being asked often by guests about what they could see in the area. She started drawing maps for them and after awhile had some printed. One thing led to another, and soon she was in contact with landscape architect Mimi Wagner and regional promoter Walt Ordway, and the three of them formed the genesis of what ultimately became the first scenic

A common Loess Hills scene, near Smithland

byway in Iowa. In 2000, it was named a National Scenic Byway, one of two in the state (the other being the Great River Road along the Mississippi River).

The main part of the route is marked with distinctive blue and white signs bearing the name "Loess Hills Scenic Byway," and always follows paved highways. There are 16 excursion loops off the main route and, while similarly marked with Byway signs, they are sometimes on gravel roads and require caution when driving on them.

Northern Area Tour

For this tour, start at the north end of the Loess Hills and work your way south. This might help those who have picked up the small guidebook Iowa's Loess Hills Scenic Byway (free at Iowa Welcome Centers in western Iowa), which proceeds in the same manner. Because you might want to visit some places and hike a few preserves, it's doubtful that you're going to drive the entire Byway in one day. Remember, you're here to relax, not set any records.

Begin in the town of Akron, the official northern terminus of the Byway, which at this point is Highway 12. As you head south, you'll see some gently rolling farmland on the left (east) side of the road and the farther south you go, the more pronounced the hills will become.

In the community of Westfield, it's easy to see that the hills just south of town are now higher and are officially Loess Hills, which means they must be greater than 60 feet in height to be considered as part of the landform. In West-

15

field, you can either continue down the Byway's main route, Highway 12, or take County Highway C38 to the east for a mile or so to meet County Highway C43, which rises up into the hills for a pleasant drive, called **Ridge Road Loop**. That reconnects to Highway 12 a dozen miles later. About four or five miles from the start of County Highway C43, you'll see a sign for Butcher Road, a four-mile shortcut back to Highway 12 if you want. Staying on Ridge Road Loop, however, will lead you to **Five Ridge Prairie**, (712) 947-4270, a county preserve with trails leading through open prairie and wooded hills.

If you remain on the main route, you'll see a sign showing the entrance to the **Broken Kettle Grasslands**, owned and operated by the Nature Conservancy, (712) 568-2596; (515) 244-5044, which gives arranged tours of this largest single tract of prairie remaining in Iowa. Along with having the 10-petal blazing star, a flower found nowhere else in the Loess Hills, Broken Kettle has one more item the rest of the hills don't have—and this may be something most readers don't want to see—the last pocket of prairie rattlesnakes in all of Iowa. However, the conservancy's workers can advise you on how to avoid the few acres of the grasslands that most of those snakes call home; mind you, they are a protected species within Iowa.

Farther to the south of Broken Kettle are the entrances to **Stone State Park** and the **Dorothy Pecaut Nature Center** (both described in chapter 3). The Byway continues down Highway 12 until it meets I-29 on the west edge of Sioux City. Following the interstate until Exit 141, the Byway turns east on First Street in the city of Sergeant Bluff and ultimately becomes County Highway D38. The Byway then meets Highway 982 at the base of some small hills and heads southeast until it meets County Highway K67 for a short stretch to Highway 141, which ascends a slope into Smithland. From there, the Byway turns south onto County Highway L12.

The Midsection

Here you can choose a route that leaves the Byway for a short while. Cross Highway 141 and stay on County Highway K67 as it passes along some very wide, gentle slopes. In a little more than five miles, K67 meets County Highway E16 where a line of hills slopes down to a point. Turn to the left onto E16 for a few car lengths where you'll meet County Highway L12. To rejoin the Byway's main route, you must turn left (north) until you are where E16 leaves L12 to the right (east). In few miles, you'll see County Highway L29 going to the right (south); follow that to Castana.

Or, when you're at the junction at County Highways E16 and L12, you can turn right (south) to go onto **Wilderness Loop**, which leads into an area where film runs like water through lots of people's cameras. Welcome to what some say is the heart of the Loess Hills. On L12, continue due south until it turns slightly to the right to go southwest. Here you'll turn onto the gravel road that leads off to the left—Nutmeg Avenue. Follow that to Oak Avenue where you'll turn right. In about a mile you'll encounter a fork in the road. Bear to the right onto 178th Street and look immediately to the left for a grassy parking area.

Park, get out and locate the hiking trails. Some of the best are those that lead to the west and begin across the road from the parking lot's entry. You may have to pass through some brush and trees but in a few moments you'll be going up and up and up into the best of the prairie-topped hills. You'll see the beauty of three preserves that come together here—the **Loess Hills Wildlife Area,** the **Turin Loess Hills Nature Preserve,** and the **Sylvan Runkel Preserve,** (712) 423-2426. With more than 3,500 acres between them, they are the largest protected area of the hills and generally reveal the hills as they were for years before European settlement began in the 19th century.

A note about hiking here: if you haven't been here before and learned your way around, it's safest to backtrack on the trail you've been using rather than come out on a road and wonder which way will return you to the parking lot.

Once back in your car, you have two choices about where to go.

1. Return to L12 where you'll wind up on the Byway's Larpenteur Road Connection that leads south into the small community of Turin. As you come into Turin you may notice a roadside marker near a depression in the ground. This is the Turin Man Archeological Site, (712) 423-1384. No longer an active site, this where the 5,500-year-old remains of four prehistoric individuals were found in 1955, and for a period of time these remains, collectively called the Turin Man, were thought to be the oldest human remains in North America. It turned out that they weren't, and there really isn't much to see at the site. On the south side of Turin, take Highway 175 to the junction of Highway 37, where you meet the Byway's main route again.

2. Upon exiting the parking lot, turn right and at the fork in the road a few yards away, take a right onto Oak Avenue. This ultimately leads to County Highway L20, the Byway's main route, which then follows Highway 175 through Castana and heads south on Highway 37.

(A note here: At the Highway 175/37 interchange, you're only seven miles from Onawa, so if you want to visit the attractions in that community, turn west on Highway 175 and see "Side Trip: To the South" in chapter 3 for details.)

Okay, now that you're at the junction of Highways 175 and 37 (no matter which way you got here), head east a little more than a mile to County Highway L16, which takes you south to Moorhead. Near town, you'll see a junction with County Highway L20. (Yes, you were on it earlier, but don't even ask how it got here. Some county highway designations just pop up willy-nilly across Iowa after you thought you saw the last of them somewhere else.) Watch on

Ingemann Danish Luthern Church, near Moorhead

the right for County Highway E54. Even though this gravel road isn't part of the Byway, take it to see one of the prettiest sights in the Loess Hills. Less than three miles east, the **Ingemann Danish Lutheran Church**, built in 1884 by Danish immigrants who settled in this area, sits picture-perfect in a bowl formed by the hills, which are mostly prairie in this area. The church is usually open if you want to visit it.

When you leave the church, it's best to return the way you came. Without trying to sound like a Stephen King plot is afoot in the countryside, to go any other way when you don't know the roads that wind through these hills is folly. So when you're back at County Highway L16, turn to the right and in less than a mile you'll enter Moorhead where, in its small downtown, you'll find the **Loess Hills Hospitality Association**, 119 Oak Street, (712) 886-5441; (800) 886-5441, a combination information center and gallery of locally made items related to the hills. It's also a good place to pick up some books about the Loess Hills if you want to learn more about them. Nearby, the **Moorhead Cultural Center**, 109 Oak Street, (712) 886-5384, displays items reflecting the culture, art, and history of the region.

From Moorhead, go south on Highway 183 where, about two miles later, you'll see the turnoff to **Preparation Canyon State Park**, (712) 243-2829, which is located in the deep woods of the hills. If you want to see one of the best overlooks in the interior of the Loess Hills and you feel adventurous enough to try your hand on the back roads, go to the first paved road on the right (west) just beyond the turnoff to Preparation Canyon. Follow the signs that point the way to the lookout of the **Loess Hills State Forest**, (712) 456-2924. In three miles, the road turns to gravel shortly before you reach the lookout. Again, the best way back to the Byway is the way you came.

Highway 183 soon leads into Pisgah where the Loess Hills State Forest Visitor Center, 206 Polk Street, (712) 456-2924, features displays about the hills' geology and Loess Hills artwork. It's also a good place to pick up information and directions to other locales in the hills.

Again you have some options on how to continue:

1. Take **Orchard Ridge Loop** by following County Highway F20 east out of town to County Highway L23 and south to Magnolia, where you rejoin the main Byway.

2. Take the **Fountainbleau Loop** by following County Highway F20 west out of Pisgah. In about four miles you'll come upon the parking area on Murray Hill, one of the better overlooks across the Missouri River valley. Park there and hike up the rise ahead of you. The trail is deceptive because the rise isn't the highest point but in fact a ridge that, when crossed, reveals a higher rise beyond it. Eventually you'll reach the true crown of the hill; it's not arduous but it takes awhile and it's across open prairie. Along the way you'll see yucca and wildflowers that don't grow anywhere else in Iowa but in these hills. You may also meet a few little lizards and frogs skedaddling across the ground, but nothing more harmful.

    From the parking lot, Fountainbleau Loop runs south along the base of the bluffs on Larpenteur Road, which is gravel, and then turns east to return to Pisgah. Allow about 45 minutes to drive this 9-mile route if you're stopping at Murray Hill.

3. Continue down the Byway's main route, Highway 183.

So, what's a traveler to do with these options? Try this: stop at the Loess Hills State Forest Visitor Center, go to Murray Hill, eat at the cafe in Pisgah, and then head south on Highway 183.

Eventually Highway 183 comes out of the hills and runs along the base of some big bluffs until it joins Highway 127 for a short distance. Along the way you'll see a sign pointing to **Small's Fruit Farm**, (712) 646-2723. From about midsummer on, you can get fresh produce here and in the fall you're welcome to pick your own apples and pumpkins. Of course, if you don't want to pick anything, there's plenty waiting for you in the farm's store, which also serves up cider, hot fruit pies, and other desserts.

From here the Byway passes through Magnolia on Highway 127 and goes down to Logan where it meets Highway 30, which you'll take west toward Missouri Valley. Just a note: You're on a section of the Lincoln Highway, the first transcontinental auto route across the United States.

In five miles you'll see the **Harrison County Historical Village** and **Iowa Welcome Center** (see the "Side Trip" in chapter 5 for details about this site) as you approach Missouri Valley. Right after the village and welcome center, the Byway turns onto County Highway F58, which goes due east until it meets County Highway L34, which goes south.

About six miles later L34 meets I-680 and now there's another choice between staying on the Byway's main route (L34) or going on a loop. To take the **Hitchcock Loop**, head west on I-680. When you see what looks like a rest stop with a lookout tower, pull in, get out, walk up the tower, and count yourself blessed because the people on eastbound I-680 don't have a turnout or a lookout tower, which means they're missing the wonderful view you're enjoying of the Loess Hills.

Return to I-680 and go north on I-35, staying in the right-hand lane so you can immediately take Exit 72, where you'll go east into the small town of Loveland. You'll rejoin Highway 183 again and travel south along the base of the bluffs. At the very small, almost nonexistent community of Honey Creek, the Byway enters the hills and climbs through a nice valley. As you pass the crest, watch on the right for a sign pointing the way to the **Hitchcock Nature Area** (see the "Side Trip" in chapter 5 for details), which is soon to become one of the major nature centers in the Loess Hills.

Continuing south on Highway 183 again, you'll see signs telling you that the Hitchcock Loop is turning onto County Highway L36. An option here is to leave the Byway again by continuing south on Highway 183. You'll pass the entry to **Mount Crescent Ski Area** (see the "Side Trip" in chapter 5 for details), then go through the town of Crescent and on into Council Bluffs itself. You'll rejoin the Byway at the first stoplight you meet, at the intersection with Highway 6, also called Kanesville Avenue. From here, turn right (west) and follow the signs through the city (see chapter 5 for details). Eventually you'll find yourself leaving town on Highway 192, the South Expressway, and then on Highway 275. That will take you east briefly and then turn south to follow the base of the hills in a large arc around part of the Missouri River floodplain.

Southern Area Tour

Suddenly the Byway will veer left to go south directly into the hills on its way to Glenwood. If you watch carefully for the first gravel road on your left (east) as you go south, you'll see Ashton Road. By turning onto that road, you'll wind around a bit—generally going east and north—and after a mile or so you'll come across the humble little **Salem Lutheran Church**. Built in 1867 by German immigrants and restored since then, it's open at most times and features a pump organ and an old cemetery across the road.

Back on Highway 275, about four miles south of Ashton Road you should see signs pointing the way to the **Pony Creek Loop**. By going on Deacon Road, you'll wander into **Pony Creek Park**, (712) 527-9685, where a nice lake nestled between the hills baits fisherman to lob their lines into its waters. Or, you can just continue down Highway 275 to Glenwood.

For those going into Glenwood: when you enter the town and come to an area that's more commercial than residential, watch for Sharp Street and take it to the east (left). Keep going through the downtown of this county seat; in a few more blocks you'll cross Keg Creek and be in **Glenwood Lake Park**. On your left (north) you'll see the **Indian Earth Lodge**. Built with tree trunks and branches and covered with dirt like many of the shelters constructed here hundreds of years ago, the lodge can be seen on guided tours offered by the **Mills County Historical Museum**, (712) 527-5038, which is on the right hand side of the road. Besides the lodge, the museum has other historical structures as well as a fine collection of arrowheads, spear points, pottery shards, and more that were used by the Indians who inhabited this area in prehistoric times.

Also at the park is a lake with trails around it and the 750-seat, open-air **Davies Amphitheater**, (712) 527-3334, where family entertainment is offered on summer weekend evenings for a nominal fee.

Back at Highway 275, you'll head south from Glenwood and now will have the opportunity to go on the **Waubonsie Loop** rather than the main route of the Byway. Shortly after turning east on Highway 30 you can depart the four-lane highway for the two-lane County Highway L45. In a while it will turn to gravel but it's a nice drive through the hills and, 14 miles later, rejoins the Byway just north of the community of Tabor.

In Tabor, turn west (right) onto Orange Street and go to Center Street. There you'll find **Todd House**, 705 Park Street, (712) 629-2675, a small, unpretentious frame house that faces the city park. It was built as a parsonage in 1853, which makes it one of the earliest buildings in western Iowa. Look closely at the upper floor. There's a window in the middle, visible from the outside but not inside the house. This hidden room was a stop on the Underground Railroad for runaway slaves fleeing southern states to seek freedom in Canada.

South of Tabor, the Byway jogs onto County Highway J18 to go to Thurman at the base of the hills. Now it's time for another departure from the Byway. Instead of going south on County Highway L44, keep going through town on Highway 145 until you see County Highway L44 heading north.

In a couple of miles you'll see **Forney Lake** off to your left (west). A dirt road leads along the south side of the lake where there are several pullouts to view the lake with the Loess Hills in the background. It's rather peaceful here. Scan the trees for bald eagles, which are making a comeback in this area. You may discover a half dozen or so in the high branches and see them dive for fish in the lake.

*D*own South

All good things must come to an end and when you leave the lake, you'll be heading on the last section of this tour. Return to Thurman and get back on

County Highway L44, the main route of the Byway, which runs along the base of the Loess Hills. The first paved road going off to the right (east) up into the hills is County Highway J34, which leads to Sidney. Take it and soon you'll be entering into the courthouse square of this Norman Rockwell town. Go three-quarters of the way around the square, park, and visit **Penn Drug**, 714 Illinois Street, (712) 374-2513, the oldest soda fountain and drug store in the U.S. continuously owned by one family (since the days of the Civil War). Penn Drug is a great place to stop for ice cream treats and its specialty, homemade lemonade.

Well, from here the Byway folks want you to go on the **Pleasant Overview Loop** but you might better enjoy going south on Highway 275 and west on Highway 2. In about two miles you'll arrive at **Waubonsie State Park**, (712) 382-2786, which has some pretty overlooks within a short walk of the parking lots. Once a prairie, the park is heavily wooded now and is just gorgeous when the leaves change color in the fall. Because lots of people come here on the fall weekends, think about coming on a weekday. You might find you're the only folks in the park besides the ranger. There are campgrounds, picnic areas, and lots of trails. By the way, at the entrance to the park is a small stand for **Mincer Orchard**, (712) 382-1484; it's open on Saturdays and Sundays in the fall from 1-6 p.m. if you're a lover of apples, pumpkins, and such.

Inside the Battle Hill Museum, Battle Creek

From the park, take Highway 2 west to the base of the hills where you'll head south on County Highway L44 once more and roll along the Byway into the border town of Hamburg. Even though the Byway continues another mile or so to the state's southern border with Missouri, Hamburg is basically the end of the line and what better way to draw your journey to a close than to stop at the soda fountain in **Stoner Drug**, 1105 Main, (712) 382-2551. For those of you who loaded up at Penn Drug in Sidney, well, perhaps you should have been warned that these two great soda fountains are so close to each other—but hey, what a way to end this drive.

SIDE TRIP

What's this? A crazy suggestion for a side trip after a drive like the Loess Hills Scenic Byway? Well, crazy it's not, when you see what's in store.

Remember when you were southbound below Sioux City and you entered the little town of Smithland? Well, that's where you begin this side trip, by going east on Highway 141 to Mapleton. There, you turn north on Highway 175, which, 17 miles later, rolls into Battle Creek, home of the **Battle Hill Museum of Natural History**, Highway 175 E, (712) 365-4414. Located in two former schoolhouses and a garage that look quite unpretentious from the outside, the museum is jammed packed—and quite well-organized—with more than 4,000 natural specimens. One would not think about seeing a giraffe here—or an elephant skeleton—but here they are displayed along with many other full-size mounts. There's a Burmese python that was found south of town in 1996, and a small limestone cave under the buildings. This is one roadside stop you shouldn't miss. It's open on summer Sundays from 1-4 p.m. and at other times by appointment.

LODGING (From north to south on the Byway)

Sioux City
(See "Lodging" in chapter 3.)

Mapleton
Maple Motel, Highway 41/175, (712) 882-1271. Nine miles off the Byway from either Smithland or Castana. Restaurant, lounge. $

Missouri Valley
(See "Lodging" in chapter 5.)

Council Bluffs
(See "Lodging" in chapter 5.)

Glenwood
Western Inn, 707 S. Locust Street, (712) 527-3175. Near restaurants on south edge of town. $

BED AND BREAKFASTS (From north to south on the Byway)

Sioux City
(See Bed and Breakfasts in chapter 3.)

23

Battle Creek

The Inn at Battle Creek, 201 Maple Street, (712) 365-4949; (877) 365-4949. Twenty-four miles off the Byway from Smithland, near the Battle Hill Museum of Natural History, but worth the drive. An 1889 Queen Anne Victorian home in the city, spectacularly redone, with a restaurant. Five rooms. $-$$

Moorhead

Loess Hills Hideaway Cabins & Campground, 33774 Plum Avenue, (712) 886-5003. Four cabins. $

Castana

The Dormitory Inn, 130 4th Street, (712) 353-6797; (877) 553-6797. An inn built in the 1880s as classrooms and a dormitory for a school. Seven rooms. $$

Turin

The Country Homestead B&B, 22133 Larpenteur Road, (712) 353-6772; (888) 563-7455. Near the Loess Hills Wildlife Area north of town. Two rooms. $$-$$$

Logan

Blue Bird Run Farm, 2460 Norton Avenue, (712) 644-3102. A small farmstead with ride-along guide service in the Loess Hills. Organically grown fruits and vegetables. Three rooms. $$

Missouri Valley

(See "Side Trip" in chapter 5.)

Council Bluffs

(See chapter 5.)

Tabor

The Victorian Inn, 807 Main Street, (712) 629-5605. On the Byway and near the historic Todd House. Four rooms. $

Thurman

Plum Creek Inn, 505 Harris, (712) 628-2191; (800) 829-0646. In town, near Waubonsie State Park. Three rooms in the main house and two bedrooms in a small cottage. $$$-$$$$

DINING (From north to south on the Byway)

Sioux City

(See "Dining" in chapter 3.)

Mapleton

Maple Motel, Restaurant and Lounge, the intersection of Highways 141 and 175, (712) 882-1271. Nine miles off the Byway from either Smithland or Castana.

Battle Creek

The Inn at Battle Creek, 201 Maple Street, (712) 365-4949; (877) 365-4949. Twenty-four miles off the Byway from Smithland. It's a B&B with a full-service restaurant serving very fine food.

Pisgah

Old Home Fill 'er Up and Keep on Truckin' Cafe, Main Street, (712) 456-2727. Café-style food. On the main route through town.

Logan

Old Theatre Restaurant and Lounge, 308 E. 7th Street (Highway 30), (712) 644-2994. Closed Sundays.

Missouri Valley

Gurney's Restaurant, 229 S. 6th Street, (712) 642-2580. South of town on Highway 183.

Crescent

(See "Dining" in chapter 5.)

Council Bluffs

(See "Dining" in chapter 5.)

Glenwood

Oriental Palace, 91/2 Vince Street, (712) 527-5901.

 Pub Restaurant & Lounge, 612 S. Locust, (712) 527-3020.

Sidney

Penn Drug, 714 Illinois Street, (712) 374-2513. On the town square. Light lunches with soda fountain treats.

INFORMATION

Western Iowa Tourism Region, 103 3rd Street, Red Oak, IA 51566, (712) 623-4232; (888)-623-4232; www.traveliowa.org

Chapter 3

Sioux City: Triple Play

Located where the Missouri River takes a great turn to the west, the Sioux City area seems to have a preoccupation with the number three. Three states meet here: Iowa, South Dakota, and Nebraska. So do three rivers: the Missouri, the Big Sioux, and the Floyd. And three cities abut each other here: Sioux City, Iowa; South Sioux City, Nebraska; and North Sioux City, South Dakota. For the most part, this tour will take you through Sioux City, Iowa, the southern hub of a region called Siouxland that extends up to Sioux Falls, South Dakota.

The South Side

You should start your tour by approaching Sioux City from the south and taking Exit 141 off I-29, which is the way to the Sioux Gateway Airport. When you reach Harbor Drive, take a left and follow the signs to **Mid-America Air Museum**, 6715 Harbor Drive, (712) 252-5300; admission. Housed next door to the Iowa Air National Guard, the museum has a few military jet fighters and several private aircraft, including gliders, in a nearby hangar, but the heart of the museum, in the opinion of some, is its collection of aviator uniforms from throughout the years.

North of here is where the region's recorded history began, at the **Sergeant Floyd Monument**. To get to it from I-29, take Exit 143 (the next one north of the airport), turn to the right, where you'll meet South Lewis Boulevard (also Highway 75), and take a left. Go north about one mile.

A brick obelisk sits atop a bluff overlooking the Sioux City area. The nation's first National Registered Landmark, it marks the burial site of Sergeant Charles Floyd, the only member of Lewis and Clark's Corps of Discovery to die during their journey. Some say he died of a burst appendix but no one knows for sure. In addition to the nice view from the monument, there are well-done interpretative signs.

One of the 30-foot statues at Trinity Heights in Sioux City

𝓘nto the City

From here, take Highway 75 north, turn left on 11th Street, then take a right on Floyd Boulevard. In less than two miles you'll see the sign for **Trinity Heights**, 33rd and Floyd Boulevard, (712) 239-8670; free. The drive into this place is less than appealing but the road takes you to what has become Sioux City's most visited spot. Thirty-foot-tall statues of the Virgin Mary and Jesus Christ dominate this pastoral setting of open lawns and flower gardens set on a hillside. Between the statues are buildings housing the gift shop and a life-size wooden sculpture of the Last Supper made by a resident of the area.

When you leave the grounds, take a right on Floyd Boulevard until you reach 27th Street, which heads to the west. While 27th Street goes all the way to Jackson Street (where you want to ultimately end up), be aware that at one point there is a jog to the right for about half a block before 27th Street resumes going west again. Turn right on Jackson and find the **Sioux City Public Museum**, 2901 Jackson, (712) 279-6174; free, on the northwest corner of 29th and Jackson.

Located in the former mansion of a financier who built his home with pink-gray Sioux quartzite, the museum is a great place to learn about the history of Sioux City and the surrounding region, including seeing exhibits about the Lakota, Omaha, and Winnebago tribes.

Farther south and on the east edge of downtown is **Historic Fourth Street** (between Virginia and Iowa Streets), an old warehouse district that's still evolving into a nice area of shops and restaurants that can take a couple hours to explore. A block west of the historic district is what looks like a modern version of a covered railroad station platform—look for **Farmers Markets** there on Saturday mornings. And just to the west of there is the **Sioux City Convention Center**, 801 4th Street, (800) 593-2228, where the **Sioux City Tourism Bureau** is located and brimming with information.

Government buildings aren't often on the must-see list, but the **Woodbury County Courthouse**, 620 Douglas Street, (712) 279-6611; free, is definitely worth a stop. The largest municipal building in the nation designed in the Prairie School style (inspired by architect Frank Lloyd Wright), the courthouse was built in 1917 and is magnificent inside and out. Expect to be surprised by the beautiful architecture and artwork of the interior courtyard, which has a stained-glass dome ceiling (which is quite a trick considering a tower is up there ... see if you can figure it out).

On the south side of downtown is the ultra-modern **Sioux City Art Center**, 225 Nebraska Street, (712) 279-6272; free. A beautiful blend of tan brick, glittering steel, and shimmering green glass, the center is a piece of art in itself and kids especially like to play on the drum-shaped atrium's spiral floor pattern. Exhibits include artworks from the permanent collection as well as traveling exhibits. Studios provide space for visiting artists who conduct workshops and a gift shop is on the main floor.

*T*he Riverside

Farther south, **Chris Larsen Jr. Park** lies alongside the Missouri River and may be the only large city park on the Missouri River in this part of the Midwest. Other cities on the Missouri may call themselves "River City" but Sioux City is the only one that really plays up the river and rightfully has earned that title.

Entering the park on its east end, one immediately sees the *Belle of Sioux City*, 100 Larsen Park Road, (712) 255-0800; (800) 424-0080, a riverboat casino that's open year-round and cruises daily during the summer. Loaded with slot machines and table games, the *Belle* is open 24 hours a day.

One can either drive west through the park, or hike, bike, or rollerblade on the paved trail that goes the length of the park to connect with another trail system that goes for miles beyond. Along the trail you'll encounter a children's playground and the **Anderson Dance Pavilion**, (712) 279-6111, scene of many planned and impromptu concerts during the summer. Just beyond the pavilion is a small, quiet place where a statue of an airman carrying a small boy to safety stands near a colonnade. This is the **Flight 232 Memorial**, which honors those who survived and those who died in the crash of United Flight 232 at Sioux City's airport in July 1989.

Sergeant Floyd Riverboat Museum and Iowa Welcome Center

At night, this area of the park is dominated by the **Veterans Memorial Bridge**, which connects South Sioux City with Sioux City and is bathed in blue light.

Just beyond the bridge is another boat, the *Sergeant Floyd*, 1000 Larsen Park Road, (712) 279-0198; free, that anchors the park's west end. A riverboat museum and **Iowa Welcome Center** all rolled into one, the *Sergeant Floyd* was once a survey boat for the U.S. government on the Missouri River and hosted President Harry S. Truman at one time. Now, she serves up an excellent study of watercraft that have used the Missouri, all the way from dugout canoes and keelboats to the legendary sternwheelers and modern tows. Also inside the boat is a statue of Sergeant Floyd (remember him?) that is no mere fanciful depiction. When the unfortunate Floyd's remains had to be moved in 1857 from the edge of a deteriorating bluff, a cast of his skull was made. The cast was used by a modern-day forensic specialist to create the statue bearing an authentic likeness of the man. By the way, there's plenty of information here about the regional attractions in this three-state area.

Just across the river, in South Sioux City, is the **Scenic Park Aquaplex**, at the east end of E. 4th Street, (402) 494-7543; admission. Located alongside the river, it has the nation's one and only figure-eight water slide and it's more than 100 feet long ... wowee!

From the *Sergeant Floyd*, it's an easy jaunt to I-29 again where, going west, you get off at the next exit onto Highway 12. Going north, you'll notice **Riverside Sports Complex** where another aquatic center is waiting to cool you off.

Otherwise, about four miles north of the interstate exit, you'll reach the entrance to the **Dorothy Pecaut Nature Center**, 4500 Sioux River Road, (712) 258-0838; free, just north of a small business area. This center is one of the few dedicated to explaining the geography, flora, fauna, and fossils of Iowa's Loess Hills and it does so in a fine way, including a walk-through view at what's under one of those hills.

Less than a mile from the turnoff to the nature center is **Stone State Park**, 5001 Talbot Road, (712) 255-4698; free. Just inside the entry you'll come to a fork in the road. If you're planning to picnic, take the low road. But if you want views, go to the right for the high road that traverses the ridges of the park's hills, providing many good overlooks of the Big Sioux River valley to the west.

SIDE TRIPS

To the North

To begin this side trip, head north of Sioux City on Highway 75 until you reach Le Mars about 25 miles up the road. Continue on the highway through the community to the **Ice Cream Capital of the World Visitor Center**, at the junction of Highways 75 and 3, (712) 546-4090; admission, on your right. Operated by Wells Dairy, which makes more ice cream in Le Mars than is made in any other place in the world, the center gives a history of the origins of ice cream and describes how it is made nowadays. There's also a very interactive

Ice cream memorabilia on display at the Ice Cream Capital of the World Visitor Center, Le Mars

room at the end of the self-guided tour that's quite a hit with the kids. Just beyond that (also accessible without having to go through the museum) is a 1920s-style ice cream parlor that serves it all—sundaes, sodas, floats, phosphates, banana splits, and special concoctions. These dishes don't serve up the typical golf-ball sized scoops of ice cream … we're talking baseball-sized scoops here. A regular sundae of two scoops is about $2.50 and you just might want to have a friend along to help eat it. Besides all types of ice cream flavors and toppings, the soda fountain also serves yogurt and fat-free and sugar-free ice cream as well.

Once you waddle away from the soda fountain, resume your northward trek on Highway 75 but only to the north side of Le Mars where you'll take Highway 60. About 10 miles up Highway 60 is a sign pointing to Orange City, which is another five or so miles up County Highway K64.

Note the names on some of the signs as you approach this community and you'll quickly deduce that this region was settled by the Dutch in the 1870s. And if you need confirmation, there's the **Old Mill**, a replica of a small Dutch windmill, standing outside the headquarters of Diamond Vogel Paint, 1020 Albany Place SE, (712) 737-8880; free. If the mill's not open, just ask at the nearby office for a key and let yourself in for a visit.

Continue on into town on County Highway K64—which becomes Albany Avenue—until you reach 2nd Street, where you'll go one block to the downtown. One glimpse of the Dutch-style store fronts leaves absolutely no doubt that the Dutch are still here and proud of their heritage. Naturally, it doesn't take too much imagination to guess what's for sale in the **Dutch Bakery** and the **Dutch Meat Market**. Look carefully around the intersection of First Street and Central Avenue, downtown's main drag, and you might spot the windmill-shaped phone booth.

On the south side of downtown is the **Old Factory**, 110 Fourth Street SW, (712) 737-4242. Located in a building where wooden shoes were actually made, this gift shop handles delft, lace, tile, and foods imported from Holland. And yes, it still carries wooden shoes—in 20 sizes.

An excellent time to visit Orange City is during the **Tulip Festival**, (712) 737-4510, held the third weekend of May each year. Tulips are in bloom everywhere and the residents don Dutch clothing of a century ago to wash the streets, hold a parade, and generally have a good old time.

To the South

Driving about 30 miles south of Sioux City on I-29 to Exit 112 takes you to **Lewis and Clark State Park**, (712) 423-2829; free, which is a few miles west of the interchange. The park fronts Blue Lake, an oxbow lake that was once the channel of the Missouri River, which changed its course frequently before the big dams were built in the Dakotas in the 20th century. In 1804 Lewis and Clark passed through this region, and a group of volunteers has built replicas of the keelboat and pirogues (vessels much like large rowboats) used by the explorers and put them on Blue Lake.

The park itself is a nice place to relax with a hike, picnic, campout, dip in the lake, or just fishing off the dock.

Note: The second weekend of each June is the **Lewis and Clark Festival**, (712) 423-1801, in which buckskinners and other reenactors celebrate the passage of the explorers through this area. If conditions are right, the keelboat and pirogues take to the water during the festival.

Casino Omaha, No.1 Blackbird Lane, Onawa, (712) 423-3700; (800) 858-8238, has slots and progressive blackjack, craps, roulette, and poker tables. A buffet restaurant, lounge, and gift shop are also at the casino, a short drive from the state park.

Another casino, **WinnaVegas**, three miles west of I-29 at Exit 127, (712) 428-WINN; (800) 468-9466, is near Sloan, which is between Onawa and Sioux City. It also has slot machines, table games, a restaurant with a buffet and menu options, plus a snack bar and lounge.

To the east of Exit 112 is the city of Onawa, which boasts of having the world's widest Main Street as well as being the first community to make an Eskimo Pie. You can learn more about that and quite a few other things regarding this region, including Loess Hills pottery, at the **Monona County Historical Museum**, 47 12th Street, (712) 423-2776; free. On the east side of town is the **Monona County Arboretum**, 318 E. Iowa Avenue, (712) 423-2400; free, which not only has about 300 different trees and shrubs but also presents displays of the mixed grass and short grass prairies that once covered most of the Loess Hills off to the east (see chapter 2 for more information on the hills).

LODGING

Le Mars

AmeriHost Inn, 1314 12th Street SW, (712) 548-4910; (800) 434-5800. Near Highway 75 and the Ice Cream Capital of the World. Indoor pool. Near restaurants. $$-$$$

Sioux City

AmericInn, 4230 S. Lewis Boulevard, (712) 255-1800; (800) 634-3444. Near I-29, Highway 20, airport, and Sergeant Floyd Monument. Indoor pool, Jacuzzi, continental breakfast. $$-$$$$

Best Western City Centre, 130 Nebraska Street, (712) 277-1550; (800) 528-1234. Downtown near the Sioux City Art Center. Outdoor pool, coffee shop, restaurant, and lounge. $-$$

Comfort Inn, 4202 S. Lakeport, (712) 274-1300; (800) 228-5150. East side of Sioux City near the Southern Hills and Mayfair shopping malls and Highway 20. Indoor pool, continental breakfast. $-$$$

Hamilton Inn, 1401 Zenith Drive, (712) 277-3211; (800) 274-3211. Hamilton Boulevard Exit (149) on I-29, near Dorothy Pecaut Nature Center and Sergeant Floyd Riverboat Museum and Iowa Welcome Center. Indoor and outdoor pools, coffee shop, restaurant, and lounge. $$-$$$

Hilton Sioux City, 704 4th Street, (712) 277-4101; (800) 593-0555. Downtown and connected to other business and retail buildings with pedestrian skyways. Indoor pool, coffee shop, restaurant, and lounge. $$-$$$

North Sioux City, South Dakota

Comfort Inn, 1311 River Drive, (605) 232-3366. Near I-29 just west of Sioux City. Indoor pool, continental breakfast. $$-$$$

Country Inn & Suites, 151 Tower Road, (605) 232-3500; (800) 456-4000. Near I-29 just west of Sioux City. Indoor pool, hot tub, two-room suites, continental breakfast. $$-$$$

South Sioux City, Nebraska

Marina Inn, 4th and B Streets, (402) 494-4000; (800) 798-7980. Best view of the Missouri River and Sioux City, Iowa. Indoor and outdoor pools, restaurant, lounge, some private patios. $$$

BED AND BREAKFASTS

Sioux City

English Mansion B&B, 1525 Douglas Street, (712) 277-1386. Just north of downtown area. Full breakfast and evening desserts in a 1894 mansion. $$$-$$$$

Rose Hill Inn B&B, 1602 Douglas Street, (712) 258-8678. On the north side of downtown. Full breakfast. $$-$$$$

DINING

Sioux City

El Fredo Pizza, 523 West 19th Street, (712) 258-0691. Pizza, pasta, and barbecue with a comedy show. Call for reservations on Friday and Saturday evenings.

Green Gables Restaurant, 400 Pierce Street, (712) 258-4246. Family-style restaurant famous for homemade soups and pies, and ice cream sundaes.

Kahill's, South Sioux City, 4th and B Streets, (402) 494-5025. In the Marina Inn. Full menu. Riverside view.

King Sea, 512 5th Street, (712) 255-0222. Downtown. Seafood, Szechwan and Mandarin dishes. Lunch buffet.

Luciano's Italian Bistro, 1019 4th Street, (712) 258-5174. In Historic Fourth Street District. Italian cuisine.

Minerva's Restaurant & Bar, 2901 Hamilton Boulevard, (712) 252-1012. Food prepared in wood-burning stove.

Victorian Opera Company, 4th and Court, (712) 255-4821. Restaurant and gift shop in a restored downtown building.

INFORMATION

Sergeant Floyd Riverboat Museum and Iowa Welcome Center, 1000 Larsen Park Road, (712) 279-0198.

Sioux City Convention and Tourism Bureau, 801 4th Street, Sioux City, IA 51102, (712) 279-4800; (800) 593-2228; www.siouxlan.com/ccat

Western Iowa Tourism Region, 103 3rd Street, Red Oak, IA 51566, (712) 623-4323; (888)-623-4232; www.traveliowa.org

Chapter 4

Elk Horn and Kimballton: Velkommen

On the way to Elk Horn up Highway 173 from I-80, signs will make it clear that you're approaching a Danish community. In fact, it's about as Danish as you can get without flying to Denmark. Then what, you ask upon entering Elk Horn, is a Dutch windmill doing here?

That's what a lot of people have puzzled over as they enter the community-aren't all windmills Dutch? But the Danes had them too—and still do in many areas. The one you see as you drive into Elk Horn was built in 1848 in Norre Snede, Denmark. In the 1970s, the citizens of Elk Horn and the surrounding area—descendants of Danes who started settling here in 1867—decided they needed a symbol of their heritage so they purchased it, dismantled it, shipped it across the Atlantic, and rebuilt it as the community's Bicentennial project. Besides being a touchstone for the locals, the windmill became a tourist attraction, not a bad thing for a rural community of 664 residents that was, like so many others, having trouble making ends meet.

The **Danish Windmill**, as the 60-foot-tower with 66-foot-wide red wings is called, is part museum and part **Iowa Welcome Center**, 4038 Main Street, (712) 764-7472; (800) 451-7960. In the museum, admission, which is the windmill itself, your tour begins with a short video that answers most questions about how the windmill came to Elk Horn. Guides can answer the rest as they lead you into the mill afterward.

Instead of just being a showpiece, the mill actually grinds wheat and rye that's sold in the welcome center, which is in the building attached to the base of the windmill. Because the windmill's manager travels to Denmark every year, what you find for sale here is what Danes are buying back home, except you don't have to spend the airfare. Everything that's Danish, from Legos and chocolates to B&G and Royal Copenhagen figurines, is here.

North of the windmill is the **Danish Inn**, 4116 Main Street, (712) 764-4251, where the menu lists not only American dishes but those loved by Danes in-

The Danish Windmill in Elk Horn

cluding *Moredard* (pork stuffed with apples and prunes), *frikaddeler* (meatballs), *medisterpolse* (sausage), *rodkall* (red cabbage), and *smorrebrod* (open-face Danish sandwiches)

Even the local grocery has Danish breads, meats, and cheese for sale. At the **Danish Bakery**, 4234 Main Street, (712) 764-2151, a few blocks walk away, expect to find all those pastries that have made Denmark famous (and some people chubby).

And just to further emphasize that you're in Danish territory, red and white Danish flags flutter next to the red, white, and blue almost everywhere you look. Even the sidewalk benches are painted with the Danish colors.

On the west edge of town is the **Danish Immigrant Museum**, 2212 Washington Street, (712) 764-7001; (800) 759-9192. Not just about the immigrants who came to this area, the museum is national in scope and encompasses the story of all Danes who came to America, plus their descendants. Located in an A-frame building that evokes images of Danish farm buildings, the museum's main floor has exhibits on the lives of the early Danish immigrants. Luggage trunks stenciled with Danish names once held clothing and other dear possessions of those who came to America. Records of a *folkschule* that was started in Elk Horn to properly educate young Danish-Americans about their heritage can be seen here. A piano that belonged to Victor Borge, perhaps the most famous Danish-American, is also here.

Upstairs at the museum are records of Danish families that have grown and spread across America over the years, so if you think you have any Danish blood, this is the place to verify it.

A nice adjunct to the museum, **Bedstemor's Hus**, 2015 College Street, (712) 764-6082, is back in town. Representing the house of a young Danish immigrant family between 1910 and 1920, Bedstemor's Hus (which translates as "grandmother's house") shows a blend of American and Danish cultures.

Each year Elk Horn hosts two major events. On Memorial Day weekend, there's **Tivoli Fest**, a springtime celebration. The parade is much like many others in small towns but what sets this event apart are the Danish dances that are usually held in the field just south of the windmill. In brightly colored native dress, the dancers dip, whirl, and twirl through intricate moves to snappy tunes.

The other event is **Jule Fest**, held on Thanksgiving weekend to celebrate the winter holidays. Once more, the town is decked out for visitors.

Kimballton

Elk Horn may be the largest Danish rural community in the United States, but it's not the only one. **Kimballton** is just three miles north up Highway 173. Two items are worth seeing here. The first is a gilded replica of the **Little Mermaid** statue that graces the Copenhagen harbor as a remembrance of the main character in a Hans Christian Andersen fairy tale. She's easy to find in a small circular fountain at the north end of town, which is only a few blocks long.

The second item is the **General Store Museum**, 112 N. Main, open from 1-4 p.m. Wednesdays to Fridays, June-August, and also easy to find on the town's short main street. If it weren't for the modern clothes you're wearing, you'd swear you've been transported back a century or so because things here are as they were then.

SIDE TRIPS

To the East and West

Kimballton lies close to the middle of the **Western Skies Scenic Byway**, one of a series of pleasant drives in Iowa. Traversing west central Iowa, from Missouri Valley on the west end to Stuart on the east end, this byway takes in wide expanses of open fields and farmland that appear to roll on forever. Look for the colorful and distinctive Iowa Scenic Byway signs on Highway 44 on the north side of Kimballton.

To the South

About 15 miles southwest of Elk Horn is Walnut (Exit 46 on I-80), which proudly calls itself Iowa's Antique City. About 20 stores, representing about 250 dealers, sell a variety of antiques ranging from the small, such as baby spoons and bottle caps, to the large, such as oak back bars and soda pop machines. There are also specialty stores selling items such as quilts and, on a year-round basis, Christmas decorations. With all these stores, it's easy to spend at least half a day browsing. The shops are open from 9 a.m. to 5 p.m., Monday-Saturday, and from noon to 5 p.m. on Sunday.

The Walnut Welcome Center, 607 Highland Street, (712) 784-2100, located a half block from the main street, is a good source of information about the

A portion of the Western Skies Scenic Byway

community. Make sure to look at the murals of old-time products painted on some of the buildings. They're part of a special art project that involved bringing professional sign painters to town to demonstrate their skills.

From Walnut, take County Highway M47 to the south about 12 miles and turn left (east) on Highway 6. Now there are two ways to get to your next destination: **Hitchcock House,** (712) 769-2323.

1. Go into the town of Lewis, about seven miles east of the M47/Highway 6 intersection, and double back about a mile, following the signs.

2. When you're on Highway 6 and see County Highway M56 on your left (about 6.5 miles from the M47/Highway 6 intersection), turn right onto a gravel road going south. That T's into another gravel road; take that to the right (west) about a quarter-mile and follow the signs that lead you down the first road on your left (south), which is the turnoff to Hitchcock House.

This brownstone, two-story home built in 1856 by the Rev. George Hitchcock was a stop on the Underground Railroad for runaway slaves coming up the nearby Nishnabotna River from southern states. The hidden room in the basement is now easily seen in this restored structure, which is furnished as it was 150 years ago.

Also, take note of what's happening just down the hill from the house along the Nishnabotna River to the east. On the east bank of the river, a small structure that's undergoing restoration is one of the oldest buildings in western

Iowa. A ferry house on the Pioneer-Mormon Trail, this simple frame building was the spot where thousands of travelers boarded a boat across the "Nish" on their way west for several years before a bridge was built in the area.

Just south of town is **Cold Springs State Park**, (712) 769-2372, a pleasant place to visit, picnic, and camp.

The best way to return to Elk Horn from here is to first return to Lewis, then take Highway 6 to the east where it meets Highway 83. Take that to the left (west) for a short distance to Highway 173, which heads north to I-80 and then Elk Horn.

To the North

Traveling through the beautiful countryside north of Kimballton for about 35 miles up County Highway M66 brings you to Manning, another community rich with ethnic heritage, this time German. In the last few years the residents did what Elk Horn did in the 1970s—return to their homeland and bring back something linked to their past. In this case, it's the **Hausbarn**, a combination house and barn that, at the age of 350 years, was dismantled in the village of Offenseth in Germany and brought to the east side of Manning, (712) 655-3131; (800) 292-0252. Animals were quartered in one area while the owners lived in a corner of the barn, walled off from the rest of the structure, which is covered with a thatched roof. It's a safe bet to say it's unlike any other structure you will see in America. By the way, its Web site, http://pionet.net/~kuselb/hframe.htm,

The Hausbarn in Manning

39

is very interesting in that it's in Deutsche und Englische and shows photos of the barn being constructed.

From Manning, go east on Highway 141 for seven miles to Highway 71, which will lead you south to Audubon, the seat of Audubon County.

Downtown, you'll find **Hansen's Galleries**, 223 Broadway, (712) 563-3335, featuring the creations of local artist Clint Hansen. As a graphic designer, Hansen has been illustrating commercial works for companies like IBM, GM, Coca-Cola and others, primarily using his scratchboard technique. He even designed a commemorative coin for the U.S. Olympics in Atlanta. The gallery—which has a Model A pickup as its centerpiece—displays his more personal works, which are mostly oils of subjects ranging from farms to lighthouses to bears.

When it comes time to leave town, you'll notice something you more than likely won't see anywhere else—a 45-ton concrete statue of a Hereford bull with a 15-foot span of horns. That's **Albert**, billed as the world's largest bull. Built to honor the region's strong cattle industry, Albert stands about 30 feet high at the shoulder.

A bit farther south is something else you don't see often, a collection of windmills. That's the **Nathaniel Hamlin Park and Museum**, a mile south of Audubon on Highway 71, (712) 563-9594. Named after the county's first settler, the park has at least 18 windmills, all in working order, as an homage to the wind-driven machines that helped water the West. The museum has antique machinery of various sorts and the world's largest collection of nails, which will teach you that nails are more extraordinary than you thought.

LODGING

Atlantic

Econo Lodge Motel, I-80 and Highway 71, (712) 243-4067; (800) 553-2666. Adjacent to I-80 a few miles north of Atlantic. Outdoor pool. Close to Audubon. $

Super 8, 1902 E. 7th Street, (712) 243-4723; (888) 243-2378. On the east side of the downtown area. Continental breakfast. $-$$

Elk Horn

AmericInn, 4037 Main Street, (712) 764-4000; (800) 634-3444. An American motel in touch with the Danish heritage of the town. Indoor pool, continental breakfast. Restaurants nearby. $-$$

Walnut

Red Carpet Inn, Exit 46 from I-80, (712) 784-2233; (800) 711-5409. Adjacent to I-80 and one mile from the antique stores. Restaurants next door. $-$$

Super 8, 2109 Antique City Drive, (712) 784-2221; (800) 800-8000. Adjacent to I-80 and antique stores. Indoor pool. $

BED AND BREAKFASTS

Atlantic

Chestnut Charm B&B, 1409 Chestnut Street, (712) 243-5652, In town, a quiet and secluded turreted Victorian mansion built in 1898, with nine rooms in the main house and the renovated carriage house, some with Jacuzzis. Gazebo and gardens. $$-$$$$

Elk Horn

Hansen's Kro, 2113 Park Street, (712) 764-2052; (800) 606-2052. A modern kro (Danish for house) in the middle of the community. Two rooms. Full Danish breakfast. Children welcome. $$

Joy's Morning Glory, 4308 Main Street, (712) 764-5631; (888) 764-5631. A 1912 home within walking distance of the downtown businesses and attractions. Breakfast served in the dining room, on the front porch or in the backyard. $-$$

Walnut

Antique City Inn B&B, 400 Antique City Drive, (712) 784-3722. Located in a Victorian home built in 1911, it has a wraparound porch with a swing so you can watch the world go by. A block from the antique stores. Four rooms and two suites. Breakfast on the back porch, weather permitting. $-$$

Clarks County Inn B&B, 701 Walnut Street, (712) 784-3010. A 1912, two-story home with antiques within an easy walk of the town's antique stores. Three rooms, landscaped deck. $$

Veranda View Guesthouse, 50517 Highway 83 S, (712) 784-2267. An 1892 two-story farm home with guest rooms in the quiet of the country. Breakfast on the veranda if the weather's fine. Three rooms. $-$$

DINING

Elk Horn

Danish Inn, 4116 Main Street, (712) 764-4251. American and Danish meals.

Danish Bakery, 4234 Main Street, (712) 764-2151. Traditional Danish and American pastries, breads, and European coffees.

Simply Sweet, (712) 764-4030. Homemade soups, sandwiches, and pies. Close to the windmill.

Walnut

Aunt B's, 221 Antique City Drive, (712) 784-3681. Among the antique shops. Basic small restaurant food with good specials.

Glenn's Food and Pub, 214 Antique City Drive, (712) 784-3063. Sandwiches and luncheon fare.

Sandy's, 213 Antique City Drive, (712) 784-2190. A tavern restaurant among the antique shops.

Villager, 2117 Antique City Drive, (712) 784-2200. Near the interstate. A good stop for well-made food. Evening and Sunday buffets.

INFORMATION

Danish Windmill Museum and Visitor Center, 4038 Main Street, Elk Horn, IA 51531, (712) 764-7472; (800) 451-7960; www.danishwindmill.com

Walnut Welcome Center, 607 Highland Street, Walnut, IA 51577, (712) 784-2100.

Western Iowa Tourism Region, 103 N. 3rd, Red Oak, IA 51566, (712) 623-4232; (888) 623-4232; www.traveliowa.org

Chapter 5

Council Bluffs:
Gateway to the West

I'll confess right away to being careful here because Council Bluffs is where I live. One wrong move and my next address will be a post office box in Antarctica. Still, as a writer, I have a responsibility, so here goes.

Downtown

Although the city's earliest buildings are gone, perhaps the closest thing to them one can see is the **Kanesville Tabernacle**, 222 E. Broadway, (712) 322-0500, a replica of the first Mormon Tabernacle. Erected in the 1990s, this log structure is close to where the original was built in the 1840s by the Mormons who elected Brigham Young as the first president of their church here. Members of the Church of Jesus Christ of Latter-day Saints are at the site and you might anticipate some proselytizing.

Some structures built in the latter half of the 19th century are just a block or so to the west, forming part of the downtown area on Broadway, the major drag of the Bluffs, as the city is also called (along with "CB"). By going a few blocks farther west on Broadway and then traveling south on Main until you reach the **Haymarket** area (where a concrete watering trough for horses remains at a triangular intersection), you will easily cover the original downtown area—and the present downtown too. Not many businesses and homes were built west of here for several years because one never knew where the wide Missouri—the last major river to be tamed in the United States—might cut a new channel each spring when it carried heavy runoff from melting snows in the Rocky Mountains thousands of miles away.

In 1869, as he was directing the expansion of the Union Pacific Railroad, Grenville Dodge built a three-story brick mansion alongside a bluff at a cost of $35,000. Now called the **Historic General Dodge House**, 605 3rd Street, (712) 322-2406, the mansion is open Tuesday-Sunday (closed in January). It

Ruth Ann Dodge Memorial in downtown Council Bluffs

represents the best of its era and its period furniture and decorations reveal the lush life that privileged residents enjoyed back then. The highlights of the house—located about three blocks east of the Haymarket area—are the dining room and the twin parlors where opposing mirrors create images of infinity. However, some younger visitors are more fascinated by the bathroom, which contains the decorative bowl of the city's first flush toilet! Ask your guide to turn on the six-foot-tall German music box that uses platter-sized metal disks to create melodious tunes—call it a forerunner of today's CD players.

On the north edge of downtown, the general's wife is remembered at the **Ruth Anne Dodge Memorial** in Fairview Cemetery on Lafayette Avenue. Fashioned after an image Mrs. Dodge talked of having in a dream, the statue of an angel standing on the prow of a boat was designed by Daniel Chester French, creator of the Lincoln Memorial. The statue, which some locals call "The Black Angel," has inspired a number of legends; but, as far as anyone knows, none of the whispered rumors of a quick doom for visitors have ever come true (nor has anyone spoken of any agonizingly slow exits).

Although Council Bluffs was the nation's fifth-largest rail yard with eight railroads and six depots in the 1940s, sadly, only one of those stations remains, the Rock Island Depot. Built in 1899, it now houses **RailsWest Museum,** 16th Avenue and S. Main, (712) 323-5182, open Tuesday-Sunday, Memorial Day to Labor Day. Dedicated to the city's railroad history, the museum houses a station manager's office, railroad artifacts, and a large HO-scale model train layout. Outside sit two short trains headed by antique steam locomotives.

A few blocks north of the depot—back in the downtown area—is another reminder of the city's past, the 1885 **Squirrel Cage Jail**, 226 Pearl Street, (712) 323-2509, open Wednesday-Sunday, June through August, and weekends only in May and September. One of three such jails left in the nation, this brick building contains a three-story, drum-shaped set of cells that revolved within a barred cylinder. On each floor a single opening permitted the jailers to open only one cell at a time when they rotated the "squirrel cage." While efficient for controlling inmates, it was deemed a fire hazard and closed in 1969. It is now a museum.

Next on the trip north up Pearl Street is the old **Carnegie Library**. Don't worry about an address because you aren't going to miss this impressive building just across the alley from the old jail. Although not open at the time this book went to press, the Carnegie is slated to open in October 2002 as the new headquarters of the Union Pacific Railroad Museum.

Less than a block north of the jail is **Bayliss Park** (bounded by Pearl Street, Willow Avenue, 6th Street, and 1st Avenue), a downtown park with a water fountain of constantly shifting sprays accompanied by changing lights in the evening, making for colorful entertainment. Various types of music are performed by bands on the shaded lawn throughout the summer, and in the winter the park is brilliant with colorful lights and lighted sculptures. If you visit Bayliss, watch for the black squirrels that have become a mascot of the city (and mind you, city laws prohibit the harassment and capture of black squirrels).

If you want more live music on a year-round basis, there's no other place than **Acorn Supply**, 329 16th Avenue, (712) 325-9282. As they've done since 1984, owners David and Harry Frank push aside the feed sacks every Saturday afternoon and turn their agricultural store into an outstanding country music jam spot with tunes ranging from old favorites to original compositions. If you just want to listen, sit among the antiques and don't worry about that odd feeling near your ankles—it's probably one of the chickens or small pigs checking you out. However, if you're so inclined, bring your own fiddle, guitar, spoons to tap on the knee—or whatever—and join in. Once you do, you're entitled to autograph one of the store's white-washed bricks.

The East End

Two miles east of Exit 8 on I-80, **Westfair**, 22984 Highway 6, (712) 322-3400; (402) 393-0900, also provides live music during the summer at the county fairgrounds on the east edge of the city. With a natural amphitheater, Westfair has been drawing big-name performers and big crowds since the mid-1990s. By the way, Pottawattamie County is so large—it's the largest county in Iowa—that it has two county fairs, one in the east end of the county and one at Westfair.

While the subject is music, no music lover should overlook **Kanesville Kollectables**, 530 S. 4th Street, (712) 328-8731. In an old brown brick downtown building, this music store buys and sells used cassette tapes and compact discs but its main stock in trade is thousands upon thousands of 45- and 78-rpm vinyl platters. The collection can cause the casual browser to get lost in musi-

Dairy Queen
Nostalgia

Several of the eating places in this book are listed at the end of each chapter. But there's one place in Council Bluffs that deserves special mention. It's the nation's oldest existing Dairy Queen, 1634 W. Broadway, (712) 322-8801, located just west of the Broadway viaduct. The 10th Dairy Queen ever built, it retains its original ice cream cone sign atop the building and is definitely a treat from decades ago.

cal memories for a few hours. Those in the know consider this to be one of the better treasure troves of records in the Upper Midwest. Comic books occupy a few rooms here too.

West of downtown and past I-80 is the Council Bluffs Airport, where a detachment of the **Confederate Air Force**, (712) 322-2435, a group dedicated to maintaining historical aircraft in flying condition, has a hangar open to the public every Wednesday evening and all day Saturday. The showpiece is a P-51 Mustang, perhaps the best propeller-driven aircraft used by the Allies in World War II. There are also two light observation aircraft (depending on air show engagements, the aircraft are not always on hand) along with a small museum of aviation artifacts and a squadron of scale model aircraft of all types. The airport is about two miles east of the intersection of McPherson and Valley View Drive. (Note that the name Confederate Air Force is due to change, but at the time of this printing the new name is not known.)

The South Side

On CB's south edge is its prime outdoor recreation area—**Lake Manawa State Park**, 1100 South Shore Road, (712) 366-0220. Here, at a 1,529-acre lake that was part of the Missouri until the river changed its course (which it did often until dams were built in the Dakotas beginning in the 1930s), you can sun on the beach, fish, sail, take a power boat for a spin, golf at a nearby course, hike a nature trail, and roll down bike paths. The place that children like best is **Dream Playground**, a large and wonderful wooden labyrinth where they can roam through bridges, platforms, watch towers, ladders, tunnels, and more and never get tired of playing (okay … sometimes they get tired, but never bored).

Not far from the lake are other attractions. The closest is the **Council Bluffs Drive-In**, 1130 W. South Omaha Bridge Road, (712) 366-0422, an outdoor movie theater that's been showing flicks since 1950 and is one of the few original outdoor screens left in the nation.

Another attraction is the **Western Historic Trails Center**, 3434 Richard Downing Avenue, (712) 366-4900, just south of the South 24th Street exit of I-80. The facility honors the major trails that have crossed this region—Lewis

A portion of the 63-mile Wabash Trace Nature Trail

and Clark, Pioneer-Mormon, California and Oregon—as well as more modern "trails" such as the Lincoln Highway and the interstates. Of particular note are the entry's paver stones engraved with famous names often associated with the Old West. Alongside the walk is a wall of polished stone that's cut to show a cross-section of the terrain stretching from the Mississippi River near St. Louis to the Pacific Ocean. The center has an **Iowa Welcome Center** and a gift shop. Outside, a trail leads through woods and wildflowers to a riverside perch.

(Just a note here about a future development in Council Bluffs that will occur near the Western Historic Trails Center, at the western junction of I-80 and I-29. Called the Mid-American Recreation and Convention Complex, this $114 million project will have a 7,500-seat sports arena, conference center, indoor aquatic park, hotels, and restaurants. So watch for this to develop in the upcoming years.)

East of Lake Manawa, about a half-mile south of the junction of Highways 92 and 275 and near the Iowa School for the Deaf, is the northern trailhead of the **Wabash Trace Nature Trail**. Once a route for the Wabash Railroad, the trail is now used by hikers, rollerbladers, and bicycling enthusiasts (along with equestrians on some designated segments). The longest hike-bike trail in Iowa, the Wabash ends at the Missouri border 63 miles to the southeast after traversing fields, woodlands, hills, and valleys, crossing various rivers and streams on trestles, and passing through several small communities. Plans exist to connect the Wabash with the hike-bike trail that links Lake Manawa State Park and the Western Historic Trails Center. For information about the Wabash, contact one of the city's bike shops: **Endless Trail Bike Shop**, 506 S. Main, (712) 322-9760; **True Wheel Cycling and Fitness**, 120 W. Broadway, (712) 328-0767; or **Extreme Wheels**, 1851 Madison, (712) 388-0800, which also rents in-line skates.

Just north of Lake Manawa and close to the western junction of I-29 and I-80 are the city's three casinos. Two of them are **Harrah's** (formerly Harvey's), 1 Harvey's Boulevard, off the 9th Avenue exit of I-29, (712) 329-6000; and **Ameristar**, 2200 River Road, off the Nebraska Avenue exit of I-29, (712) 328-8888. Both have large hotel/convention center complexes and restaurants with live entertainment. They also have casinos, which are located on riverboats that ply the Missouri River on summer mornings. The third casino, **Bluffs Run**, 2701 23rd Avenue, (712) 323-2500, which also has slots, restaurants, and an RV park, has a racetrack that features greyhound races every day except Monday.

Council Bluffs also has some of the great outdoors within its city limits. Atop a ridge of the Loess Hills overlooking the Council Bluffs-Omaha metro area is **Fairmont Park** (at the top of Park Avenue), which has playground equipment and trails that wind through wooded scenery. **The Narrows Park** (on River Road North, which is best reached by going north at the 25th Street exit of I-29) is alongside the Missouri, putting you practically at water level with one of our nation's more famous waterways. Some people come just to kick back, picnic, and watch the water glide by and others use it as a starting point to ride bikes or hike the levee that surrounds the western part of the city. And then there's **Big Lake Park** (just east of the 16th Street/I-29 interchange)

Artifacts from the *Bertrand* steamboat on display at the DeSoto National Wildlife Refuge where Canada geese and duck favor a lake and a nearby marsh. For information on these and other Council Bluffs parks, contact the city's Parks Department at (712) 328-4650.

That just about wraps up your visit to Council Bluffs but if you want a good overview of the city, check out two places in particular. One is the **Lincoln Monument.** On a bluff just north of the downtown area (at the west end of Lafayette Avenue and not far from the "Black Angel"), this brick platform is where Abraham Lincoln stood in 1859 and foresaw the nation's first transcontinental railroad. The other is the **Lewis and Clark Monument** (go north on 8th Street and follow the signs), which is on the north edge of town near Big Lake Park. Although the explorers did not actually visit this site, the plaza that overlooks the wide valley of the Missouri River nevertheless commemorates their passage, which forever changed the United States.

SIDE TRIP

To the North

North of Council Bluffs lie several attractions. One that's very popular is the **Hitchcock Nature Area**, about five miles north of the community of Crescent on Highway 183, (712) 545-3283. Located in the Loess Hills about 20 minutes north of downtown CB, Hitchcock has a limited nature center (due to expand in the next few years) explaining these unique hills and the Pottawattamie County Conservation Board, (712) 328-5638, often hosts educational programs here for all ages. Paths, including a handicapped accessible boardwalk, lead through woodlands and prairie. A quiet place to stroll and watch the different wildlife of the region throughout the seasons, Hitchcock is also where one can enjoy cross-country skiing and tubing down an old tractor trail.

A few miles south of Hitchcock is **Mount Crescent Ski Area**; main entry is off Highway 183, north of Crescent, (712) 545-3850. Sure, some people joke about downhill skiing in Iowa but uncounted skiers have learned their moves here and continue to enjoy the slopes, which range from novice to expert. Snowboarders and tubers have their own runs and a lodge has refreshments, equipment, and lessons.

North of Hitchcock is the community of Missouri Valley, home of another **Iowa Welcome Center**, about three miles east of town on Highway 30, (712) 642-2114, which is part of a complex encompassing a gift shop with Iowa-made items and the **Harrison County Historical Village**. A roadside attraction from years ago, the village remains up to date with a modern museum and interpreters who tell the history of log cabins, a store, a church, and a one-room school that were once in other parts of the county.

West of Missouri Valley is **DeSoto National Wildlife Refuge**, about five miles west of I-29 at the Highway 30 exit, (712) 642-4121. This is a great place to watch up to half a million snow geese—plus other waterfowl, hawks, and eagles—that pause here during their annual fall migration and can be viewed from the comfort of the lakeside galleries in the visitor center. The refuge also has the cargo of a riverboat that sank in the Missouri more than a century ago. Taking supplies to the Montana gold fields, the sternwheeler *Bertrand* hit a snag on April 1, 1865, and slowly sank without loss of life. However, most of its cargo was claimed—and preserved—by the mud at the bottom of the river. Thus, when salvagers found the boat in 1965, they opened a window on the everyday items of a century before. Now, you can walk along the glass walls of a climate-controlled room and examine everything from hundreds of pickaxes and shovels destined for the minefields to gleaming kerosene lanterns, brass door knobs, fancy fabrics, bottles of various food stuffs, and more.

To see what the Missouri River was like before it became a riprap-lined race-way, you should visit an adjunct of DeSoto Refuge called **Boyer Chute**. As the snow geese fly, it's just across the river from the main body of DeSoto, but you must drive 18 miles to reach this wonderful waterway edged with trees and prairie. Six miles of trail lace the grounds and there are no amenities here other than pit toilets. To reach Boyer Chute, drive five miles west to Blair, Nebraska, from DeSoto's entrance on Highway 30, then south on Highway 75 to the community of Fort Calhoun. Follow the signs to Fort Atkinson, which also lead to Boyer Chute.

Here's a final historical note: These bottomlands of the Missouri River are approximately where Lewis and Clark met with the Indians in 1804, just below the nearby bluffs on the Nebraska side of the river. That's right, this is the "Council Bluff" they described in their journals, about 20 miles upstream and on the opposite side of the river from the city now bearing that name.

As you go to and from Boyer Chute, there's no way you can miss **Fort Atkinson State Park**, open Memorial Day to Labor Day, and weekends in May, September, and October. A Nebraska State Parks permit is required, which can be purchased at the visitor center, (402) 468-5895. In the 1820s this was the nation's largest fort and the reconstruction is enhanced on the first Saturday of every summer month when reenactors bring the old fort back to life.

LODGING

Council Bluffs

Ameristar Casino Hotel, Nebraska Avenue exit on I-29, (712) 328-8888; (877) 462-7827. AAA 4-diamond facility on west edge of city. Close to interstates and Omaha with a view of the Missouri River. Four restaurants. $$$-$$$$

Harrah's Casino Hotel, 1 Harvey's Boulevard, (712) 329-6000; (800) 427-8397. West edge of the city near Omaha and interstates with a view of the Missouri River. $$$-$$$$

Settle Inn, 500 30th Avenue, (712) 366-5555; (888) 980-5555. At the Lake Manawa Power Center on the south side of the city. Theme rooms, indoor pool. $$-$$$$

Western Inn, Exit 5 on I-80, (712) 322-4499; (800) 322-1842. West side of city near Mall of the Bluffs and Council Bluffs airport. Continental breakfast, indoor pool. Near restaurants. $-$$

Missouri Valley

Days Inn, Highway 30 and I-29, (712) 642-4003. Near DeSoto National Wildlife Refuge and Loess Hills Scenic Byway. Indoor pool, continental breakfast. Restaurants nearby. $-$$$

BED AND BREAKFASTS

Council Bluffs

Historic Shea House, 309 S. 8th Street, (712) 328-1872. An 1887 Queen Anne home near downtown. Two suites. $$$$

Missouri Valley

Apple Orchard Inn, 2925 Monroe Avenue, (712) 642-2418. On Highway 30 next to Harrison County Historical Village and Iowa Welcome Center. Near Loess Hills National Scenic Byway. A 26-acre working apple orchard. Three rooms. $$-$$$

DINING

Council Bluffs

Beverlee's, 1 Harvey's Boulevard, (712) 329-4703. Atop Harrah's Casino with the best view of the area and the Omaha skyline. Contemporary American cuisine.

Diane's Deli on the Park, 105 Pearl Street, (712) 322-3354. Downtown opposite Bayliss Park. Homemade sandwiches and daily specials.

Duncan's Cafe, 501 S. Main in the Haymarket area, (712) 328-3360. Big, old-style breakfasts and lunches in a family-run cafe.

Fireside Steakhouse, 2701 23rd Avenue, (712) 323-2500. Top-of-the-line restaurant at Bluffs Run Casino with casual dining.

Great Wall Express, 502 E. Broadway, (712) 323-1541, and 900 Woodbury Avenue, (712) 323-9622. The East Broadway location is downtown and the other is near the Mall of the Bluffs. Both are primarily take-out Chinese.

Lansky's, 1131 N. Broadway, (712) 329-5400. East side of town. Sandwiches, pasta, pizza, and carryout.

Pizza Counter, 520 E. Broadway, (712) 323-7245, and 610 W. South Omaha Bridge Road, (712) 366-0593. Downtown. Small eating area. Carryout.

Runza Hut, 2146 W. Broadway, (712) 322-8935. Another fast-food place, but different. Started in Lincoln, Nebraska, this restaurant serves the East European runza—a spicy hamburger with cabbage, rolled and baked in dough.

Scott Street Pub, 25 Scott Street, (712) 328-7275. Downtown. Sports bar with tavern food.

Szechwan Chinese Restaurant, 2612 W. Broadway, (712) 325-1782. West side of town. Chinese cuisine. Seating and take-out.

Waterfront Grill, 2200 River Road, (712) 328-8888. At Ameristar Casino, the only AAA 4-Diamond casino in the nation.

Crescent

Iowa Feed & Grain Company, Exit 66 on I-29, (712) 545-3190. North of Council Bluffs on I-29. Good meals and specials.

Pink Poodle, 633 Old Lincoln Highway, (712) 545-3744. In the middle of the small town of Crescent up Highway 183, about six miles north of Council Bluffs. Steaks and prime rib.

INFORMATION

Council Bluffs Convention and Visitors Bureau, 7 N. 6th Street, Council Bluffs, IA 51503, (712) 325-1000; (800) 228-6878. www.councilbluffsiowa.com

Harrison County Historical Village and Welcome Center, 2931 Monroe Avenue, Missouri Valley, IA 51555, (712) 642-2114.

Western Iowa Tourism Region, 103 N. 3rd., Red Oak, IA 51566, (712) 623-4232; (888) 623-4232. www.traveliowa.org

Chapter 6

Omaha:
Right Next Door

Now you're probably wondering why Omaha, Nebraska, is in a book about Iowa.

The answer is simple: not mentioning Omaha is like ignoring an elephant standing next to you. With a population approaching half a million people, Omaha is the largest metropolitan area in or abutting Iowa. Because of its size, Omaha deserves a guidebook all by itself, but you'll have to do with an abbreviated version here.

Downtown

A good place to start your visit to Omaha is where it all began—at the Missouri River—and head west from there. At Omaha's eastern edge is the **Heartland of America Park**, an urban park at 8th and Douglas Streets. From its parking lot under the I-480 bridge, walk up the hill and then go left (east) onto a paved trail that leads to a small platform overlooking the Missouri. The view is pretty basic: some pleasure boats and the trees and a casino on the Iowa side of the river, but you're standing where Omaha began. Now, turn your back on the river and start walking toward the city you see spread out before you.

As you walk along the lake in the park, you have the best view of Omaha's downtown skyline, framed by the lake in the foreground and accented by the lake's fountain, which puts on colorful light displays at night. A tour boat takes visitors around the lake for a nominal fee. Also, the pavilions and the park are the sites on some summer weekends of concerts and other events.

In the distance is the city's tallest building which is also its newest, the First National Center, to be completed in 2002. Just to the left of it is the Woodmen of the World Tower, which was the city's tallest building for more than three decades. Closer, on the opposite side of the lake, those low red-brick buildings are the headquarters for ConAgra, the nation's second-largest food processor.

Fountain at Heartland of America Park, downtown Omaha

Though they look like they're part of the park, they're not, so be respectful of that private property.

Tip: You might want to forgo returning to your vehicle and just keep walking, primarily because parking near the park is easier than in some of the areas you're about to visit.

When you exit the park on its west end, take the right-hand path that leads to a pedestrian bridge across 9th Street to the **Gene Leahy Mall** (bounded by 9th, 14th, Douglas, and Farnum Streets). Here, a waterway passes through a five-block-long mix of concrete steps, stones, grassy slopes, gardens, sidewalks, sculptures, and trees to end at an amphitheater near the Omaha Public Library. Just past 10th Street and around the far side of the elegant, old, white Burlington Building, two huge metal slides built into the side of a hill are a hit with kids (and plenty of adults too), especially those armed with wax paper to make them really fly.

Walk the length of the mall if you want but return to 11th Street and head south two blocks to Howard Street, the heart of Omaha's most-visited attraction, the **Old Market**. A cluster of old brick warehouses a century ago, the area was revitalized in the 1960s and is now a menagerie of restaurants, pubs with live music, clothing stores, art galleries, and shops that offer everything from year-round Christmas items and kites to music CDs and Persian rugs. On pleasant evenings, it's nice to sit outside some of the eateries and watch the world go by, including the horse-drawn carriages that provide rides through the area and along the Gene Leahy Mall. Parking can be difficult here, especially on weekend evenings.

Tip: Parking spaces can usually be found at the lot at the southwest corner of 10th and Jackson Streets. This may sound odd but a good time to visit the Old Market can be determined by looking at the schedule of the University of Nebraska football team. If the Cornhuskers are playing an evening game that's televised, the Old Market is virtually yours because so many fans are glued to their TV sets.

At 10th Street, go south again up the long viaduct and you'll reach a large, white, art deco building that was the Union Pacific Depot. Restored to its original splendor, the depot is now the **Durham Western Heritage Museum**, 801 S. 10th Street, (402) 444-5071; admission. Permanent displays tell the histories of the city and its railroads. Kids, including the grown ones, love to walk through the posh private passenger cars that belong to the Union Pacific. One exhibit that should not be overlooked is the Byron Reed Coin Collection. Valued at $7 million, it's known mostly for its coins, including the rarest of the rare, such as one of the original eight U.S. silver dollars minted in 1804. The collection also has an impressive array of important documents, maps, autographs, and manuscripts. Traveling exhibits in the museum have ranged from dragons and Western lore to Princess Diana's dresses.

For a bit of seagoing history—that's right, here in the landlocked Midwest—turn around on 10th Street and go north, crossing Dodge Street and following the signs to Eppley Field, Omaha's main airport. On the way, note the turnoff to **Freedom Park**, 2497 Freedom Park Road, (402) 345-1959; admission. There you will find a World War II minesweeper called the USS *Hazard* (the largest warship to ever travel up the nation's inland waterways), a submarine, and a landing craft. The first two are displayed on land, while the landing craft, also used in World War II, rests in the Missouri River. All are open to visitors, and the visitors center has more displays, along with several outside exhibits of aircraft and naval armament.

Now it's time to return downtown, where you'll turn west on Dodge Street for a stop at the **Joslyn Art Museum**, 2200 Dodge Street, (402) 342-3300; admission.

With an extra set of galleries built in the 1990s, the Joslyn has been able to host large exhibits, including one about the wonders of ancient

Interior of the Durham Western Heritage Museum

55

Egypt and a collection of colorful works by glass artist Dale Chihuly. Works in the permanent collection range from the Old Masters to contemporary creations but you should really zero in on the art of the American West, the Joslyn's forte. The museum has the largest collection of works by Swiss artist Karl Bodmer, who delineated the scenes and inhabitants of the Upper Midwest in the 1830s. Other famous artists whose portrayals of the American West hang in the Joslyn include Thomas Hart Benton, Grant Wood, Frederick Remington, and Alfred Jacob Miller. Besides a gift shop, the Joslyn also has a fine cafeteria with seating in a large atrium between the original and new galleries.

Tip: The museum opens its doors free to the public from 10 a.m. to noon every Saturday.

Go West

After visiting the Joslyn, go west on Dodge again for a long jaunt of 108 blocks (yes, you've retrieved your car by now). As you pass 132nd Street, follow the signs for **Boys Town**, (402) 498-1140, the home for boys started in the 1930s by Father Edward Flanagan and made famous in the movie of the same name. In its early years, miles of open land separated Boys Town from Omaha, but urban sprawl now encases the campus, which officially changed its named to Girls and Boys Town in August 2000 because 60 percent of its youngsters are girls. The best way to learn about this place is to stop at the visitors center but also meander down a nearby lane to find the statue of one boy carrying a smaller one on his back with the inscription below: "He ain't heavy, he's my brother."

. . . and South

You're at the west end of your Omaha tour, so head east on Dodge until you reach I-680. Go south, then east on I-80. In less than 10 miles you'll reach Exit 454 where you take the 13th Street northbound ramp. Once on 13th Street go north to Bancroft Street and take a right. Follow that all the way to the end of Bancroft where you'll enter the **Omaha Botanical Gardens**, 100 Bancroft Street, (402) 346-4002. What began as a small effort years ago has blossomed into a very beautiful place that's just finishing a $16 million expansion, which includes a wonderful visitors center. As one might imagine, the grounds are loaded with gardens of all types, featuring colorful flowers to shade-loving hostas and everything in between.

Now it's time to go to **Henry Doorly Zoo**, 3701 S. 10th Street, (402) 733-8401; admission. Because of the one-way streets here, it's not as close as you might think. Return to 13th Street from the gardens and go south. After passing Rosenblatt Stadium (more about that site in a moment), turn left at Bert Murphy Drive, which curves around to put you right at the entrance to the zoo. Parking might be easier if you use Rosenblatt's Stadium's parking lot, just west of the zoo entrance. (And note that if you want to visit the zoo during the

Tunnel through the aquarium at the Henry Doorly Zoo

College World Series in early June, you might as well use a hot-air balloon because parking spots will be hard to come by. Plan for another weekend.)

As you approach the main gate of this nationally ranked zoo you'll see a gigantic, geodesic dome. Scheduled to open in April 2002, it will house the world's largest indoor desert. When the project is complete, it will feature seemingly barren landscapes that are actually alive with various creatures surviving in some of the harshest conditions in the world. An additional treat, not yet highly publicized, is that the world's largest nocturnal exhibit, built under the desert exhibit, will open in 2003.

Also in the zoo is another superlative, the world's largest indoor jungle. Featuring habitats of Asia, Africa, and South America, the Lied Jungle requires you to watch where you walk because golden marmosets, bats, iguanas, and colorful birds may cross your path from time to time. Other animals such as river otters, pygmy hippos, monkeys, and spotted leopards are in safe enclosures. Penguins will delight you in the Walter and Suzanne Scott Aquarium, where you walk though a long glass tunnel that affords an underwater look at the world of a coral reef. Large rays and sharks pass over your head.

After all this, don't overlook other parts of the zoo: its large cat house (as in large lions, tigers, and leopards), walk-through aviary, 3/4-scale steam train, IMAX Theater and various animals ranging from flamingos and sea lions to elephants and gazelles. It's easy to spend most of a day here.

Tips: If your family might visit the zoo more than once a year (it's open year-round), consider buying a family pass. It may be cheaper than paying two rounds of gate admissions and is good for discounted tickets at the zoo's IMAX Theater and the Wildlife Safari Park about 35 minutes to the west on I-80.

Enter the zoo about 4 p.m. Nothing's cheaper but there are fewer visitors and you can stay on the grounds until dusk. If you get into the jungle before its doors close at 6 p.m. you can sometimes be the only visitors there and, because many of the animals know it's feeding time, they are easier to see.

Throughout much of the baseball season, **Rosenblatt Stadium**, 13th Street and Bert Murphy Drive, is home to the Omaha Royals, (402) 734-2550, a Triple-A farm team of the Kansas City Royals. If you're unhappy with big-league prices, then visit a baseball stadium like this where everything's more reasonably priced and you can be closer to the action.

The break in the Royals' summer season occurs for ten days each June, when Rosenblatt hosts the College World Series, (402) 554-4404, the second largest NCAA Division I event after the Final Four of college basketball. The World Series tickets are hard to get sometimes but are worth the effort, especially for the championship game. Similarly, expect difficulty in finding accommodations during this time.

To wrap up this tour, head farther south on 13th Street to Bellevue Boulevard, which is just across the Omaha city limits in neighboring Bellevue. Continue down the boulevard until you arrive at the entrance to **Fontenelle Forest**, 1111 Bellevue Boulevard N, (402) 731-3140; admission. A brand new visitors center at the head of the trails in the upland forest area explains the history of the forest and gives a good understanding of the region's flora and fauna. A few miles away and accessible by car down paved and gravel roads is the forest's wetlands nature center, on the floodplain of the Missouri River. About 17 miles of trails—including about two miles of handicapped-accessible boardwalks—lead through this 1,311-acre preserve and one trail leads past the site of an 1830s trading post that gave birth to Bellevue, Nebraska's oldest city.

SIDE TRIP

This side trip is easy and well worth the extra effort. Go west on I-80 to Exit 426, where three top-notch attractions are found about 30 miles from downtown Omaha.

Overlooking the Platte River, **Mahoney State Park**, (402) 944-2523, may be one of the youngest in Nebraska's state park system, but it's been drawing more visitors than any other state park in the past few years. That's because it's within a 30-40 minute drive of Nebraska's most populous areas and it has great amenities—hiking trails, horseback rides, modern housekeeping cabins, a large lodge with restaurant and convention facilities, swimming complex, miniature golf, and more. The only drawback is that you cannot spend only a Friday or a Saturday night at the cabins; you must stay both. Only during the rest of the

One of more than 30 aircraft on display at the Strategic Air and Space Museum, southwest of Omaha

week can you reserve just one night. A Nebraska parks permit is required; it can be purchased at the entrance.

Next door to the park is the **Strategic Air and Space Museum**, (800) 358-5029; admission, which tells the story of America's prime peacekeeping force, the Strategic Air Command. Two large galleries house about three-dozen aircraft; the third gallery features aircraft being restored, a gift shop, snack bar, library, and theaters. Among the aircraft are a World War II B-17 Flying Fortress, a rare F-85 Goblin parasite fighter, the large 10-engine B-36, and the high-flying SR-71 Blackbird spy plane. There are also a Soviet-built MiG-21 fighter and a British Royal Air Force Vulcan bomber among other airplanes.

Also at Exit 426 is **Henry Doorly Zoo's Wildlife Safari Park**, (402) 944-9453; admission, a 360-acre drive-through park populated by wildlife that have inhabited Nebraska for years. It is easy to spot the larger animals, such as buffalo, white-tailed deer, pronghorn antelope, and elk, but the smaller species require patience and a keen eye.

LODGING

Downtown

Best Western Redick Plaza Hotel, 1504 Harney, (402) 342-1500; (888) 342-5339. Art deco furnishings. Near Orpheum Theater. Restaurant and lounge. $$$$

Doubletree Downtown Hotel, 1616 Dodge, (402) 346-7600; (800) 222-8733. Near federal offices, banks, and Civic Auditorium. Indoor pool, restaurant, lounge. $$$$

Embassy Suites Downtown, 555 S. 10th Street, (402) 346-9000; (800) 362-2779. Close to the Old Market and Durham Western Heritage Museum. Indoor pool, complimentary breakfast, restaurant. $$$$

Hilton Garden Inn, S. 10th Street between Dodge and Douglas Streets, (800) 445-8667. Between the Old Market and the soon-to-be-completed Omaha convention center, this Hilton is to open in early 2002. Indoor pool. Small casual breakfast restaurant. $$$$

Holiday Inn Express, 3001 Chicago, (402) 345-2222; (800) 465-4329. On the west edge of downtown, near the Joslyn Art Museum, midtown Omaha and I-480. Complimentary breakfast. $$

Courtyard by Marriott, 101 S. 10th Street, (402) 346-2200; (800) 321-2211. Former warehouses converted into a classy hotel. Close to Gene Leahy Mall, Heartland of American Park and the Old Market. Indoor pool, restaurant, lounge. $$$$

Sheraton Omaha Hotel, 1615 Howard, (402) 231-6000; (800) 325-3535. Sited in a historic hotel with a courtyard and near the Orpheum Theater. Restaurant and pub. $$$$

South of Downtown
Comfort Inn at the Zoo, 2920 S. 13th Court, (402) 342-8000; (800) 228-5150. Closest accommodations to Rosenblatt Stadium and Henry Doorly Zoo. Within walking distance of the College World Series. $

Airport Area
Wingate Inn-Omaha Airport, 1201 Avenue H, (712) 347-6595; (800) 228-1000. Near Eppley Airfield and downtown. Indoor pool, continental breakfast. $$-$$$

Bellevue
Settle Inn & Suites, 2105 Pratt Road, (402) 292-1155; (800) 218-9602. Near major highways, Offutt AFB, sites in Bellevue and 6 miles from Rosenblatt Stadium and Henry Doorly Zoo. Complimentary breakfast, indoor pool. $$

Quality Inn & Suites, 1811 Hillcrest Drive, (402) 292-3800; (800) 228-5151. Rooms around an indoor courtyard with pool. Near Offutt AFB and 6 miles from Rosenblatt Stadium and Henry Doorly Zoo. Restaurant, lounge. $$

DINING

Old Market

Butsy Le Doux's, 1014 Howard Street, (402) 346-5100. A hard name to handle but great Creole food.

French Café, 1017 Howard Street, (402) 341-3547. Black and white decor with continental meals.

Indian Oven, 1010 Howard Street, (402) 342-4856. Indian Tandoori cuisine in East Indian decor. Sidewalk tables in pleasant weather.

M's Pub, 422 S. 11th Street, (402) 342-2550. A tight place with a walk-around bar. Continental cuisine. Sidewalk tables in pleasant weather.

Omaha Prime, 415 S. 10th Street, (402) 341-7040. Upscale steakhouse. Everything's à la carte.

Tamam, 1009 Farnum Street, (402) 344-2722. American and Mideastern cuisines with vegetarian, beef, chicken, lamb, and seafood dishes.

Upstream Brewing Company, 514 S. 11th Street, (402) 344-0200. Brew pub and restaurant with walk-around "Cheers"-type bar. Billiards room.

Downtown

Flatiron Café, 1722 Street Mary's Avenue, (402) 344-3040. In the unique triangular Flatiron Building. Upscale New American meals.

Dixie Quicks Luncheonette, Inc., 103 S. 15th Street, (402) 346-3549. Southern-style cooking.

Lo Sol Mio Ristorante Italiano, 3001 S. 32nd Avenue, (402) 345-5656. Some say this is the finest Italian dining in Omaha.

Maxine's, 1616 Dodge Street, (402) 346-7600. On top the Doubletree Hotel. Panoramic views.

South of Downtown

Bohemian Café, 1406 S. 13th Street, (402) 342-9838. Offering American and Czechoslovakian meals since the 1920s. Live accordion music on Friday and Saturday evenings.

Joe Tess', 5424 S. 24th Street, (402) 731-7278. Fresh seafood.

Johnny's Café, 4702 S. 27th Street, (402) 731-4774. Omaha's original steakhouse.

West Omaha

Center Street Cafe Espresso, 3522 Center Street, (402) 346-8680. Home-made soups and bread for sandwiches, muffins.

Charlie's on the Lake, 4150 S. 144th Street, (402) 894-9411. Fresh seafood.

Gallaghers, 10730 Pacific Street (in Shaker Place Mall), (402) 393-1421. Elegant dining specializing in Cajun.

Gorat's, 4917 Center, (402) 551-3733. Longtime steakhouse with good reputation.

Imperial Palace, 11201 Davenport Street, (402) 330-3888. Chinese cuisine. This restaurant that's just southwest of I-680 and Dodge looks like it came directly from China.

L'Orient, 11036 Elm Street, (402) 391-2021. Rockbrook Shopping Center. Asian-American cuisine.

McKenna's Blues, Booze and BBQ, 7425 Pacific Street, (402) 393-7427. The name says it all.

Bellevue

Amarillo BBQ, 303 N. Fort Crook Road, (402) 291-7495. Texas-style BBQ. Unpretentious on the outside; Texas outback interior.

Edelweiss German Restaurant, 2211 Capehart Road, (402) 291-3090. Just west of Offutt AFB. German cuisine.

Nettie's Fine Mexican Food, 7110 Railroad Avenue (402) 733-3359. Home-made chili, chips, beef, and chicken dishes.

Siam Cuisine, 11796 S. 25th Street, (402) 292-7215. West of Offutt AFB. Thai cuisine.

Stella's, 106 Galvin Road South, (402) 291-6088. Neighborhood lounge known for the metro area's best hamburgers and cheeseburgers.

INFORMATION

Greater Omaha Convention and Visitors Bureau, 6800 Mercy Road, Suite 202, Omaha, NE 68106, (402) 444-4660; (800) 332-1819; www.visitomaha.com

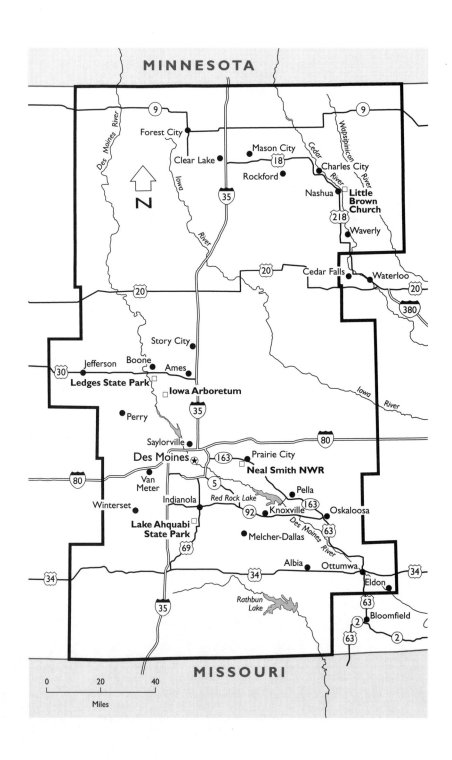

MINNESOTA

9

Forest City

Clear Lake ● ● Mason City

Rockford ●

18

Charles City □
Nashua □ **Little Brown Church**

35

218

Waverly ●

N

20

Cedar Falls ● Waterloo ●

20

380

30

Story City ●

Jefferson ● Boone ● Ames ●

Ledges State Park □

□ **Iowa Arboretum**

35

Perry ●

Saylorville ●

80

Des Moines ⊛

163

Prairie City ●
□ **Neal Smith NWR**

80

Van Meter ●

5

Pella ●

Winterset ● Indianola ● *Red Rock Lake*

92

Knoxville ● 163 Oskaloosa ●

Lake Ahquabi State Park □

69

Melcher-Dallas ●

63

Albia ● Ottumwa ●

34

34

35

Rathbun Lake

Eldon ●

63

2 Bloomfield ●

63

2

MISSOURI

0   20   40

Miles

Section II

Central Iowa
In the Middle of It All

Chapter 7

Mason City and Clear Lake: The Music Man and the *Lady of the Lake*

The Mason City-Clear Lake region is a wonderful area to visit. It may be due to the architecture of Mason City, its riverside park, the waters of Clear Lake itself, or any of the other charming qualities about this section of north-central Iowa. Visit and decide for yourself. Even though the two towns are relatively close to each other—10 miles apart—it's best to describe them separately.

Mason City

For this tour, approach Mason City from I-35, taking Exit 194. New visitors might think about taking Exit 190, but they shouldn't. That leads to the new four-lane, eastbound segment of Highway 18, which is more of a bypass south of the city.

Instead, take Exit 194, which leads to Highway 122, another four-lane road that had been the main entry to Mason City until the new segment of Highway 18 was built.

First-time visitors, now at the bottom of the exit ramp, may wonder, "Where's the city?" Well, it's nine miles to the east. So, let's get going.

Your first stop is the **Kinney Pioneer Museum**, Highway 122, (641) 423-1258; admission, which is very visible at the turnoff to the Mason City Airport. This private museum has rooms decorated to look like they did a century ago, including a doctor's office, a dentist's office, a sweet shop, and the bedroom and parlor of a private residence. Collections of fossils and dolls are here along with four antique autos including the nation's sole surviving Colby Car, the last of 900 made in Mason City between 1911 and 1914. New to the museum is a former studio from KGLO radio, where some broadcasts will still originate from time to time. Outside are a one-room schoolhouse, log cabin, 1912 black-smith shop, and a wooden jail from nearby Rockwell.

Continue toward Mason City on Highway 122, which becomes 6th Street, a one-way heading east until you reach South Federal Way, which is also Highway 65. Here, turn left (north) and cross Willow Creek where the road swerves to go around the South Bridge Mall, the city's main retail center.

By now you should see the Music Man Square. It's impressive and you will want to visit it but hold off for a bit. Take a right on 1st Street SE for a couple blocks to S. Pennsylvania Avenue where you take a left. In about the middle of the block is the **Meredith Willson Boyhood Home**, 314 S. Pennsylvania Avenue, (641) 423-3534; open May-October, Thursday-Sunday, 1-4 p.m., other times by appointment by calling (641) 424-0700; admission. This is where the composer of "The Music Man" was born and spent his early years, acquiring a taste for small town living that he immortalized for millions of people to enjoy through his hit musical. Inside, the 1895 house is presented like it would have looked when young Willson lived there almost a century ago.

Now you can go next door to **Music Man Square**, 308 S. Pennsylvania Avenue, (641) 424-2852 and (800) 228-6262; admission. This is a new $10 million multifaceted center that was completed in the summer of 2001. Those who know the movie *The Music Man* may feel very familiar with the entry; that's because it is the Warner Brothers set that was used in the film. There's a place for barbershop quartets, children to play and a reunion hall that resembles an old high school. And if the kids want to try out their voices, a recording studio is waiting just for them.

The Stockman House in Mason City

If you want more of Meredith Willson, go south to 2nd Street SE, turn left (east), and follow it two blocks where you must turn north. Park and hop out for a walk on the **Meredith Willson/Music Man Footbridge**, a pedestrian walkway that spans Rock Glen, a beautiful rocky gorge that flanks Willow Creek as it cuts through the city. Some people prefer to turn around on the far side and just walk back across the bridge but you might want to take the long way back to your car and do some sightseeing along the way, always bearing left when you meet another road. You'll need about 15-20 minutes if you don't stop.

For those who are walking, you'll pass through a very nice residential area until you reach E. State Street where you should go left to cross a street bridge over Willow Creek again. However, instead of turning left at Rock Glen to return to your starting point on this walking tour, take a right onto 1st Street NE.

Within sight of the intersection is the **Stockman House**, 530 1st Street NE, (641) 421-3666; admission. A two-story wood frame and cement stucco house with one-story wings, this Prairie-style structure was the first house Frank Lloyd Wright designed in Iowa (early in his career in 1908). It spawned a cluster of similarly designed houses in the region by other Prairie-style architects, including William Drummond, Barry Byrne, and Walter Burley Griffin, who did six of the homes (not to mention Canberra, the capital of Australia). These are most easily seen by walking through the adjacent **Rock Glen-Rock Crest** area, a national historic district. Please mind that, except for the Stockman House, the homes are private residences.

While on the subject of architecture, go downtown for a look at two more buildings, a buff-colored hotel and a bank that were also designed by Wright. On the southwest corner of S. Federal Avenue and W. State Street is what was called the City National Bank, which now houses a retail business on its lower floor and offices upstairs. Just to the west is the Park Inn, a former hotel that now is occupied partially by the **Mason City Convention and Visitors Bureau**, 15 W. State Street, (641) 422-1663; (800) 423-5724. Currently, neither building is really set up for visitors although you can go in some parts of them.

Tip: While at the CVB, pick up the $4 book designed to lead you on a walking tour of the city's architectural and historical sights. It's a good buy.

Now that you've had your study of architecture, check out the **Charles H. MacNider Museum**, 303 2nd Street SE, (641) 421-3666; free, the city's art museum. Housed in an English Tudor mansion near Rock Glen, the MacNider has extensive galleries for a museum in a community this size and a nice collection of artwork. What impresses visitors here is the collection of master puppeteer Bil Baird's puppets, which range from small string-controlled horses to spacecraft and larger-than-life suits that Baird used to wear.

A few blocks north of the downtown area is **Stebens Children's Theater**, 616 N. Delaware, (641) 424-9802; admission. If you have children with you, you should take in one of its productions—sung, danced, and acted by children, for children—that are staged from September through April.

If you want to go to a park, take a hike, or ride a bike for that matter, Mason City's parks are really nice quiet spots. In East Park (out on East State Street), Willow Creek meets the Winnebago River in a pretty scene. There are also plenty of trails, especially the **River City Trails** which, at last count, wander about 11 miles across the city and up north to **Lime Creek Nature Center**, 3501 Lime Creek Road, (641) 423-5309; free, also accessible by driving about two miles north of the city on Highway 65. The center has live animals and mounted specimens on display with trails that lead through prairie, forest, and wetlands.

In case you didn't bring any small wheels with you, check out **Bennetts Bikes and Fitness**, 30 E. State Street, (641) 424-4151, and **Wayne's Ski & Cycle**, 4700 4th Street SW, (641) 423-2851, which rent a variety of bikes and in-line skates or, if you're visiting in winter, cross-country skis.

Clear Lake

The best way to go to Clear Lake from Mason City is to simply reverse the way you came. Go west on Highway 122, pass under I-35, and at N. 8th Street (which is also Highway 107), take a left. Now things can get a bit dicey because the streets in Clear Lake shift near the lake itself and more than a few visitors have found themselves turned around, so pay attention.

To reach the lake, go south on N. 8th Street and turn right on Main Avenue. The street will gently bend left but stay on it and you'll be at the lake and the city park with its band shell in just a few blocks. Park anywhere you can, walk down to the free public beach, pull off your socks and shoes, and enjoy the feel of the sand between your toes—a sensation people don't often experience in Iowa. Since this is a public beach, you can take a swim here too.

Big events occur in the city park during the summer. DixieFest, one of Iowa's larger traditional jazz celebrations featuring regional performers, takes place on the last weekend in July in conjunction with Clear Lake Art Sail, which features the creations of painters, sculptors, photographers, and potters. LakeFest, the Iowa story-telling festival, also happens here, along with free concerts at 7:30 p.m. on Saturdays and 3 p.m. on Sundays from mid-June to mid-July.

Near the park's waterfront is the *Lady of the Lake*, Lakeview Drive and First Avenue N, (641) 357-2243; admission, a double-deck excursion boat that cruises around the lake on Saturday and Sunday afternoons and weekday evenings.

"That'll Be the Day . . . "

Continue up N. Shore Drive until you see the **Surf Ballroom**, 460 N. Shore Drive, (641) 357-6151. If you're unfamiliar with this place, welcome to rock 'n' roll history: this is the last place Buddy Holly, J. P. "The Big Bopper" Richardson, and Ritchie Valens played before they died in a plane crash north of the Mason

The *Lady of the Lake* at the dock on Clear Lake

City Airport on February 5, 1959. Name the tunes you want to hear and they're being played here—jazz, country, folk, bluegrass, polka, swing, big band, and, most definitely, rock. Check the schedule for what's on tap or just drop in during the day to see the place. It's filled with big band and rock 'n' roll mementos, including autographs penned on some of the walls by famous, near-famous, and soon-to-be famous artists. Tours can be arranged for a nominal fee.

There's just one more bit of history here and that's back toward downtown Clear Lake, so return down N. Shore Drive and take a left at 1st Avenue N. In four blocks you'll see the **Clear Lake Fire Museum**, 112 N. Sixth Street, (641) 357-2613; donations welcome. It's open only on weekend afternoons (now aren't you glad you bought a book about weekend trips in Iowa?). A modern building that resembles an old firehouse, the museum houses antique fire-fighting gear including a 1924 pumper and an 1883 hand-pulled hose cart.

After you've visited the museum, take a short walk down the street to where N. 6th and N. 8th Streets form a very small triangular-shaped park. You'll see something that's rather unusual: a sailboat sundial where the wooden sails point to the right time.

If you want to reflect on life, go east until you reach South 24th Street; turn south on it and go to12th Avenue S. Turn left (east) and just before you reach the interstate you'll see a small dirt road going off to the right (south). Take that to the tiny **Guardian Angel Roadside Chapel**, no phone; free. Open sunrise to sunset, this tiny chapel has been visited by thousands of people over the years and has pews, windows, and a choir rail salvaged from a nearby church.

What about going on the lake? you ask. Sure. It's Iowa's second-largest natural lake, measuring 2 ½ by 7 miles. To take advantage of these spring-fed waters, visit **Clear Lake Boats and Powersports**, 15296 Raney Drive, in PM Park, (641) 357-5293, which rents personal watercraft, pontoon boats, ski boats, fishing boats, and paddle boats as well as water skis, tubes, and wakeboards. You can watch the Clear Lake Yacht Club's regattas and races on Saturdays and Sundays.

As for fishing, you should find something here to please your palate—walleye, panfish, muskie, northern, perch, crappie, catfish, bullhead, and carp. Fishing licenses can be purchased at various shops in the area as well as the **Iowa Department of Natural Resources**, 1203 N. Shore Drive, (641) 357-3517.

For outdoor fun, there's **Clear Lake State Park**, (641) 357-4212, on the lake's southeast corner, with a sandy beach, picnic areas, and a campground. Also, **McIntosh Woods State Park**, (641) 829-3847, is across the water on the northwest shore where camping, picnicking, and a beach occupy a peninsula jutting into the lake.

SIDE TRIPS

To the North

Going west on Highway 18 out of Clear Lake, you'll meet Highway 69 going north to Forest City, about 25 miles from Clear Lake. As you approach Forest City's south side you'll notice **Winnebago Industries Visitor Center**, 1316 S. 4th Street, (641) 585-6936; (800) 643-4892; free. If the name Winnebago sounds familiar, it should. It's the name emblazoned on many RVs traveling our highways,

The Fertile Mill and dam in the town of Fertile

and this is where they've been manufactured since1958. The visitors center conducts 90-minute tours of the production plant of the world's largest RV manufacturer at 9 a.m. and 1 p.m., Monday-Friday. No tours are given on weekends.

To return to Clear Lake and Mason City, leave Forest City by going east on Highway 9. Along the way you'll see the entrance to **Pilot Knob State Park**, (641) 581-4835, a nice place to relax for awhile and hike some trails (one of the trails connects the park with Forest City in case you want to hoof or bike the four miles between the town and the park). Some say this is the second highest spot in the state. You'll certainly feel above it all in the stone observation tower that takes you higher than the trees for a look across the countryside.

Farther east, the town of **Fertile** lies south of Highway 9. If you crave additional quiet time, take 1st Street to the south, cross the Winnebago River, and turn into a small, tree-filled park that fronts the river. Across the river is the red Fertile Mill, which is privately owned and not open to the public but it and its dam make a nice backdrop for anyone visiting this park.

Once you're relaxed and want to go on, continue east on Highway 9 until you reach I-35 where you'll go south to the exits for Clear Lake and Mason City.

To the East

To begin this side trip, head east on Highway 122 out of Mason City. Eventually it will merge with Highway 18 and you'll take that four-lane highway to **Charles City**.

For tractor buffs, Charles City is where the gasoline tractor industry was born and the best place to learn about this is the **Floyd County Historical Society Museum**, 500 Gilbert Street, (641) 228-1099; admission. Among the displays is a 1913 Hart-Parr, one of the earliest gasoline-powered tractors made; they were manufactured in Charles City for many years. While in town, get a walking tour booklet from the **Chamber of Commerce**, 610 S. Grand Avenue, (641) 228-4234, so you can see some of the rich architectural heritage of this community. There are more Prairie-style houses, including one by Frank Lloyd Wright (all are private residences). Check out the **Historic Suspension Bridge** (pedestrians only), which crosses the Cedar River where Illinois Street meets Riverside Drive. Also, stop in the **Charles City Art Center**, 301 N. Jackson Street, (641) 228-6284; free, to see what's on exhibit there.

At Charles City, latch onto Highway 218 to go to Nashua, 11 miles to the south. Once there, turn east onto Highway 346. In a couple of miles, just around a gentle curve and on the left is a small brown church, but it's not an ordinary one. This is the **Little Brown Church**, (641) 435-2027; free, that people sing about, and if you're here on a weekend you might find a wedding in progress. If you do, just walk around the grounds for a while—they're pretty—and when the wedding is over, visit the inside of this little church, which was built between 1860 and 1864. What's interesting is that William S. Pitts, who wrote "The Church in the Wildwood," did so after being inspired while passing this spot—but that was *before* the church was built. Later, he revisited the scene and saw that a little brown church had indeed been built there.

Immediately adjacent to the church is **Old Bradford Pioneer Village**, (641) 435-2567; admission, which contains a grouping of agricultural equipment and more than a dozen buildings from the region, including the office of William Pitts.

Retrace your route west on Highway 346 and return to Charles City on Highway 218. There, take Highway 14 west out of town. In seven miles you'll meet Highway 147, which continues west into the small community of Rockford (population 842). Pass through the town and you'll find County Highway B47 at the west end, which will lead you to **Fossil and Prairie Park**, 1257 215th Street, (641) 756-3490; free, one mile west of town. Located alongside the Winnebago River, this is one of the richest spots in the state for finding 350-400-million-year-old marine fossils of the Devonian Period of the Paleozoic Era. Collecting fossils for personal use is permitted and it's so easy that no tools are needed—just flipping a rock with the toe of your shoe may reveal a fossil you can keep. Kids love this place. Adjacent to the fossil beds (which were first uncovered by workers mining clay for a brick works company in the 1870s) is a 50-acre native prairie where more than 100 prairie plants have been documented. A visitor center that opened in the spring of 2001 has museum-quality displays explaining the site, and a trail that leads back to Rockford passes an old quarry and beehive kilns where bricks were once made.

From the park, go west to County Highway S70 and turn north until you reach either Highway 18 or Highway 122, both of which return you to Mason City.

LODGING

Charles City
Hartwood Inn, 1312 Gilbert Street, (641) 228-4352; (800) 972-2335. South edge of town. Outdoor pool, continental breakfast. $

Lamplighter Motel, 1416 Gilbert Street, (641) 228-6711; (888) 245-5616. South edge of town. Indoor pool, continental breakfast. $

Clear Lake
AmericInn Motel, I-35 at Exit 194, (641) 357-8954; (800) 634-3444. On northeast edge of city. Indoor pool, continental breakfast. $-$$$$

Best Western Holiday Lodge, I-35 at Exit 194, (641) 357-5253; (800) 606-3552. On northeast edge of city. Indoor pool, restaurant, continental breakfast. $$

Heartland Inn, 1603 S. Shore Drive, (641) 357-5123; (800) 334-3277. On the lake near downtown. All lakefront rooms. Indoor pool, continental breakfast. Near public beach. Dock. $$$-$$$$

Park Inn, 15297 Raney Drive, (641) 357-2574. A 1922 lodge with a cottage by the week, hotel-style rooms by the night, and weekly rentals of apartments. Public park nearby. Dock, lake access, beach. Restaurant on site since 1917! $-$$

Forest City
Super 8 Motel, Highway 69 S, (641) 585-1300; (800) 800-8000. South of town. Continental breakfast. $-$$

Village Chateau Motor Inn, 1115 Highway 69 N, (641) 585-4351. North of town. Outdoor pool. $

Mason City
Country Inn & Suites, 4082 4th Street SW, (641) 423-1770; (800) 456-4000. On west edge of town on Highway 122. Rooms and suites. Indoor pool. $$-$$$$

Days Inn, 2301 4th Street SW, (641) 424-0210; (800) 329-7466. On west edge of town on Highway 122. Continental breakfast. $-$$$

Hanford Inn, 3041 4th Street SW, (641) 424-9494; (800) 424-9491. On west edge of town on Highway 122. Restaurant, indoor pool. $

Holiday Inn, 2101 4th Street SW, (641) 423-1640; (800) 859-2737. On west edge of town on Highway 122. Restaurant, indoor pool. $$-$$$$

Super 8 Motel & Suites, 3010 4th Street SW, (641) 423-8855; (800) 800-8000. On west edge of town on Highway 122. Indoor pool, continental breakfast. $-$$$$

BED AND BREAKFASTS

Charles City
Sherman House, 800 Gilbert Street, (641) 228-6831. An 1888 house overlooking the downtown and the river. Other meals beside breakfast available. Inquire about children. Four rooms. $$$$

Clear Lake
Blessing on Main, 1204 Main Avenue, (641) 357-0341. Victorian atmosphere. Close to downtown. Two rooms. $$$

Holstad B&B, 33 Sunset View Drive, (641) 357-3593. Near Surf Ballroom and lake. Bicycles available. Two rooms $-$$

Larch Pine Inn, 401 N. 3rd Street, (641) 357-7854. An 1875 Victorian home on a large wooded lot. Breakfast is served on the veranda. About a block from the lake and near the city park. Guest parlor and kitchenette. Bicycles available. Three rooms. $$-$$$

Norsk Hus By-The Shore, 3611 N. Shore Drive, (641) 357-8368. Two-BR suite on the lake. Norwegian-American atmosphere. Patio, dock. Two rooms. $$$-$$$$

North Shore House, 1519 N. Shore Drive, (641) 357-4443. One-room suite on the lake. Updated 1920s cottage with nautical theme with decks and docks. $$$$

Oakwood House, 15256 Ash Street, (641) 357-3336. New home overlooking Clear Lake. Recreation room, fireplace, dock. Three rooms. $$-$$$

Forest City
1897 Victorian House, 306 S. Clark Street, (641) 585-3613; 585-3465. Queen Anne home with antiques plus carriage house. Near shops, bike trail, restaurants. Five rooms. $$-$$$$

DINING

Clear Lake
Barrel Drive-In, 206 Highway 18 E, (641) 357-2600. Drive-in food, lunch, and dinner. Open in the summer.

Boathouse Grill, 468 N. Shore Drive, (641) 357-8688. Fine dining near the Surf Ballroom.

Ge-Jo's By-The-Lake, 12 N. 3rd Street, (641) 357-8288. Italian cuisine for lunch and dinner. Outside patio seating. On the City Square.

Half-Moon Café, 701 Buddy Holly Place, (641) 357-9339. Seafood, steaks, prime rib for lunch and dinner. Steakhouse atmosphere. Near the Surf Ballroom.

McKenna's Blues, Booze and BBQ, 444 N. Shore Drive, (641) 357-1443. The second of a chain of two—the other one is in Omaha. You can expect this place to live up to its name in a very fine way on all counts.

Park Inn, 15297 Raney Drive, (641) 357-2574. On the south side of the lake and part of a resort with a reputation for fine homemade food, daily specials, and pies. Great aromas when you walk in.

Sandbar Restaurant and Linden House Tea Room, 211 N. 4th Street, (641) 357-3733. Lunch and dinner in a quiet retreat.

Starboard Market, 310 Main Avenue, (641) 357-0660. Nice place for lunch in the downtown area. Homemade salads, soups, sandwiches, and desserts.

Mason City
4th Street Diner, 3041 4th SW at the Hanford Inn, (641) 424-9494. On the west edge of town. Diner atmosphere.

Lorados, 18 S. Federal Avenue, (641) 424-8060. Mexican cuisine in downtown area.

Max Seas Restaurant, 1828 S. Taft Avenue, (641) 424-0438. Serves seafood south of downtown.

Marjorie's Tea House, 320 S. Pennsylvania Avenue, (641) 421-8066. Tea room near Meredith Willson Boyhood Home.

Peachtree, 2101 4th SW at the Holiday Inn, (641) 423-1640. West edge of town.

Yin Yin Restaurant, 118 N. Federal Avenue, (641) 424-9039. Chinese cuisine. North of downtown.

INFORMATION

Central Iowa Tourism Region, PO Box 454, Webster City, IA 50595, (515) 832-4808; (800) 285-5842; www.iowatourism.org

Charles City Chamber of Commerce, 610 S. Grand Avenue, Charles City, IA 50616, (641) 228-4234.

Clear Lake Chamber of Commerce/Convention and Visitors Bureau, 205 Main Avenue, PO Box 188, Clear Lake, IA 50428, (641) 357-2159; (800) 285-5338; www.clearlakeia.com. This CVB also broadcasts a listing of events on AM 1200 on the radio and has recordings of events on (800) 469-LAKE.

Mason City Convention and Visitors Bureau, 15 W. State Street, Mason City, IA 50401, (641) 422-1663; (800) 423-5724; www.masoncitytourism.com

Chapter 8

Boone and Ames: A Study in Contrasts

Boone, the Railroad Town

Sitting almost in the middle of the state, Boone has been a railroad town since its birth in 1865. Thus, its largest attraction—and one of the biggest attractions in the state as well—is, fittingly, a railroad.

Located west of downtown is the **Boone and Scenic Valley Railroad**, 225 10th Street, (515) 432-4249; (800) 626-0319; admission. It began almost as a hobby for railroad enthusiasts and has blossomed into an effort that not only preserves trains from another era but entertains thousands of visitors every year. At the depot, you can board a tour train for a 15-mile round trip, or settle into the dining or dessert train, both of which travel 22 miles before they return to the station. The trains, which are often pulled on weekends by the last steam locomotive made in China, are composed of cars that date back to the 1920s and travel across two bridges that soar high above the valleys below. One is the highest interurban bridge in the nation—quite a revelation for those who think Iowa is all flat land. Ride the passenger cars if you like, but many think the caboose has the best seats on the train.

You also might want to ride the railroad's 1915 electric trolley; it travels downtown from 11 a.m. to 4:30 p.m. Saturdays and Sundays in the summer. Children under 13 ride free.

A bit closer to downtown Boone is the **Mamie Doud Eisenhower Birthplace**, 709 Carroll Street, (515) 432-1896; admission. Home to the woman who married a young army officer named Dwight D. Eisenhower, who went on to become one of the nation's best generals and best-loved presidents, the yellow frame house reflects how it looked during Mamie Doud's early years here. Inside are furnishings from her family, a small museum, gift shop, and library. Outside are Mamie's 1962 Valiant and a 1949 Chrysler she and Ike gave to one of her uncles.

Chinese-built steam locomotive at the Boone and Scenic Valley Railroad in Boone

Downtown are the **Boone County Historical Center**, 602 Story Street, (515) 432-1907, and the **Boone County Museum**, 1004 Story Street, (515) 432-6217, which, respectively, tell the stories of the county and city from prehistoric times to the present. There is also a walking tour of historic structures; maps are available at the **Boone Chamber of Commerce**, 806 7th Street, (800) 266-6312.

In addition to being home to the highest interurban railroad bridge in the nation, Boone has another superlative railroad structure—the **Kate Shelley Memorial High Bridge**, three miles west of the city on Avenue J. Nearly 2,700 feet long, it stands 185 feet above the Des Moines River, making it the longest and highest double-track railroad bridge in the U.S. Kate Shelley was 15 years old when she braved a storm to warn an oncoming train that a bridge was out and became a national heroine. Her story is told at the **Kate Shelley Railroad Museum and Park**, 1198 232nd Street in Moingona, (515) 432-1907, open Saturday and Sunday afternoons, Memorial Day–Labor Day. The site features a restored depot and a Rock Island Rocket passenger car, house items related to young Kate's life, and some railroad memorabilia. It is operated by the Boone County Historical Center near the small community of Moingona, about five miles west of Boone on Highway 30 and then a short distance to the south. Watch for directional signs.

After visiting the Kate Shelley museum, return to Highway 30, head east to where County Highway R23 (opposite Story Street, which goes north into Boone) leads south to **Ledges State Park**, 1519 250th Street, (515) 432-1852, about 3.5 miles away. A longtime favorite of visitors to central Iowa, the Ledges, as they're known locally, is where 100-foot sandstone bluffs overlook the valley

Prairie flowers at the Iowa Arboretum, south of Boone

of the Des Moines River. It's a great place to picnic, walk around on the trails or along the river, and explore a small canyon.

Not all that far from the Ledges is the **Iowa Arboretum**, 1875 Peach Avenue, outside of Madrid, (515) 795-3216; admission. If you're leaving the Ledges to go the arboretum, it might be best to get directions from a park ranger. Otherwise, the route to the arboretum is well marked by signs on Highway 30. Visiting the arboretum is worth the effort for its hundreds of types of trees, flowers, and shrubs. Trails on the 378-acre arboretum wander across open prairie and through areas heavily shaded by trees. A butterfly garden, flower gardens, and an educational center are also on the property. Guided tours can be arranged in advance.

*A*mes, the College Town

Only a short distance away is Ames, virtually a sister city of Boone. As almost any Iowan knows, this is the home of **Iowa State University** and, as most of those who've attended classes here can attest, one of the prettiest campuses found anywhere. The heart of the campus is the tall campanile that plays melodies on the hour. Near it is another landmark, **Memorial Union**, (515) 292-1111. Like the student unions of many other campuses, this one has rooms for lectures, arts and crafts studios, food service, a recreation center, and such. But unlike some others, Memorial Union has the **Maintenance Shop**, (515) 294-2772 (office); (515) 294-2969 (concert information). This cozy (200-seat) venue presents live entertainment, from locally and nationally known musicians to small stage productions, almost in your lap. Among those who have performed here are Arlo Guthrie, Leo Kottke, Muddy Waters, Smashing Pumpkins, Chick Corea, Buddy Miles, Suzanne Vega, and Taj Mahal.

The union also has hotel-style rooms on three floors to accommodate overnight guests. If this is your first stop at the university, pick up a campus map at the union's main desk.

Just outside the union is *The Four Seasons*, one of several sculptures and bas-reliefs created around the campus by famed sculptor Christian Petersen, a Danish immigrant who was artist-in-residence here for many years.

If you're interested in the history of the university, visit the **Farm House Museum**, (515) 294-7426; free. (Most students, faculty, and staff simply call this gray stucco, two-story structure, "the Farm House.") The first building erected when the campus opened as the State Agricultural College and Model Farm, the Farm House was home to various staff members, including two presidents. Now, it's maintained as it appeared in those early years.

As for visiting ISU, it's sad to say that some things never change here and finding a parking space never gets easier. The best recommendation is to use the parking ramp that's right next to Memorial Union and go from there.

Parking is a bit easier at **Iowa State Center**, a complex of buildings east of the main campus, as long as there's not a big affair happening in one of the buildings, notably the Hilton Coliseum, which hosts large collegiate sporting events. Also here is **C. Y. Stephens Theater**, the main performing arts hall for the campus, and the **Fisher Theater**, a more intimate space for smaller productions. To learn what events are happening at these buildings, contact Iowa State Center at (515) 294-3347; (877) 843-2368; www.center.iastate.edu/calendars/index.html.

Note: If you're near Fisher Theater, you might spot, on the southeast corner of Beach and Lincoln Way and almost hidden by the trees, an original marker of the Lincoln Highway, which is now Lincoln Way in Ames.

To the south of the center is Jack Trice Field and Cyclone Football Stadium. Beyond that is **Reiman Gardens**, 1407 Elwood Drive, (515) 294-4817; free, a botanical center that's been expanding and improving over the years. Besides having wetlands, herb, and rose gardens, this colorful retreat also has a children's garden, a small hardwood forest, and a horticulture learning center, plus rose trial gardens. Plans exist to expand the center by building a town and country garden, butterfly house, and a conservatory, so look for this beautiful place to grow even more.

Finally, for a different look at central Iowa, go south on Elwood, pass under Highway 30, and take Airport Road, the first street on your left (east). Go toward the airport and take a right (south) when you see a road going down toward a cluster of small hangars (if you reach the terminal, you've gone too far). You'll find yourself at the hangars of **Silent Knights**, (515) 233-5963; fee, a soaring club whose members will take you into the sky for a ride you'll never forget, because their aircraft have no engines! Excepting the powered tugs, all the aircraft are gliders. Call ahead to make arrangements.

SIDE TRIPS

To the North

Seventeen miles directly north of Ames on either Highway 69 or I-35 is **Story City**, home of the famous **Story City Antique Carousel**, 618 Broad Street, (515) 733-4214; admission. Located in North Park which is on the east side of downtown, the 1913 Hershel-Spillman carousel spins around kids of all ages on hand-carved wooden animals while tunes play from a 1936 Wurlitzer band organ. The carousel operates from noon-6 p.m., Monday, Tuesday, and Thursday; noon-9 p.m., Wednesday, Friday, Saturday, and Sunday, from Memorial Day to Labor Day; and noon-8 p.m. on weekends in May and September. Nearby, the **Story Theater/Grand Opera House**, 512 Broad Street, (515) 733-4551, is the oldest continually running theater in Iowa. You can view its majesty when movies are playing on the weekend or arrange a tour if you want to see it at another time.

To the West

By heading west out of Boone on Highway 30, you'll come to **Jefferson** in about a half hour, just south on Highway 4. The first thing here to catch your attention is the 14-story **Mahanay Bell Tower**, Wilson and E. Lincoln Way, (515) 386-2155; admission; open from 11 a.m.-4 p.m. daily, Memorial Day to Labor Day. The tower rises high above the courthouse square, located a couple blocks east of Highway 4 on E. Lincoln Way. Besides being a carillon, the tower is an observation platform with a view of central Iowa.

Reiman Gardens on the Iowa State University campus, Ames

A few blocks away is a rarity, the **Jefferson Telephone Company Museum**, 105 W. Harrison Street, (515) 386-4141; free; open from 8 a.m.-4:30 p.m. daily. Located in offices of the Jefferson Telephone Company, this is one of the few such museums in the nation. It's not a long visit but it certainly educates you about the history of telephones, and its phones, operator consoles, and switching gear show you how many ways you could reach out and call someone over the years.

Jefferson is also the northern trailhead of the **Raccoon River Valley Trail**, (515) 386-5674, which ends in the western suburbs of the Des Moines metro area, 57 miles to the southeast.

LODGING

Ames

Comfort Suites, 2609 Elwood Drive, (515) 268-8808. All suites. Fitness center, complimentary breakfast. Near Iowa State Center. $$-$$$$

Holiday Inn Gateway, Highway 30 and Elwood Drive, (515) 292-8600; (800) FOR-AMES. Large complex with landscaped gardens and waterfalls. Indoor pool, restaurant. Close to airport. Near Iowa State Center. $$$-$$$$

Howard Johnson Express Inn, Highways 69 and 30. (515) 232-8363; (800) 798-8363. Outdoor pool. $-$$

Iowa State Memorial Union, ISU campus on Lincoln Way, (515) 292-1111. Restaurant. In same building as Maintenance Shop. $-$$

Boone

American Inn, 1215 S. Story Street, (515) 432-4322. Near Highway 30. Indoor pool, restaurant, continental breakfast. $

AmeriHost Inn Boone, 1745 SE Marshall Street, (515) 432-8168; (800) 434-5800. Near Highway 30. Indoor pool, continental breakfast. $$-$$$$

BED AND BREAKFASTS

Boone

Barkley House B&B, 326 Boone Street, (515) 433-1424; (877) 376-5600. Near downtown and Mamie Doud Eisenhower House. Evening dessert and full breakfast. Four rooms. $$-$$$

Bluebird B&B, 1372 Peony Lane, (515) 432-5057. Country setting about five minutes from Boone. Two rooms. $$

Hancock House B&B, 1004 Hancock Drive, (515) 432-4089; 1915 Mission-style house. Near large city park. Three rooms. $$

DINING

Ames

Aunt Maude's, 547 Main Street, (515) 233-4136. Near downtown. Upscale. International cuisine.

Battle's Bar-B-Q, 112 Hayward Avenue, (515) 292-1670. Near campus. Barbecued meats with homemade sauces and beans.

Dutch Oven Bakery, 219 N. Duff, (515) 232-9244. Bakery with bread, pastries, soups, and sandwiches. Near downtown.

Hickory Park, 1404 S. Duff, (515) 232-8940. South end of town. Known for barbecue and ice cream specialties.

Lucullan's Italian Grill, 400 Main, (515) 232-8484. Italian cuisine in downtown area.

Mandarin-Chinese Restaurant, 415 Lincoln Way, (515) 233-5300. Chinese cuisine close to downtown.

Ruttles, 531 S. Duff, (515) 233-1952. Doo-wop atmosphere and 1950s-style food.

Shoppes on Grand Tea Room, 517 Grand, (515) 233-6010. Light lunches and desserts near downtown.

Boone

Colorado Grill, 1514 Marshall Street, (515) 433-7020. South end of town near Highway 30.

Gables and Gardens Tea Room, 721 Carroll Street, (515) 432-5930.

Tic Toc Restaurant and Flame Lounge, 716 Keeler, (515) 432-5979. Near downtown.

Story City

Cottage on Broad, 104 Broad Street, (515) 733-4376. Downtown location.

INFORMATION

Ames Convention and Visitors Bureau, 1601 Golden Aspen Drive, Suite 110, Ames, IA 50010, (515) 232-4032; (800) 288-7470; www.acvb.ames.ia.us/

Boone Chamber of Commerce, 806 7th Street, Boone, IA 50036, (515) 432-3342;(800) 266-6312; www.booneiowa.com

Chapter 9

Des Moines: Where Everything Is Capital

Des Moines may not be a huge city, but since it's the capital of Iowa there's a lot more happening here than in a comparably sized city, which makes this the longest tour of the book.

So, instead of simply proceeding from one side of the city to the other, as we do in the other chapters, we're going to divide Des Moines into seven manageable sections: Government of the People, History of the People, Family Fun, Sporting People, Blooming Things, Special Districts, and Evening Time. Some items will overlap and notes will be included to direct you to the other sections when that occurs.

Government of the People

One of the biggest structures to catch your eye as you approach the downtown area is that building with the big golden dome that shimmers in the sunlight. You have it right, that's the **State Capitol**, E. 9th Street and Grand Avenue, (515) 281-5591; free. The easiest way to approach it is to leave I-235 at the E. 6th exit, go south to Grand Avenue and turn left (east) to go toward the Capitol. There are other ways but this one gives perhaps the grandest approach of the Capitol's main facade, which is dominated by the 80-foot-diameter main dome that rises 275 feet above the ground and cost $400,000 to regild in the late 1990s. About 100 ounces of gold leaf that is 1/250,000 of an inch thin was used to cover the dome.

Completed at a cost of nearly $3 million in 1886 after 15 years of construction, the Capitol is graced by small copper-topped domes with gold trim at the four corners of the building. Set upon a hill east of downtown, this massive building certainly casts its presence over the city.

Des Moines's bustling downtown

You can arrange guided tours that last about 40 minutes or walk through the building on your own. Walk up the front steps and you're on the first floor, containing the offices of the governor, lieutenant governor, and several members of the governor's cabinet as well as the Supreme Court chamber, each very impressive in its own right. At the center of the floor, where you can look up at the clouds painted on the interior of the massive dome high above, are display cases holding flags carried—and captured—by many Iowa units that fought in various wars. There also are dolls dressed in the inaugural gowns of Iowa's First Ladies. Nearby is a large scale model of the USS Iowa and on the east side of the floor is the Grand Staircase, made of gleaming wood and granite steps, which leads to the other floors.

On the second floor are the chambers of the House of Representatives and the Senate. The former has warm tones and a chandelier with more than 5,000 crystals in it while the latter has a decor that's cooler in appearance and brass chandeliers made in France. You can ascend to the visitors' galleries via circular staircases or, if the legislators are not in session, visit the main floor of the chambers themselves.

Also on the second floor is the beautiful Iowa State Law Library. It's marked by four ornamental balconies bearing more than 20,000 books that are reached by open circular staircases. Best of all, the library isn't restricted to the justices—you're welcome there too.

At the center of the second floor is a staircase that winds its way up to a balcony where you can get a good look at the lunettes and statues arrayed around the interior of the dome, as well as an excellent bird's eye view of the floors below. If you don't like heights, this isn't a place for you.

Outside the Capitol are a number of monuments and statues. At the west entrance is the best-known one, a statue of Abraham Lincoln with his son, Tad, the only statue of a president in a family situation. Other monuments and statues, most located in a park-like setting directly south of the Capitol, honor Civil War soldiers and sailors, those who fought in Korea and Vietnam (that's the shiny, curved wall that reflects the Capitol), peace officers, Christopher Columbus, and a sister-state friendship program with Yamanashi prefecture in Japan. Miniature replicas of the Statue of Liberty and Liberty Bell are in the park too.

East of the Capitol is the largest memorial, the **World War II Memorial Plaza**. Focused around a large torch, the memorial has paving stones with the names of famous battles while adjacent panels describe the U.S. involvement in that war.

Down the hill to the west, close enough that you can walk to it, is the **Iowa Historical Building**, 600 E. Locust, (515) 281-5111; free. An orderly assembly of what looks like large granite boxes with glass panels, this museum has collections and displays depicting pre-recorded times as well as the written history of Iowa. In the main lobby, three antique, historic aircraft hang suspended above your head, while in galleries you can examine Native American artifacts, feel the tight confines of a coal mine, see how horses helped develop Iowa's agriculture and learn why so many insurance companies have established their headquarters in the Hawkeye State. Another exhibit called Patten's Neighborhood looks at the lives of African-Americans in Iowa from the 1920s to the 1960s. The newest exhibit, which opened in late 2000, focuses on little-known and well-known items, from aircraft to zippers, that changed the lives of Iowans in the past century. The museum has a gift shop and a cafeteria with a terrace.

The Iowa State Capitol, Des Moines

Now it's time to head west on Grand Avenue. Right after you pass through downtown, note the construction along Grand between 10th and 15th Streets. Called **Gateway West**, this area is being developed into apartments, retail businesses, and public spaces, including ponds, open plazas, spaces for sculptures, and possibly a library.

Continue west on Grand until you're just past 23rd Street where, on the left, you can see the governor's mansion, **Terrace Hill**, 2300 Grand Avenue, (515) 281-3604; admission, at the crown of a hill filled with trees covering a lush lawn. Turn into Forest Drive and proceed toward the mansion, but make your first stop at the mansion's carriage house. Built in 1869 in the Second Empire style of architecture as the home of Benjamin Allen, a local banker, Terrace Hill passed into the F. M. Hubbell family 15 years later. They, in turn, gave it to the state in the early 1970s to serve as the governor's official residence. Since then, many improvements have been made to the mansion, built originally at a cost of $250,000 when the typical family home cost $5,000.

Visitors to Terrace Hill take guided tours that begin in the carriage house, located just west of the mansion. On the first floor of Terrace Hill, you walk through halls and rooms with ceilings more than 14 feet high, which allows the Drawing Room to showcase a seven-and-a-half foot chandelier, something that couldn't be accommodated easily in most modern homes with eight-foot ceilings. Other rooms on the tours are the Reception Room, Library, Dining Room, and Sitting Room. A stained-glass window glows over a landing up the main staircase to the second floor, which has guest bedrooms, a conference room in the tower, and the offices of the governor and First Lady. The third floor holds the private residence of the governor's family and is not part of the tour.

History of the People

From Terrace Hill it's easy to continue this tour of historic places. Keep going west on Grand Avenue until you see the signs directing you south on 42nd Street to **Salisbury House**, 4025 Tonawanda Drive, (515) 274-1777; admission. The trip will take only a few minutes. If you feel like you have arrived at the estate of an English king, small wonder—the builders of this house in the 1920s went to great expense to have it resemble the King's House in Salisbury, England, which reflects the Tudor, Gothic, and Carolean styles of architecture. Also, many components, such as the woodwork, rafters, and flint, date back to 16th-century England, giving an authentic touch to the house. Visitors to the 42-room mansion take guided tours that last about an hour and 15 minutes. It's best to contact Salisbury House to verify tour times prior to your visit, although you're welcome to walk around the 10-acre grounds and gardens on your own when the house is open.

From Salisbury House, continue west on Grand Avenue (on the way, you'll pass the Science Center of Iowa, at 4500 Grand Avenue, and the Des Moines

Art Center, at 4700 Grand Avenue; see the Arts and Science section later in this chapter for more on these). As you come down a hill you'll enter the suburb of West Des Moines. Stay on Grand, which begins to swing to the southwest. After about two-and-a-half miles, turn left (east) on Fuller Road. Within a block or so you'll find the **Jordan House**, 2001 Fuller Road, (515) 225-1286; admission. Built in 1848 by the town's first settler, this country mansion was a stop on the Underground Railroad for runaway slaves seeking temporary shelter as they fled north to Canada in the years before the Civil War. Now, displays related to the Underground Railroad and the early years of this home, West Des Moines, and the many railroads that coursed through this community can be seen in the house.

For the next stop on this tour, return to Grand Avenue and keep going to the southwest. In less than three miles you'll reach I-35, which you should take north. Get off at Hickman Road, the second exit past the major intersection with I-80 and I-235. Turn right (east) at the bottom of the exit ramp and then immediately enter the grounds of the Living History Farms, 2600 NW 111th Street, (515) 278-5286; admission, on the left (north) side of Hickman. Things may seem confusing for a moment because a large restaurant is located at that same turn, as well as an Iowa Welcome Center and two motels, but just go beyond the turnoffs for these and you'll reach the entrance to the farms.

When you pass through the entrance of **Living History Farms** you enter the frontier town of Walnut Hill. The town is fictional although 18 buildings from across the state have been gathered to create this small business district that includes a blacksmith shop, general store, doctor's office, bank, law office, school, pharmacy, and millinery. At the foot of the hill in Walnut Hill is the ecumenical Church of the Land, a comparatively new structure that nonetheless fits with the other buildings. It sits where Pope John Paul II spoke during his visit to Des Moines in 1979, the first time a pope had visited the U.S. west of the Mississippi.

In Walnut Hill, you can catch a ride on tractor-drawn trailers to the working farms, starting with the 1700 Ioway Village. Here, you can see stick and bark huts, called tcakiduthan, that provided shelter for the Ioway Indians, who raised their crops in a small garden by hand

What's in a Name?

There is no definitive explanation as to the meaning of the name Des Moines. Some say it means "river of the monks," although it's doubtful that monks were living here when the river leading through the city, which starts near Keokuk, was first seen by French explorers. Others say it means "river in the middle," which, if one looks at the rivers in the interior of Iowa, it certainly is. However, no one is really certain about the translation. As for the pronunciation, the s's aren't sounded out at all. Just call the place De Moin.

with tools fashioned from bone, antler, and metal obtained from trading with the newly arrived people from the east. If you think these methods of farming are passé, consider that the Ioway surrounded their corn with squash and pumpkin, the leaves of which prickled the noses of raccoons and covered the ground so thoroughly that deer were afraid to step into them. Two crop thieves were thus averted from the corn.

You'll walk to the 1850 Pioneer Farm, similar to those created by the early settlers on the Iowa frontier, with log structures and rudimentary farming practices. Then it's on to the 1900 Horse-Powered Farm with its buildings that are similar to those still seen across the Iowa countryside. Throughout all the farms, men and women do just what was done in their respective eras as they plant gardens, harvest the fields, chop wood, shuck corn, can food, spin wool, and more.

In the summer of 2001 the farms introduced a new program called "Get a Grip on History." Visitors are handed cotton canvas work gloves upon entering and given a schedule of hands-on events at the different farms in which they can participate if they want. Among the events, which change daily as real farm chores do, are tanning hides, making bone tools, mending fences, making shingles (a very popular task, it turns out), shelling corn, baking biscuits, and threshing and winnowing in the fall.

Tip: If you're in Des Moines between November and the end of March and want a meal that you're sure to remember, contact Living History Farms for a **1900 Farm Traditional Dinner**. You're picked up by a horse and wagon in the evening at Walnut Hill and taken to the 1900 Farm where you are served a meal cooked on the wood-burning stove. The typical fare includes roast pork or baked chicken; real mashed potatoes and gravy; fresh-baked yeast rolls with homemade jams, jellies, and butter; and side dishes. For dessert, fruit pie and cake round out the meal … not to mention your stomach. After dinner, your hosts take you on a tour of the nearby barn by lantern light.

On your way out of the farms, consider stopping at the **Iowa Welcome Center**, 11121 Hickman Road, (515) 334-9625. Besides having lots of information about all of Iowa, this welcome center is a very good source for information for Des Moines-area places and events. There's also a gift shop featuring Iowa products.

From the welcome center, get back on I-35/80 and head north about eight miles to Exit 131. At the bottom of the ramp, take Merle Hay Road to the left (north) and follow the signs to **Camp Dodge**, headquarters for Iowa's National Guard. More signs there will direct you to the **Iowa Gold Star Museum**, 7700 NW Beaver Drive, (515) 252-4531; free. Telling the history of Iowans who have served in the nation's military as well as the Iowa State Patrol, the museum describes how Iowa's 113th Cavalry Group landed on the beaches of Normandy and later liberated the prisoners of Dachau in World War II. Other units include the 34th Infantry Division, which set a U.S. record for being in continuous com-

While many people would understandably assume that the first interaction between European-Americans and Native Americans in Iowa occurred on the state's east side, a little-known conflict between those two groups took place deep inside the state's present boundaries during the early 1700s.

In the 1730s, relations between the French and the Sauk Indians on the western shore of Lake Michigan had been strained by nearly half a century of war. Raids upon each other were bloody. Thus it was no surprise that when a French officer named Nicolas Coulon de Villiers entered a Sauk village in the Green Bay, Wisconsin, area in late 1733, he was killed by its inhabitants. Soon afterward, the Sauk left Lake Michigan and banded with their allies, the Fox, as they headed into present-day Iowa.

To avenge de Villiers's death, the French government in Quebec ordered an expedition of 84 Frenchmen and about 200 Iroquois, Huron, and Potawatomi allies to set out from Montreal to pursue and punish the Sauk and Fox. Under the command of Captain Nicolas de Noyelles, the small army moved out on August 14, 1734. In the Detroit area, a number of Ottawa joined de Noyelles's force, which left there on January 2, 1735. In the dead of winter, the French-led expedition crossed the Mississippi River and was somehow able to track where the Sauk and Fox had been, but time and again de Noyelles was too late to catch them.

Two months after leaving Detroit, the French force at last found the Sauk and Fox camped on a tributary of the Mississippi River, and the French and their allies attacked. But de Noyelles's forces found themselves trapped and besieged for four days by a far greater number of Sauk and Fox than they had anticipated. Finally, convinced the Sauk and Fox had been "punished," de Noyelles told them his forces would leave them in peace if they agreed to end their alliance with one another. Although they had the upper hand, the Sauk and Fox agreed and de Noyelles's forces returned to the east. The Sauk and Fox, however, remained together over the years in Iowa, where they settled. Even after they were later forced by the U.S. government to leave Iowa, many subsequently returned to buy property near the towns of Tama and Toledo in eastern Iowa so they could live once again upon their own land. Today, many of the descendants of the Sauk and Fox, now called the Meskwakie, live on that land, which is not a reservation but is called the Meskwakie Settlement.

The battle fought between Indians and whites on the prairie 40 years before the Battles of Lexington and Concord half a continent away took place on the Des Moines River near where downtown Des Moines now stands.

bat for 517 days in North Africa and Europe. Besides exhibits in the museum, outside are several military vehicles, two helicopters—a UH-1 troopship and a Cobra attack helicopter—and a Bradley armored fighting vehicle, representing equipment from World War II, Korea, Vietnam, and Desert Storm.

Also, although this doesn't fit the historical theme of this tour, Iowa's largest swimming pool, (515) 276-1106, is here at Camp Dodge and open to the public. You should also note that, while you're at Camp Dodge, you're practically on top of Saylorville Lake, a reservoir and recreation area formed on the Des Moines River (and covered under "Family Fun" in this chapter).

Tip: Although not complete at this time, you should note that plans exist to open another museum related to the region's military history at Fort Des Moines, on the metro area's south side near Blank Park Zoo. Called the **Fort Des Moines Black Officers and WAC Memorial Park**, (888) 828-FORT, the project plans to convert a barracks at the former fort into a hall honoring the black officers who trained there in World War I and the members of the Women's Army Corps who received their education there during World War II. Plans exist to implement this project in four phases, with the dedication occurring sometime in 2001 or 2002.

From Camp Dodge, return to I-35/80 and head south back to the big interchange with I-235 where you'll go east toward downtown Des Moines. Leave I-235 at the Martin Luther King Jr. Parkway exit and head south. After a few blocks, turn left (east) on Woodland Avenue. In six blocks you'll come upon **Hoyt Sherman Place**, 1501 Woodland Avenue, (515) 244-0507; free, but admission for some theater presentations. Although this 1877 home has had a fine arts gallery and concert hall added onto it, you still get a good sense of how life was for an upper-class family of the late 19th century in Des Moines. Rich woodwork abounds in the entry, parlors, library, and dining room. The added-on gallery displays fine artwork and the concert hall hosts a wide range of events from poetry readings to concerts by bands, orchestras, and chorales.

A bit more than two blocks away and also in the **Sherman Hill National Historic District** is the **Wallace House**, 756 16th Street, (515) 243-7063; free, home of Henry Wallace, agriculture leader and editor of *Wallaces Farmer*. Now headquarters of the Wallace House Foundation and the Sherman Hill Association, which use some of the Italianate Victorian home's first floor for conferences, the house still has some portions from its early years that remain in fine condition, including the front and middle parlors, library, dining room, and kitchen.

*F*amily Fun

There's fun for everyone in a big city, and Des Moines is no exception. Let's start in the metro area's northeast corner, in the town of Altoona, where you can visit Iowa's largest amusement park, **Adventureland**, Exit 142 on I-80, (515) 266-2121; (800) 532-1286; admission. This is where you go to get

One of four roller coasters at Adventureland, Iowa's largest amusement park, in Altoona

splashed in the log ride, hurtled on four roller coasters (each with a different style), flung by the Space Shot, raised high in the Ferris Wheel, and much more. In all, about 100 rides offer fun for everyone from the little tykes to the thrill seekers. Live entertainment is also staged on the grounds. It's safe to say you can spend a day at this great place—and many do.

Located a few miles away is a place you're guaranteed to get wet, **White Water University Fun Park**, 5401 E. University Avenue, (515) 265-4904; admission. An aquatic park with a wave pool, four water slides, tube runs, children's play area, and a three-foot-deep lazy river, White Water University also has a miniature golf course and the state's only twin-engine-powered go-carts. To get here from Adventureland, just go south on NE 56th Street and turn right (west) on E. University Avenue (Highway 163).

If you're in the area in August, you must visit the **Iowa State Fair**, E. 30th and University Avenue, (515) 262-3111; (800) 545-FAIR (June-August); admission, less than 30 blocks to the west on University Avenue. Immortalized as the epitome of state fairs in books, movies, and on stage, the Iowa State Fair is the largest event in the state, drawing an average of 900,000 visitors over its 11-day run each year. Action ranges from carnival rides on a 10-acre Midway that dances with light at night and barns with prize-winning livestock to the grandstand's live entertainment by the nation's top performers and endless industrial exhibits.

To get on with more family fun, get back on University Avenue heading east and go south on Highway 65, part of a four-lane outer belt around the metro area. Highway 65 joins Highway 5, which you'll stay on instead of following 65 when it heads south. Leave Highway 5 at Exit 96, which is SW 9th Street. At the bottom of the ramp, turn right (north) and in a short distance you'll be at the **Blank Park Zoo**, 7401 SW 9th Street, (515) 285-4722; admission. Kids and adults can learn about more than 800 animals from five continents. One exhibit features a walk through Australia while another takes you through an aviary with free-flying birds. There's even a child-sized exhibit for the kids to climb through, allowing them to poke their heads up in the middle of a prairie dog town with the furry little burrowers just inches away on the other side of a glass enclosure.

New at the zoo in the summer of 2001 was the **Myron and Jackie Blank Discovery Center**, a wonderful indoor exhibit that has visitors follow the path of water from its origins as snow in a chilly alpine setting, through a cave flowing past tropical snake pits, plunging over waterfalls near a butterfly garden into the Amazon basin that's rocked by thunder, and finally washing into a 65,000-gallon coral reef. All along the way, real animals highlight the very interactive exhibit.

*A*rts and Sciences

When you have dragged yourself and the kids away from the zoo, return to Highway 5 and go west until Highway 28 peels off to the right (north) as the boundary between Des Moines and West Des Moines. Turn right (east) on Grand Avenue and travel to the **Des Moines Art Center**, 4700 Grand Avenue, (515) 277-4405; free, itself quite a work of art. If you think the building ap-

The Des Moines Art Center on Grand Avenue

pears disjointed, well, you're right but that's because three noted architects designed each segment of the center as it was built. Eliel Saarinen designed the original portion and I. M. Pei did the second section. If you back away from the building to the south in nearby Greenwood-Ashworth Park, you'll see windows form the letters P E I in the south wall. Finally, Richard Meier designed the last addition in the center's northwest corner, a gleaming white, very modern structure that sharply contrasts the bricks used in the other areas.

Of course, architecture alone doesn't an art center make and this art center has plenty on the inside in the way of paintings, photographs, sculpture, and other media in its permanent collection, including works by Picasso, Monet, Jasper Johns, Roy Lichtenstein, John Singer Sargent, Andy Warhol, and Edward Hopper. The museum has a gift shop, an auditorium that hosts film series among other events, and a restaurant that has earned top ratings from the Des Moines Register. It serves lunches and, on Thursday evenings, reservation-only dinners.

Also in Greenwood-Ashworth Park is the **Science Center of Iowa**, 4500 Grand Avenue, (515) 274-4138; admission. This is a place of discovery for all ages, with 27 permanent exhibits. For example, you can watch an image of your voice, create energy while you pedal, try a different type of roller coaster, and learn that Bernouli has nothing to do with spaghetti. The Sargent Space Theater is a 42-foot-wide planetarium that does double duty offering educational star shows and, for pure entertainment, laser light performances set to music. (Note: See the "History of the People" section of this chapter for details on the nearby Salisbury House.)

From Greenwood-Ashworth Park, go east on Grand Avenue, then take 42nd Street north to I-235. There, go west and turn north at the junction with I-80/35. Leave the interstate at Exit 131 and go north on Merle Hay Road. You will eventually join NW Beaver Road and then follow the signs to **Saylorville Lake**, 5600 NW 78th Avenue, (515) 964-0672; free, but a fee for swimming and camping. Eventually you'll arrive at the visitors center on the east end of the dam, which is a good place to get information about all the camping, swimming, boating, hiking, biking, and a lot more that you can do at this 6,000-acre lake, which is a dammed portion of the Des Moines River. Besides this U.S. Army Corps of Engineers-administered area, the region has two other large recreational areas. One is **Lewis A. Jester County Park**, 11407 NW 118th Avenue, (515) 323-5300; camping fee, on the lake's west side, with campsites, trails, and a golf course. On the east side of Saylorville is **Big Creek Recreation Area**, Highway 415, (515) 984-6473; camping fee, which surrounds Big Creek Lake, a branch of Saylorville Lake, and also has campsites, picnic areas, and a swimming area.

If you haven't brought your own boat, find **Big Creek Marina and Boat Rental**, Highway 415, (515) 984-6083; fee, on the east side of Big Creek Lake, where you can rent houseboats, sailboats, kayaks, canoes, water bikes, and paddle boats. The marina also offers sailing lessons.

Similarly, if you want to bike around here, check out **Polk City Bike Rentals**, 1021 S. 3rd Street, Polk City, (515) 984-6737; fee, which has bicycles, including recumbents, as well as trailers for towing small children. The shop is located near the 23-mile-long **Saylorville-Des Moines Trail**, (515) 237-1386.

The metro area features a number of trails, including the 7-mile **Clive Greenbelt Trail**, (515) 223-6230; **Great Western Trail and Bill Riley Bike Trail**, 17 miles from Des Moines to Martensdale, (515) 323-5300; **John Pat Dorrian Trail**, 5.7 miles, (515) 237-1386; **Jordan Creek Trail**, 9 miles, (515) 222-3444; **Two Rivers Walk**, 6.2 miles, which passes the Iowa State Capitol, Des Moines Botanical Center, and parts of downtown Des Moines; and **Raccoon River Valley Trail**, 57 miles long from Clive to Jefferson, (515) 465-3577.

Also note that you're very close to **Camp Dodge**, which has a wonderful swimming pool and the **Iowa Gold Star Museum** (both described in the "History of the People" section of this chapter).

Sporting People

Fans of professional sports will find that Des Moines certainly has its share. At **Sec Taylor Stadium**, 350 SW First Street, which is on the south side of downtown, you can enjoy fine minor league baseball played by the **Iowa Cubs**, (515) 243-6111; (800) 464-2827; admission, a Triple-A farm team of the Chicago Cubs. One of the nice things about baseball on this level is that it's like major league baseball used to be. At Sec Taylor, fans are close to the action, can talk with the players, and don't have to pay exorbitant ticket prices.

The **Iowa Barnstormers**, an indoor arena football team, play in the Veterans Memorial Auditorium, 833 5th Avenue, (515) 323-5444, on the north side of downtown. The team's offices are located at 319 7th Street, Suite 222, (515) 282-3596.

Also playing at Vets (as the auditorium is locally known) are the **Des Moines Dragons**, offices: 2753 99th Street, Urbandale, (515) 276-5559; admission, which won the championship of the International Basketball Association during its 1999-2000 season.

In the western part of the metro area, the **Des Moines Buccaneers** play ice hockey at the Metro Ice Sports Arena, 7201 Hickman Road, Urbandale, (515) 278-9757; admission. A top team with the United States Hockey League, the Buccaneers have been playing since 1980. They are the only junior league hockey team to win the national championship three times in a row.

And not far away, the **Des Moines Menace**, offices: 6400 Westown Parkway, West Des Moines, (515) 226-9890; admission, plays soccer at Cara McGrane Memorial Stadium, located on the grounds of Hoover High School at 50th and Aurora in Urbandale. A member of the Heartland Division of the United Soccer Leagues, the Menace has twice advanced to the National Final Four Championships since the team was formed in 1994.

While in the western metro area, think about making a short trip just out-side the city limits to the small town of **Van Meter** (population 931), which is barely a mile south of Exit 113 on I-80, 10 miles west of the I-80/35/235 junc-tion in West Des Moines. When you come into Van Meter you'll see what first appears to be a plain but attractive brick building. Upon closer examination you'll notice a brick bas-relief mural featuring a baseball pitcher in different scenes. And in front of the building is the step of a pitcher's mound and the pentagonal shape of home base. Welcome to the **Bob Feller Hometown Ex-hibit**, 310 Mill Street, (515) 996-2806; admission, a museum dedicated to Hall of Famer Bob Feller, who went from hometown hero to a long career with the Cleveland Indians. His uniforms, trophies, special awards, and more are here, including a display on his departure from pro ball to face combat in the U.S. Navy during World War II. Occasionally Feller shows up at the museum to greet visitors and fans.

Finally, at any time of day or night throughout the year you can visit **Prairie Meadows Racetrack and Casino**, Exit 142 off I-80 in Altoona, (515) 967-1000; (800) 325-9015, on the metro area's northeast side. Along with having 1,500 slot machines in the casino, Prairie Meadows hosts live horse races featuring thoroughbreds and quarter horses from spring through fall and offers simul-casting throughout the year. A restaurant, cocktail lounge, and concessions are on the premises.

The Des Moines Botanical Center on East River Drive

Blooming Things

If there's one place in Des Moines that's colorful throughout the year, it's the **Des Moines Botanical Center**, 909 E. River Drive, (515) 323-8900; admission. On the east bank of the Des Moines River and under a glass-and-steel geodesic dome, the center has about 15,000 plants from tropical, semi-tropical, and desert climes. Displays change with the seasons and birds fly freely through the interior of the dome. The center has a gift shop and cafe. Outside the center are expanding displays including an herb garden and a portion of **Two Rivers Walk** (see the "Arts and Sciences" section in this chapter) that connects the center to downtown and the state Capitol. To reach the botanical center, take the E. 6th Street exit off I-235 and follow the signs.

To travel to another place that's vibrant with lots of flowers, take a left out of the botanical center's parking lot and head south on River Drive to the first intersection, Grand Avenue, where you will turn right (west). Follow Grand through downtown, then follow the signs for the Des Moines airport, a route that will put you on Fleur Drive going south. After you cross the Raccoon River, take the first right (west) turn that you can and you'll enter **Waterworks Park**, Fleur Drive; free, where, near the entrance you will see a fountain surrounded by a number of colorful flowerbeds. From there you can almost ramble forever in the park, which hugs the Raccoon River for quite a distance to the west, providing lots of open spaces and tree-shaded groves.

East of Waterworks Park, across Fleur Drive, is **Grays Lake**, which has been improving slowly over the years into another recreational area. The latest improvement is a 2.2-mile-long-trail that opened in June 2001 to connect with other trails in the downtown area and Waterworks Park.

Another place you might want to visit is the rose garden behind the Des Moines Art Center in **Greenwood Park**, 42nd and Grand Avenue, which also has a pond and boardwalks. On the city's southeast side, **Easter Lake Park** has lots of open spaces perfect for flying kites, and other areas that are filled with lilac bushes, making this a beautiful and fragrant place in May and June.

Special Districts

The metro area has plenty of shopping malls for those who like to hang out at such places, but it's also blessed with three unique areas.

One is called **Court Avenue**, which, appropriately, is on Court Avenue just east of the Polk County Courthouse in the southern part of downtown Des Moines. A bit difficult to maneuver around sometimes because of the area's one-way streets, it's nevertheless a nice place to visit because of all the places to eat. They range from a coffee shop with a small art gallery and a brewpub to fine dining and restaurants with a funky flair.

Valley Junction is on the west side of the metro area, in an older section of West Des Moines. Earning its name from the many railroads that once traversed the area, Valley Junction is now centered on Fifth Street and has about 120 businesses—gift shops, antique stores, art galleries, gourmet food stores, boutiques, and more. Should you shop 'til you drop, there's even a spa where you can get your tired shopping muscles rubbed down to prepare you for another round.

To get to Valley Junction from Des Moines, take Grand Avenue to the west, turn left (south) on 63rd Street (which is First Street in West Des Moines … go figure) until you reach Elm Street. Turn right there and in four blocks you'll be in the heart of Valley Junction.

The final district has no real formal name—perhaps "Downtown" will do— but more accurately it's the **Skywalk System**. These second-story links that pass over streets between blocks and buildings make getting around downtown wonderfully easy in all weather conditions. There is no beginning, no end. Just get on and go from parking garages through department stores, around business centers, to hotels, into food courts, along specialty shops, and even up to Vets Auditorium.

Evening Time

The free **Music under the Stars** series of musical performances begins the first Sunday in June and runs for nine weeks on the west steps of the State Capitol.

More live entertainment occurs at **Firstar Nitefall on the River**, admission, at **Simon Estes Plaza**, a pretty setting on the east bank of the Des Moines River (between E. Court and E. Walnut Streets), which features the skyline of downtown Des Moines as a backdrop. These concerts take place every Thursday evening between the second Thursday of June and the first Thursday of August.

Simon Estes Plaza is also the site of Wednesday evening concerts called **Country on the River**, admission.

SIDE TRIPS

To the South

If you're in downtown Des Moines, the best way to begin this side trip is to work your way to East 14th Street, which is also Highway 69, and go south, out of town into the country. Just after you cross the Middle River, take the first left (to the east) turn that you can, turning onto Summerset Road. Go two miles to a T intersection. Turn left (north) there and go a quarter-mile to the entrance to **Summerset Inn and Winery**, 1507 Fairfax, (515) 961-3545, a combination B&B and winery. Opened in 1997, the winery raises 10 varieties of grapes on 12 acres of land, producing a variety of hybrid French and American wines.

Back on Highway 69, continue south and on the north edge of Indianola you will see the **National Balloon Museum**, 1601 N. Jefferson, Highway 65/69, (515) 961-3714; donations appreciated. It has exhibits devoted to balloon pilots, record-setting balloon flights, hot-air and gas balloons, gondolas, and various equipment that has been used in 200 years of flying balloons. One exhibit has information and photos of the World War I balloon unit that was trained and stationed in Omaha, Nebraska. The gift shop offers ballooning-related material.

If you're in the area in August, you're in for an eyeful—and a skyful—of countless hot-air balloons as they go on high to compete in the National Balloon Classic competition and, every so many years, in the National Hot Air Balloon Championships.

Just south of Indianola is **Lake Ahquabi State Park**, Highway 349, (515) 961-7101; camping fee, a small but nice place to camp, swim, picnic, and fish.

To the West

Leave Des Moines on I-80 going west until Exit 110 and you will see the **Aircraft Super-Market**, 10 Ellefson Drive, (515) 834-2225; fee for flights, just as you're leaving the interstate. Pull into this small airport and sales hangar and you can arrange a flight like you may never have had before—in an ultra-light aircraft. Flights take you over the Raccoon River Valley and other areas west of Des Moines including the bridges of Madison County to the south.

From Exit 110, head south on Highway 169 to the town of **Winterset**. For many years Winterset's most well-known spot was the **Birthplace of John Wayne**, 216 S. 2nd Street, (515) 462-1044; admission. A small, four-room house east of the town center, this is where Marion Morrison—the Duke's real name—was born in May 1907 to a pharmacist and his wife. Restored to how it looked when young Morrison lived there before heading west, the house has a collection of John Wayne memorabilia, including the eyepatch he wore in his Oscar-winning role as the sheriff in *True Grit* and the hat he wore in *Rio Lobo*. Also on hand are rare photos of his Hollywood friends and letters written by his contemporaries, including Lucille Ball, Jimmy Stewart, Kirk Douglas, Bob Hope, and Ronald Reagan.

Things in Winterset changed in 1992 when a gent by the name of Robert James Waller wrote a small book about a traveling photographer who arrived in Winterset to photograph a series of covered bridges in the area and developed a relationship with a farm wife during his short stay. The book, *The Bridges of Madison County*, not only became the best-selling hardcover book of all time, it also set this town a-spinning because so many people thought the story was true that they came to see where everything in the book had happened. Well, the only items that were true in the book were the bridges themselves and the **Northside Café**, which still serves up meals on the north side of the town square.

The Roseman Bridge near Winterset

Later, the movie of the same name came out and brought more attention to Winterset and the surrounding countryside where most of the covered bridges are found. Using the money generated by the tourism boom, local officials fixed up the bridges (almost too much in the opinion of some) and today they continue to attract visitors from near and far.

At one time Madison County had 19 covered bridges; county officials had ordered them built that way to protect the flooring timbers, which were more expensive to replace than the wood used to build the roofs and sides of the bridges. One by one, the bridges gradually disappeared from the scene until finally six remained. One, called Cutler-Donohoe, is now in Winterset City Park but the others are in the countryside, some in their original locations.

Of course, the most famous, because of their roles in the book and the movie, are Roseman, Cedar, and Holliwell Covered Bridges. Only Cedar remains open to vehicular traffic. All can be visited for free and the best way to find them is to obtain a map from the **Madison County Chamber of Commerce**, 73 Jefferson, (515) 462-1185; (800) 298-6119. Use the map and watch for signs on the roads directing you to the bridges. Visiting all of them can take a few hours.

Besides the bridges, another part of the movie can be visited: **Francesca's House**, 3271 130th Street, Cumming, (515) 981-5268; admission. Unlike the bridges, which were authentic structures, Francesca's House is fictional, having been an abandoned farmhouse that was restored for the movie and used for many of its scenes. The best way to reach the house is to go north on Highway 169 from Winterset to County Highway G4R, about two miles north of town. Turn to the right (east) there and 15 or so miles later you'll reach the house after quite a few turns in the road, which winds its way to the northeast.

To return to Des Moines from Francesca's House, continue north on G4R until you reach County Highway G14 in about a mile and take that to the east to I-35, which will lead directly to the metro area.

If you want to spend more time in Winterset, go to the south end of town and visit the **Madison County Historical Complex**, 815 S. Second Avenue, (515) 462-2134; admission. Dominated by the 1856 Kaser-Bevington House, this group of 12 buildings from yesteryear is a very pleasant place to visit.

Another fine place to see is **Pammel County Park**, Highway 322, (515) 462-3536, located southwest of town on Highway 322, which drops south of Highway 92. Located on tree-filled hills, the park has a stone tower plus camping sites and fishing.

LODGING

Altoona

Adventureland Inn, I-80/Highway 65, (515) 265-7321; (800) 910-5382. Near Adventureland and Prairie Meadows. Restaurant, indoor pool. $-$$$

Heartland Inn, I-80 at Exit 141, (515) 967-2400; (800) 334-3277. Near Adventureland and Prairie Meadows. Indoor pool, continental breakfast $$-$$$$

Downtown Des Moines

Des Moines Marriott Downtown Hotel, 700 Grand Avenue, (515) 245-5500; (800) 228-9290. Downtown. Restaurant, indoor pool. $$-$$$$

Embassy Suites on the River, 101 E. Locust Street, (515) 244-1700; (800) EMBASSY. On east side of downtown. Near Capitol, Botanical Center, and Simon Estes Plaza. Restaurant, indoor pool, continental breakfast. $$$$

Holiday Inn Downtown, 1050 6th Avenue, (515) 283-0151; (800) 465-4329. North of downtown near I-235 and Vets Auditorium. Restaurant, indoor pool. $$-$$$$

Hotel Fort Des Moines, 10th and Walnut, (515) 243-1161; (800) 532-1466. Historic downtown building. Restaurant, indoor pool. $$-$$$$

The Savery Hotel and Spa, 401 Locust, (515) 244-2151; (800) 798-2151. Downtown location in historic hotel. Restaurant, indoor pool. $$$-$$$$

Suites of 800 Locust Hotel, 800 Locust, (515) 288-5800. New hotel built in a historic building that held the Des Moines Club. Restaurant, indoor pool. $$$-$$$$

West Area

Comfort Suites at Living History Farms, 11167 Hickman Road, (515) 276-1126; (800) 395-7675. Restaurant, indoor pool, continental breakfast. $$$-$$$$

Sleep Inn at Living History Farms, 11211 Hickman Road, (515) 270-2424; (877) 233-0333. Restaurant nearby. Indoor pool, continental breakfast. $$

South Area

Comfort Inn Airport, 5231 Fleur Drive, (515) 287-3434; (800) 228-5150. Near airport and Blank Zoo. Near restaurants. Indoor pool, continental breakfast. $-$$

Hampton Inn Hotel, 5001 Fleur Drive, (515) 287-7300; (800) HAMPTON. Near airport and Blank Zoo. Near restaurants. Outdoor pool, continental breakfast. $$

Wingate Inn Airport, 6800 Fleur Drive, (515) 285-7777; (800) 557-7048. Near airport and Blank Zoo. Near restaurants. Indoor pool, continental breakfast. $$-$$$$

Indianola

Apple Tree Inn, Highway 65/69 N, (515) 961-0551; (800) 961-0551. On north edge of town. Restaurants nearby. Continental breakfast. $-$$

Super 8 Motel, 1701 N. Jefferson, (515) 961-0058; (800) 800-8000. On Highway 65/69 on north edge of town. Restaurants nearby. Indoor pool, continental breakfast. $-$$$$

Winterset

Super 8 Motel, 1312 N. 10th Street, (515) 462-4888; (800) 800-8000. Near John Wayne's birthplace and bridges of Madison County. Continental breakfast. $

BED AND BREAKFASTS

Adel

The Grey Goose, 1740 290th Street, (515) 833-2338. In countryside west of Des Moines. Near Living History Farms. Pond, fishing, hiking, and water garden. Three rooms. $$

Des Moines

Butler House on Grand Avenue, 4507 Grand Avenue, (515) 255-4096. Tudor mansion near Terrace Hill, Des Moines Art Center, and Science Center of Iowa. Seven rooms. $$$-$$$$

Carter House Inn, 640 20th Street, (515) 288-7850. Late 19th-century Italianate home in Sherman Hill National Historic District. Near downtown. Four rooms. $$-$$$

Indianola

Summerset Inn and Winery, 1507 Fairfax, (515) 961-3545. Countryside inn between Des Moines and Indianola. Iowa's largest vineyard. Four rooms. $$$-$$$$

Winterset

A Step Away, 104 W. Court Street, (515) 462-5956. Renovated 1880 commercial building near courthouse square. Near John Wayne home and bridges of Madison County. Three rooms. $$-$$$$

DINING

Downtown Des Moines

A Taste of Thailand, 215 E. Walnut Street, (515) 243-9521. Thai cuisine.

Buzzard Billy's Flying Carp Café, 100 Court Avenue, (515) 280-6060. Cajun fare in the Court Avenue district.

Landmark Grille, 10th and Walnut, (515) 243-1161. In Hotel Fort Des Moines. Fine dining.

Stella's Blue Sky Diner, 400 Locust Street, #235, (515) 246-1953. A 1950s-style diner where waitresses will pour malts and shakes into glasses you hold atop your head . . . if you want.

Midtown

Bauder's Pharmacy, 3802 Ingersoll Avenue, (515) 255-1124. Old-fashioned soda fountain that's still pumping.

Des Moines Art Center Restaurant, 4700 Grand Avenue, (515) 277-4405. Rated as one of top five restaurants in Des Moines. Serving lunches and a reservation-only supper on Thursday.

Drake Diner, 1111 25th Street, (515) 277-1111. Near Drake University. The original Drake (there are three now) with 1950s-style decor and menu.

El Patio, 611 37th Street, (515) 274-2303. Mexican food created by owners who travel to Mexico frequently. In a former house just off Ingersoll Avenue near downtown.

Noah's Ark Ristorante & Fireside Lounge, 2400 Ingersoll Avenue, (515) 288-2248. Italian cuisine.

Waveland Café, 4708 University Avenue, (515) 279-4341. Known for its breakfast menu.

West Area

Brix, 86th and Hickman, Clive, (515) 251-6867. Rated as one of top five restaurants in Des Moines. American with seafood. Reservations recommended.

Iowa Machine Shed, 11151 Hickman Road, (515) 270-6818. Near Living History Farms. Family-style, farm-size meals. Staff is dressed as farmers.

Tavern Pizza and Pasta Grille, 205 5th Street, West Des Moines, (515) 255-9827. In Valley Junction area. Known for its pizza.

East Area

Big Daddy's Barbeque, 1000 E. 14th Street, (515) 262-0352. Seating is tight with just 10 seats! Excellent food, especially the barbecue.

Iowa Beef Steakhouse, 1201 E. Euclid Avenue, (515) 262-1138. Steaks.

Indianola

Corner Sundry, 101 N. Buxton, (515) 961-9029. Fine soda fountain on the southwest corner of the courthouse square.

Crouse Café, 115 E. Salem, (515) 961-3362. Breakfast, dinner specials.

Harvest Restaurant, 107 E. Salem, (515) 962-0466. On the southeast corner of the courthouse square.

Winterset

Northside Café, 61 W. Jefferson, (515) 462-1523. On the north side of the courthouse square, made famous by the movie and book Bridges of Madison County.

Nature's Cupboard & Down to Earth, 105 N. John Wayne Drive, (515) 462-3579. Health foods, Victorian teas.

Rookies' Pub & Grille, 105 E. Madison Street, (515) 462-2226. Sandwiches, salads, dinners, and desserts.

INFORMATION

Greater Des Moines Convention and Visitors Bureau, 405 6th Avenue, Suite 201, Des Moines, IA 50309, (515) 286-4960; (800) 451-2625; www.visitdesmoines.com

Chamber of Commerce, 515 N. Jefferson, Suite D, Indianola, IA 50125, (515) 961-6269; www.indianolachamber.com

Madison County Chamber of Commerce, 73 W. Jefferson, Winterset, IA 50273, (515) 462-1185; (800) 298-6119; www.madisoncounty.com

Chapter 10

Pella and Knoxville: Going Dutch and Going to the Races

When it comes to the communities of Pella and Knoxville, you can go from the slow lane to the fast lane in mere minutes. Settled by Dutch immigrants, Pella determinedly has been recalling its heritage in the last few years, while just a few miles away, Knoxville hums with the excitement of one of the best speedways in America.

$\mathcal{P}$ella

We'll be coming into Pella on Highway 163 from the west, getting off at Exit 40, a route that brings you right into town on Washington Street. The little windmill in the park on the west end of town gives you a hint about Pella's heritage, but you get the message loud and clear when you arrive at the town square with its overwhelming Dutch look. Yes, even though some business signs are familiar and in English, the architecture of many of the buildings, including the very American Casey's, Subway, and even the Great Wall of China restaurant, is Dutch in character.

Dominating everything in the town square, **Central Park**, is the **Tulip Toren**, a set of 65-foot-tall pylons that loom above the platform used by the "royalty" during **Tulip Time Festival**, one of the largest and most colorful events in the state. During the event, held each May, Central Park is awash in colorful tulips and full of Dutch descendants wearing the fanciful clothing of their ancestral homeland.

Even without a festival, there's plenty to do in Pella, especially around the square, so park your car and work the shoe leather for awhile. To acquaint yourself with the town, visit the small **Information Windmill** at the southeast corner of the square where the guides should be able to answer most of your questions and supply helpful literature.

The park is also the focal point of **"Thursday in Pella,"** a series of weekly evening events in the summer. Each week has a different theme that celebrates the town, always family oriented, and everyone's welcome to attend.

While in Central Park, walk through it to the north, passing its antique street lights and benches, a sundial, and flower beds until you reach Washington Street, which you cross to get to the **Scholte House**, 728 Washington Street, (641) 628-3684; admission. Built in 1847 by the town's founder, Dominie H.P. Scholte, who promised his wife a home like the nice one they had left behind in Holland, the 23-room house shows the elegance of the upper class in Pella's early years. Alongside and behind the house, sculptures of Dutch figures in everyday poses watch over an extensive array of flower gardens.

The Klokkenspel in downtown Pella

If you're interested in seeing more gardens, walk up Main Street to the north a few blocks to **Sunken Gardens Park**, bounded by Main, Houston, Jefferson and Lincoln Streets; free. Similar to Central Park in that it too has a small windmill, flower gardens, antique street lights, and benches, Sunken Gardens Park is dominated by a pond in the shape of—what else?—a wooden shoe. In the spring, more than 15,000 tulips bloom here.

For a look at another historical home, walk across Main and head north four blocks to the **de Zee Meeuw House**, 1357 Main, (641) 628-3592; by appointment only; admission. Although built in the 1940s, it reflects the homes that its builders left behind in the Netherlands and includes a tower with a castle motif. Inside are braided rugs, antique furniture, and knitted curtains.

Returning to downtown, you can either walk along the east side of Main and take a close look at what the stores have to sell—some have Dutch imported gifts—or walk on the west side of the street in Central Park to view the stores' Dutch facades. Just east of the intersection of Main and Franklin is something no other town in Iowa has: a three-story **Klokkenspel**. Make sure you're here on the sidewalk at 11 a.m. or 1, 3, 5, or 9 p.m. so you can witness a wonderful performance by eight 4-foot-high mechanical figures that move to the music of a 147-bell carillon. Among the characters that put on the show are a shoemaker, street scrubbers, a blacksmith, Pella founder Dominie Scholte, and Wyatt Earp. Wait a minute! What's a Western lawman like Wyatt Earp doing here? Hang on, you'll soon find out. Four of the characters can be seen from the street side of the Klokkenspel and, if you walk through its arches, you can see the other four from a courtyard.

Keep walking east on Franklin, where you'll see the large **Pella Opera House**, 611 Franklin Street, (641) 628-8628; admission for shows. Built in 1900 and renovated in 1990, it hosts a variety of entertainment.

If you had any doubts about how Dutch the town of Pella is, at the end of the block check out the 135-foot-tall windmill looming high above you. It serves as the new entry for one of the town's longtime attractions, the **Pella Historical Village**, 507 Franklin Street (641) 628-2409; admission. Opened in late 2001, the nation's largest windmill has a base built by local folks. The upper stories were assembled in part by craftsmen in the Netherlands who accompanied the pieces to Pella to complete the windmill. Also, millers from the Netherlands came to show their Dutch-American relations how to operate what is now a fully functional windmill grinding a variety of grains. An elevator takes visitors up to the walk-around observation deck partway up the structure.

At the base of the windmill is an interpretative center about Dutch heritage and traditions and the entrance to the rest of the historical village. Here, you can pick up audiotapes to guide you on a walk past the village's 20 or so other

The Molengracht plaza, Pella

buildings. One in particular deserves special note because it was once home to a boy who grew up to be a legend of the Old West. From the age of 2 until he moved west with his family in 1864 at the age of 16, Wyatt Earp lived in the long, two-story house near the windmill while his father served as U.S. provost marshal for Marion County.

Among the other buildings are a grist mill with a water wheel, cobbler, bakery, log cabin, and church. You can examine displays of delft, a small-scale Dutch village, clothing, and everyday items from more than a century ago.

Now it's back to the Klokkenspel, where you pass through the arches again and enter a plaza with a distinctively Dutch flavor: **Molengracht**. A set of buildings clustered around a mill canal crossed by a drawbridge and flanked by colorful flowerbeds, Molengracht (which means "mill city") has several businesses in a small area: the Royal Amsterdam Hotel and Grand Café, which has fine and unusual dining, a three-screen movie theater, condos, offices, and retail business that include a jewelry store, hobby shop, and an outlet for Stam chocolates, which originated in Holland in 1916. Molengracht has underground parking, a nice convenience in an area where parking can be tight, and a rarity in a town of only 10,000 residents.

When you leave Molengracht and return to Iowa, about a block farther to the south on Main is the **Fire Station Museum**, 612 Main, (641) 628-2626; (888) 746-3882; free, but reservations for tours required. Built in 1882, this brick, two-story structure with a bell tower houses an antique fire engine in its garage and has other firefighting equipment and memorabilia as well as the city's old jailhouse.

If, by now, your children are a bit restless, there are two sites that should grab their interest. Across Main Street from the Fire Station Museum is the **Pella Public Library**, 617 Main Street, (641) 628-4268, which has an excellent children's section with its own small windmill.

Another option is to walk west on Liberty Street (right next to the library) three blocks to **West Market Park**, bounded by Liberty, Franklin, W. 2nd, and W. 3rd Streets. The little ones will know what to do once they see the wooden wonderland there, complete with bouncing bridges, towers, climbing structures, slides, soft sand, swings, and more. The whole structure is scaled for kids, so try to curb your urge to run through it yourself. For parental peace of mind, the site is enclosed by a perimeter fence. For relaxing, visit the park's butterfly garden.

Two of Pella's large corporations offer museums. About a mile east of downtown is the **Vermeer Museum**, 2110 Vermeer Road, (641) 621-7017; free, highlighting the company's agricultural and trenching equipment, including ditch diggers, underground cable installers, and stump grinders. On the south side of town, in a former railroad depot, is the **Rolscreen Company Museum**, Main and Oskaloosa Streets, (641) 628-1000; free, which illustrates the history of the Pella Corporation's window manufacturing from yesteryear to today.

Lake Red Rock

While still in Pella on University Avenue, you should take note of the trailhead of the Volksweg Trail on the city's southwest side near the water plant. This is the eastern terminus for a paved (and free) 14-mile trail that allows you to bike, hike, jog, or skate through the pretty countryside of south central Iowa to Fifield Recreational Area, a part of Lake Red Rock.

To travel from Pella to Knoxville, go south of Central Park on Main and then take a right (east) turn on University Street. That will become County Highway T15, which will take you to Knoxville, 14 miles away. The first major intersection you come to is a Y, with a sign pointing to Lake Red Rock. Following the sign will lead you to a campground at the base of the dam. If you want to go straight to Knoxville, veer to the right at the Y intersection. Then, at the following T intersection, take a left.

Lake Red Rock is one of Iowa's largest lakes. A dammed portion of the Des Moines River, the 19,000-acre lake is four miles southwest of Pella. County Highway T15 will take you to the south end of the lake, where the highway crosses the top of the dam. In this vicinity are several campgrounds above and below the dam, overlooks, nature trails, sandy beaches, boat ramps, and a marina. The **Red Rock Visitor Center**, 1105 Highway T15, (641) 828-7522; free, has an exhibit about the lake, videos on the bald eagles that frequent this region during the winter, a butterfly garden, and a deck overlooking the lake. On Saturdays at 11 a.m. and 5 p.m. and on Sundays at 11 a.m., 45-minute tours of the dam are given by a ranger of the U.S. Army Corps of Engineers; the assembly point for this tour is the North Tailwater Recreational Area, which is on the Pella side of the dam. Including **Elk Rock State Park**, 811 146th Ave, Knoxville, (641) 842-6008, which is on the south shore, more than 500 campsites are available for tents and RVs around the lake. With all of these diversions, it just might take you awhile to get to Knoxville.

Knoxville

From County Highway T15, turn right (west) on County Highway S71 a few miles south of the Red Rock dam to go to Knoxville. If you're a sprint car racing fan, you know about this place and you're smiling by now. If you don't know what sprint car racing is, this is a great place to learn—Knoxville bills itself as the Sprint Car Capital of the World.

When you reach the intersection with Highway 14, turn to the right and go north until you see the racetrack on your left. Mind you, this is no ordinary county fairground racetrack. This is the **Knoxville Raceway**, Highway 14, (641) 842-5431; admission, where the national competitions in sprint car racing are held every August, drawing about 80,000 fans from near and far. More than 150 cars from the U.S., Canada, and Australia compete in the four-day event.

The fastest that a sprint car ever made it around the half-mile oval dirt track is 14.934 seconds, a record set by Don Droud Jr. in August 1998.

During the nationals the **Knoxville Chamber of Commerce**, (641) 828-7555, runs a **Guest/Host Housing Program** that puts up fans with area families, giving the visitors an appreciation of warm Iowa hospitality.

Besides the nationals, sprint car races are held every weekend from about mid-April through early September, bringing an average of 6,000 fans to town each weekend.

Should you not be in town during the racing season, you can visit the **National Sprint Car Hall of Fame and Museum**, One Sprint Capital Place, (641) 842-6176; (800) 874-4488; admission, immediately adjacent to the racetrack. One advantage of visiting this complex is that things are a lot quieter than at the track during a race and you can get close to the sprint cars, about 25 at last count, which date from the first half of the 20th century to the present. Indeed, it is rather neat to see these beautiful speed demons in toto as they're otherwise just colorful blurs on the track. Two interesting displays are the re-creations of the garages, outfitted with original equipment, used by Hall of Fame drivers John Gerber of Davenport and Bob Trostle of Des Moines.

The Hall of Fame honors the leaders of the sport from the earliest days of sprint car racing to today. A gift shop offers everything from T-shirts and jackets to Christmas ornaments and dress ties bearing the images of sprint cars or the museum's logo.

While in Knoxville, be sure to visit the **Marion County Historical Village**, Willetts Drive, (641) 842-7274; free, open 1–5 p.m. Saturday and Sunday. It's in Marion County Park, located a couple of long blocks west of the main interchange of Highway 14 and Highway 5/92 and south on Willetts Drive. The

Atop the water tower looking down on Lake Red Rock at Cordova County Park, west of Pella

village has a number of historic buildings, including a stagecoach inn believed to be built in 1850, church, country store, schoolhouse, and a museum with agricultural equipment and artifacts from the early days of the region.

On the return to Pella, go north on Highway 14, cross Lake Red Rock on the longest and highest bridge in Iowa, and stop at Cordova County Park, 1378 Highway G-28, (641) 627-5935; (641) 828-2213; free. Operated by the Marion County Conservation Board, this park has four 1,236-square-foot, two-bedroom cabins with lofts, making this a great place to stay overnight without roughing it in a tent.

Also on the grounds are a nature trail, picnic facilities, and a converted water tower that's now the best overlook of Lake Red Rock. Encircled by a winding staircase with 170 steps that lead to the semi-enclosed but very secure viewing platform 106 feet high, this is the highest observation tower in the Midwest. A small fee is charged for going up.

From the park, you return to Pella by going east on County Highway G28, which runs straight into town.

SIDE TRIPS

To the Northwest

Leave Pella on Highway 163 to the northwest and proceed about 22 miles through Monroe to Prairie City. At the Prairie City exit, follow the signs directing you to the **Neal Smith National Wildlife Refuge**, 9981 Pacific Street, (515) 994-3400; free. This is one of the nation's newer wildlife refuges and the largest prairie restoration and reconstruction project in the nation. The place to stop first at this 5,000-acre refuge is its **Prairie Learning Center**, a large, modern visitors center where displays explain how the tallgrass prairie covered some 85 percent of Iowa when settlers arrived about 150 years ago and what's being done today to restore the prairie here. Other displays cover the great variety of prairie plants and grasses as well as the animals that inhabit the area. The center also has a very good gift shop with an excellent array of books about prairie flora and fauna plus toys, apparel, and photos.

Outside are trails that are up to two miles in length, ADA-compliant, and have interpretative stations along the way. You can expect to see big bluestem grass accompanied by plants such as blunt-leaf milkweed, rough blazing star, New England aster, and yellow coneflower, many of which were planted by restoration project volunteers. Among the wildlife you might see—or spot the tracks of—are wild turkey, rabbit, raccoon, turtle, and, in a special 1,000-acre area that's open only for auto tours, buffalo and elk.

To the South

From Knoxville, head south on Highway 14 to County Highway G76, which leads west to the town of **Melcher-Dallas** at Main and Cross Streets. Going up

Main Street here leads you to two small but interesting museums. The first is the **Melcher-Dallas Museum of Military History**, 123 Main, (641) 947-4506; free, which has a collection of uniforms, equipment, flags, firearms, photos, posters connected with the men and women who have served this nation from the 19th century to the present. Also on hand are English, Belgium, French, German, Dutch, Italian, Russian, and Iraqi military items.

A bit farther up Main is the **Melcher-Dallas Coal Mining and Heritage Museum**, Main and Center Streets, (641) 947-5651; free, which recalls the coal mining era in this region. Located in a former miner's union hall, the museum has a reconstructed coal mine, a blacksmith shop, and tools from the early days of this community.

LODGING

Knoxville

Red Carpet Inn, Highway 14 N, (641) 842-3191. Close to raceway. Continental breakfast. $-$$

Super 8 Motel, 2205 N. Lincoln Street, (641) 828-8808; (800) 800-8000. North edge of town. Continental breakfast. $-$$$$

Pella

Bos Landen Holiday Inn Express, 2508 Bos Landen Drive, (641) 628-4853; (800) 916-7888. Southwest side of city near Bos Landen Golf Resort. Indoor pool, continental breakfast. $$-$$$$

Country Inn & Suites, Exit 42 on Highway 163, (641) 620-1111. On south edge of town. Restaurants nearby. $$-$$$

Pella Motor Inn, 703 Oskaloosa Street, (641) 628-9500; (800) 292-2956. On southeast side of city. Continental breakfast. $

Royal Amsterdam Hotel, 705 E. First Street, (641) 620-8400; (877) 954-8400. In Molengracht. European flair. Restaurant, Dutch breakfast. $$$-$$$$

Strawtown Inn, 1111 W. Washington Street, (641) 621-9500. Four blocks west of Central Park. Set in historic buildings. Restaurant, breakfast. $$$-$$$$

BED AND BREAKFASTS

Pella

The Clover Leaf, 314 Washington Street, (641) 628-9045. Near Central Park. Four rooms. $$

DINING

Knoxville

Mr. C's Steakhouse, Highway 14 N, (641) 828-8909. On north edge of city.

Taso's Steakhouse, 221 E. Main, (641) 842-6583. Downtown.

Udders Steakhouse, 1265 Hayes Drive, (641) 828-7821. In the country near Lake Red Rock. Grill your own entreé. Dinner only.

Pella

De Candij Keuken (The Candy Kitchen), 709 Franklin Street, (641) 621-0008. Downtown. Candy, lunches, and ice cream.

Drive Salami's, 1205 W. Washington Street, (641) 628-3210. Family-style. Lunch and dinner.

Dutch East Indies Coffee Company, 804 E. First Street, (641) 628-9723. Downtown. Deli and gourmet sandwiches, salads, soups, and desserts. Lunch only.

Great Wall, 906 W. Washington Street, (641) 628-9855. Chinese cuisine.

The Grille on the Green, 2411 Bos Landen Drive, (641) 628-4627. Southwest of town. Lunch, dinner, and summer breakfast.

Royal Amsterdam Grand Café, 705 E. First Street, (641) 620-8400. Casual dining in the Bistro and fine dining in the restaurant. In Molengracht. Dutch, European and American cuisines. Lunch and dinner. Outside seating available on the canal.

Smokey Row Coffee House, 639 Franklin Street, (641) 621-0008. Coffee shop, restaurant, ice cream parlor.

INFORMATION

Central Iowa Tourism Region, PO Box 454, Webster City, IA 50595, (515) 832-4808; (800) 285-5842; www.iowatourism.org

Marion County Development Commission, 214 E. Main, Knoxville, IA 50138, (641) 828-2257; www.marioncountyiowa.com

Pella Chamber of Commerce/Convention & Visitors Bureau, 518 Franklin Street, Pella, IA 50219, (641) 628-2626; (888) 746-3882; www.pella.org

Chapter 11

Ottumwa:
Southern Hospitality

If you saw the movie or the television show *M*A*S*H*, you might remember that Ottumwa is the hometown of Radar O'Reilly, the company clerk at the surgical hospital with an uncanny ability to know what was going to occur before it did. Of course, Radar was a fictional character, but Ottumwa is very real—and a great place to visit and use as a base for traveling to nearby areas.

The most impressive way to enter Ottumwa is from the north on Highway 63, which brings you down a long hill with a great view of the broad Des Moines River valley ahead of you. As you descend the hill, downtown is to your left (southeast), and you should turn that way, onto 4th Street. After two blocks, turn right (southwest) onto Washington, which will take you directly to the **Wapello County Historical Museum**, 210 W. Main Street, (641) 682-8676; admission, which is in a former railroad depot, a part of which still serves as an Amtrak station.

In the museum are full-scale depictions of an early fire station, complete with a 1925 America LaFrance fire truck, and part of a Sauk and Fox Indian village. Other exhibits showcase geological and archaeological artifacts, the history of the town's agricultural industry, and a scale replica of the Coal Palace Industrial Exhibition Hall, considered one of the finest show palaces ever built. Outside are a small park with a fountain and flowers and an interesting granite horse trough with lion-head spigots, built in 1909.

From the park go southeast on Main Street toward downtown and find the **Ottumwa Convention and Visitor Bureau**, 217 E. Main, (641) 682-3465; (800) 564-5274, to obtain information and brochures for self-guided tours.

One, entitled Gateway to Ottumwa's Past, will lead you past the headstones of famous Ottumwans and 59 types of trees and shrubs ranging from Austrian pine to Japanese zelkova at the **Ottumwa Cemetery** (bounded by N. Court and Jefferson Streets, Van Ness and Park Avenues) north of downtown. Dating back to 1857, the cemetery has a wide arrangement of simple and ornate grave mark-

Waterslides at The Beach aquatic park in Ottumwa

ers, a few mausoleums, a statue of a beloved dog, and an entryway in the form of a Roman triumphal arch.

The other brochure, a self-guided walking tour of downtown Ottumwa, is worthwhile for those interested in the town's architecture and history. The 14 sites listed include the Wapello County Courthouse, which is topped by a statue of Chief Wapello, the neoclassical Ottumwa Public Library fronting Central Park, and the Benson Block which had been designed as a theater but was turned into commercial space because it lacked exits.

You might also see if there is any information available on three other historic districts in Ottumwa: Court Hill, Vogel Place, and Fifth Street Bluff Historic Districts.

Back up Main Street for about half a block from the CVB you'll find Market Street, which becomes the Church Street Bridge as it crosses the Des Moines River. Immediately after crossing the river, you'll come to **The Beach**, 101 Church Street, (641) 682-7873; admission, one of the largest aquatic parks in the Midwest. In addition to enjoying its indoor and outdoor heated swimming areas, you can soak under large mushroom-shaped pedestals spraying water, climb a tower to drop almost straight down a speed slide, wind around a curvy 340-foot body slide, bob up and down in the wave pool, do laps in a 25-yard competitive pool, paddle canoes and kayaks around a four-acre lagoon, play volleyball on sand courts and, well, just have a blast getting water-logged. Concessions are available. If you come on a warm day, count on spending hours here.

The Beach is part of a large park complex; to reach the rest of it you have to return to Church Street, turn right, and immediately turn right again onto Highway 34 heading west. Then you immediately turn left onto Wapello Street from which you can access the other portions of **Ottumwa Park,** at the intersection of Highways 63 and 34, (641) 683-0654; camping fee. Bounded by an oxbow lake, this 340-acre park has serpentine drives, ponds, picnic shelters,

playground equipment, ball diamonds, and tennis, basketball, and sand volleyball courts. You can also fish, canoe, and pedal the paddleboats at the la-
goons, and camp in an area with 335 spaces for tents and RVs. Two long trails
begin in the park; one goes to Chief Wapello's grave, about 12 miles away, and
the other to Eldon, about 25 miles away.

Country Air

To visit attractions outside of town, get back on Wapello Street and head
south through Ottumwa until the street T's into Mary Street where you will
turn right (west). As you head out of town, Mary Street becomes County Highway H41, which leads to the **Airpower Museum**, 22001 Bluegrass Road, (641)
938-2773; donations appreciated, about eight miles away. Although the name
may suggest military aircraft, this museum is dedicated to all types of aircraft,
primarily pre-1940s, and its location next to a grass airstrip gives it the ap-
propriate feel of a small 1930s airport.

In one building, the museum has a number of engines, models, a small sim-
ulator-trainer, propellers, aviation artwork, artifacts of all types, and an ex-
perimental working model of a ground-effect aircraft that rode on a cushion
of air above a flat surface. In the hangars next to that building are a number of
beautiful aircraft, ranging from a 1950 Mooney M-18C "Mite," a tiny red slip
of an airplane, and the Rose Parrakeet A-1, a biplane that's beautiful beyond
compare, to a 1931 Stinson SR(S) with a log that reveals it made a secret trip

One of the antique aircraft on display at the Airpower Museum, west of Ottumwa

117

The site of Chief Wapello's grave, east of Ottumwa

in July 1944, possibly to haul components of the atomic bomb. There's also the one-and-only Brewster Fleet B-1, made in 1939. Overall, about four dozen aircraft are at the museum.

The headquarters of the Antique Airplane Association is here along with a museum dedicated to the memory of those who were in the 6th Air Force, an almost-forgotten command that flew missions over Central America and the Caribbean during World War II.

To sample another bit of Americana, return to Ottumwa and take Highway 34 east to Highway 16, about 11 miles east of town. Take 16 south to Eldon and follow the signs to an American icon, the **American Gothic House**, 301 American Gothic Street, (515) 281-6412; free. You'll probably recognize the building the moment you see it. It's the house in the background of the famous painting by Iowa artist Grant Wood, who depicted a farmer with a pitchfork standing in front of the building with his daughter (usually mistaken for his wife). Wood sketched the house while visiting the area—he lived in and near Cedar Rapids—and later worked it into the painting, which has become one of America's best-known artworks. The site is open year-round, but the interior of the house is closed to the public; feel free nonetheless to take pictures of each other in front of the house and create your own work of art.

*I*nto the Great Outdoors

On your way back to Ottumwa on Highway 34, you'll notice a turnout near the little town of Agency to the **Chief Wapello's Memorial Park**. Many years ago this site was near the villages headed by Chiefs Wapello, Keokuk, and Appanoose. Now it holds the graves of Wapello, a Meskwakie chief who died in 1842, and his friend, Gen. Joseph M. Street, who died a couple years earlier. What's interesting about Wapello's burial site is that it is so untypical of the graves of famous people from his time. Instead of being granite and adorned with fanciful carvings, it's a pyramid of stainless steel sides that reflect the sky above.

When you get close to Ottumwa again, take Highway 63 south and in a few miles you'll arrive at **Pioneer Ridge Nature Area and Nature Center**, Highway 63 S, (641) 682-3091; free, on the left (east) side of the highway. Overlooking a nice pond that's surrounded by fields and woods is a new nature center with permanent mounts of animals that are customarily found in this region plus some permanent exhibits related to the area's natural history. Miles of trails, from handicapped-accessible to steep and difficult, lead through woods and prairie and to picnic areas and a primitive camping site. There's also a re-creation of an Indian village within the woods of this 737-acre preserve.

SIDE TRIPS

To the North

Taking Highway 63 north from Ottumwa leads you directly to **Oskaloosa**, about 25 miles to the northwest. Leave the four-lane highway at the Oskaloosa exit and remain on Highway 63 into town. There's a nice downtown square with a gazebo and a magnificent courthouse as the backdrop; on summer Thursdays there are free concerts here at 8 p.m.

About a mile north of town turn right (northeast) on Glendale Road, also called County Highway T65. Two miles up that road is **Nelson Pioneer Farm**, 2294 Oxford Avenue, (641) 672-2989; admission. Started in 1844 as a farm by Daniel Nelson, it remained active and in the family until 1958, when it was turned into a center to educate the public about farming practices in Iowa's early years. Besides the farm's buildings, including the original log cabin, the family's first frame home, meat house, summer kitchen and barn, the site also has a blacksmith shop, two post offices, a country store and an 1861 school that were all moved there. The state's only mule cemetery is here too, containing "Becky" and "Jennie," who served in the Civil War and finished their days at the farm in Nelson's care.

To the West

This is one of the book's simplest, yet most rewarding side trips. From Ottumwa, take Highway 34 west for 21 miles to **Albia**, which has what surely must be one of the prettiest town squares in the nation. Residents have taken great pride in restoring many of the 92 buildings in the business district; several, including some homes and the courthouse, are listed on the National Register of Historic Places. Descriptive plaques can be found on many of the structures. Visit the **Albia Area Chamber of Commerce**, 107 S. Clinton Street, (641) 932-5108, in the downtown area to pick up a brochure about these architectural wonders. You may find it hard to believe, but Albia was once called the ugliest town in America . . . but no more.

Almost due south of Albia is Iowa's largest lake, **Rathbun Lake**, 20112 Highway J5T, (641) 647-2464; fees for camping and swimming, a manmade reservoir of 21,000 surface acres—and 55 miles of shoreline—on the Chariton River. Around the lake are five campgrounds, three swimming beaches, numerous boat ramps, and endless trails. The U.S. Army Corps of Engineers' **Information Center**, (641) 647-2464; free, is at the south end of the dam—over which County Highway J5T runs—on the lake's southeast side. The center also has wildlife dioramas and displays on coal mining, which was once a large industry in this part of Iowa.

Rathbun Marina, 21646 Moravia Place, (641) 741-3212; fee, the closest marina to the center, has boats for rent. Also near the dam is the **Rathbun Fish Hatchery**, 15053 Hatchery Place, (641) 647-2406; free, one of the largest freshwater fish hatcheries in the nation. An elevated walkway leads through the hatchery and aquariums give you a fish-eye level of life underwater. Nature trails lead around the hatchery.

On the north side of the lake is **Honey Creek State Park**, Highway 142, (641) 724-3739; camping fee. It has camping, picnic facilities, trails, and boat ramps.

To reach the lake from Albia, drive south on Highway 5 to Moravia, turn right (west) onto Highway 142 for two miles until you reach County Highway J5T, and take that straight south to the dam.

LODGING

Albia

Indian Hills Inn, 100 Highway 34 E, (641) 932-7181; (800) 728-4286. Restaurant, indoor pool. $-$$

Oskaloosa

Comfort Inn, 2401 A Avenue W, (641) 672-0375; (800) 228-5150. West end of town. Indoor pool, continental breakfast. $-$$$$

Ottumwa

Heartland Inn, 125 W. Joseph Avenue, (641) 682-8526; (800) 334-3277. North end of town. Near restaurants. Indoor pool, continental breakfast. $$

Parkview Plaza Hotel & Suites, 107 E. 2nd Street, (641) 682-8051. Downtown. Restaurant. $-$$$$

Super 8 Motel, 2823 N. Court Street, (641) 684-5055; (800) 800-8000. North end of town. Near restaurants. Indoor pool, continental breakfast. $-$$$

BED AND BREAKFASTS
Albia
> **Arvine White House B&B**, 309 N. Main Street, (641) 932-3329; (888) 449-7791. Near downtown. Three rooms. $$

Ottumwa
> **The Cat's Meow**, 423 N. Market Street, (641) 682-6855. A 1900 mansion in historic district north of downtown. Three rooms. $$-$$$$

> **The Guest House**, 645 N. Court, (641) 684-8893; 682-8876. North side of town. Two rooms. $$

DINING
Albia
> **Albia Café**, 11 N. Main Street, (641) 932-2975. Downtown.

> **The Skean Block**, 11 Benton Avenue E, (641) 932-2159. Downtown in historic building.

> **White Buffalo Restaurant**, 100 Highway 34 E, (641) 932-7181. South end of town.

Oskaloosa
> **Hunter's,** 113 High Avenue W, (641) 673-9911. In downtown area. Specialty coffees and lunches.

> **Oskaloosa Family Restaurant**, 1802 A Avenue E, (641) 673-1480. East end of town. Family style.

> **The Peppertree**, Highway 63 N, (641) 673-9191. On north side. Suppers and Sunday brunch buffet.

Ottumwa
> **Greenbriar Restaurant,** 1207 N. Jefferson Street, (641) 682-8147. North edge of town.

> **China Restaurant**, 321 E. Main Street, (641) 682-9467. Downtown. Chinese cuisine.

> **Ching Dow Hu Restaurant**, 704 Richmond Avenue, (641) 683-3133. Near Ottumwa Park.

> **Fisherman's Bay**, 221 N. Wapello Street, (641) 682-6325. North edge of town.

INFORMATION

Albia Area Chamber of Commerce, 18 S. Main Street, Albia, IA 52531, (641) 932-5108.

Central Iowa Tourism Region, PO Box 454, Webster City, IA 50595, (515) 832-4808; (800) 285-5842; www.iowatourism.org

Oskaloosa Visitors Center, 124 N. Market Street, Oskaloosa, IA 52577, (641) 672-2591; www.oskaloosachamber.com

Ottumwa Convention and Visitors Bureau, 217 E. Main, PO Box 308, Ottumwa, IA 52501, (641) 682-3465; (800) 564-5274; www.ottumwa chamber.com

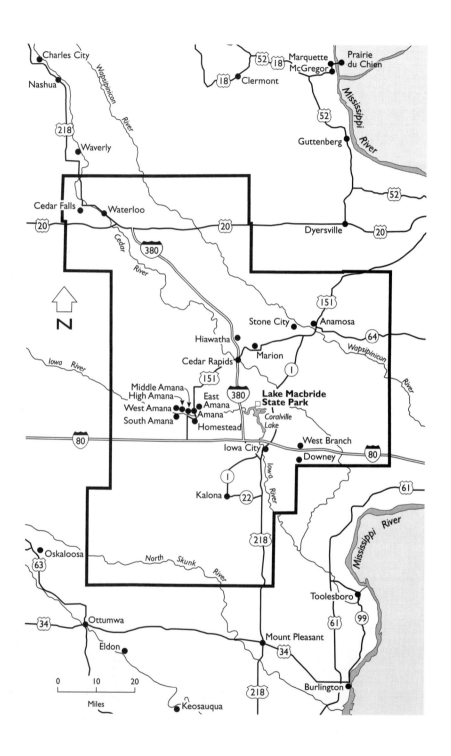

Section III

East Central Iowa
Big Cities... and a Few Small Ones

Chapter 12

Waterloo and Cedar Falls: Cities of the River

In 1845, George and Mary Hanna settled with their family alongside the Red Cedar River at a ford called Prairie Rapids Crossing. That same year, William Sturgis and a friend started another settlement about six miles upriver and called that Sturgis Falls. Five years later the names of the communities had changed. Prairie Rapids Crossing became Waterloo and Sturgis Falls became Cedar Falls. And somewhere along the line the Red Cedar River lost its colorful adjective and became just the Cedar River.

As time went on, the cities grew and bumped up against each other, ultimately forming the largest metropolitan area in northeast Iowa. Still, each city has retained its own identity, which means there are two wonderful cities to visit within a short distance of each other.

Waterloo

The larger of the cities, Waterloo has a number of attractions clustered in the downtown area on the west bank of the Cedar River and an easy way to reach them is by coming into the metro area on I-380, which turns into Highway 218 as it nears the cities. Watch for the signs showing the way to the Grout Museums and exit there, at Washington Street. Go to W. Park Avenue, turn left (west) and go a couple blocks to South Street

There are three Grout Museums, one on your left and two on your right. The main one is the **Grout Museum of History and Science and Planetarium**, 503 South Street, (319) 234-6357; admission. Opening in 1956 with only 2,000 artifacts collected by early Waterloo resident William Grout, the museum now has more than 75,000 items, many of which are used in exhibits related to the natural and cultural history of the area. There are life-size dioramas depicting a cabin, tool shed, smithy, carpenter's shop, and a general store. On the natu-

Downtown Waterloo along the Cedar River

ral side, exhibits highlight the region's plants, animals, and geology. As for things out of this world, the Grout gives visitors the means to examine the stars and planets either at its planetarium or through its telescopes. With more than 700 programs scheduled each year, the Grout offers plenty to see and do.

From the museum, you can walk to the north, across W. Park Avenue to Washington Park, where there's a small Japanese garden, and a block beyond that is another part of the Grout: the **Rensselaer Russell House,** 520 W. 3rd Street, (319) 233-0262; admission. Built in 1861, the brick house was the showpiece of the city and remains quite a place to visit today, with its Victorian parlor and furnishings from three generations of the Russells.

Immediately next door to the house is the **Bluedorn Science Imaginarium,** 322 Washington, (319) 233-8708; admission, another part of the Grout complex. Loaded with interactive exhibits and frequent demonstrations, the Imaginarium concentrates on the physics of light, electricity, motion, sound, and more. Remember looking at those little gyroscopes when you were a kid? Here, there's one so big that you can sit in it and feel the world of motion. You can also play with lightning flashing inside a glass globe, take charge of a laser light show, and compete in one of the wackier races you'll come acros—seeing whose air bubbles rise faster in tubes filled with various clear liquids.

Art is the highlight of the next stop. Drive over to Cedar Street on the west bank of the river, where sits the **Waterloo Center for the Arts,** 225 Commercial Street, (319) 291-4490; free. Among its permanent works are drawings, paintings, and prints by Grant Wood, American decorative arts, the largest public collection of Haitian art in the nation, African-American art and paintings, drawings, original prints, photographs, and sculpture by Midwestern artists. Of particular interest to children is the **Junior Art Gallery**, which over the years has arranged exhibits ranging from a prehistoric cave dwelling to a Chinese home to an Athens market scene from centuries ago.

From the art center, it's a short hop to another form of art, that of making tractors, at the **John Deere Waterloo Works**, 400 Westfield Avenue, (319) 292-7697 and 292-7668; free but call for reservations (only kids 12 and older are allowed). With four John Deere plants in the area conducting tours, you can see the entire manufacture of tractors, from the casting of parts and the subassembly of engines and drivetrains, to the final assembly of tractors of all sizes. To get to this particular John Deere plant, called the Component Works, from the art center, go one block to Commercial Street, turn right to go north, and the street will turn into Westfield Avenue where the plant is located.

Upon leaving the John Deere plant, there are two ways to drive to Cedar Falls, both with nice diversions along the way.

1. Get on Highway 218 to head west. After crossing the Cedar River, you will take the first exit to visit **George Wyth State Park**, (319) 232-5505; fee for camping. A 1,100-acre park, Wyth offers modern campsites, swimming, picnic facilities, trails, and lots of water in the form of several lakes and the Cedar River. To go into Cedar Falls from here, go west on Highway 57.
2. Continue up Westfield Avenue to a T intersection, take a left (west) onto Ansborough Avenue and just past the highway take a right (north) onto Rainbow Drive. That will turn into Grand Avenue. In a little more than three miles, you should see signs pointing the way to **Hartman Reserve Nature Center**, 657 Reserve Drive, (319) 277-2187; free. There's an interpretative center to detail the flora and fauna of the region and the preserve has miles of trails within its 287 acres that connect to others outside the preserve. To go into Cedar Falls from here, return to Grand Avenue and go west to Main Street. Turn right to go north until you come to a T intersection with 1st Street.

Cedar Falls

On the north side of 1st Street near downtown Cedar Falls is a restored, 1920s-era gas station that dispenses information, not gas and oil. It's the **Behrens-Rapp Tourism Information Station**, 1st and Clay Streets, (319) 277-8817 and 266-5149, in the center of a historical complex in Sturgis Park and full of helpful information. One brochure you might want is the Cedar Falls Walking Tour, an excellent resource for viewing the historic buildings in this city.

While at the historic complex, visit the **Little Red School House #5**, (319) 277-8817; 266-5149; donation appreciated, just a few steps away. Built in 1909,

The Little Red School House #5, Cedar Falls

the school still has the black-boards, desks, books, and a potbelly stove used by the teachers and students during the early 20th century. Tours are given from 2:30-4 p.m. on Wednesday, Saturday, and Sunday, or by appointment.

Just beyond that is the **Broom Factory**, 115 Mill Street. Although built in 1862 to produce cornstarch, the building became a broom factory in 1905 and, in a odd turn, later produced pickles along with brooms. Now a restaurant called The Broom Factory, the old pickle-and-broom business was owned by C.N. McHugh, who served as the city's mayor from 1935 to 1943 and was known as "The Pickle Mayor" because he donated pickles to many charitable events.

Also in the area is one of Cedar Falls' most-visited attractions, the **Ice House Museum**, 1st and Franklin Streets, (319) 277-8817 and 266-5149; donation appreciated. Built in 1921, the icehouse stored up to 8,000 tons of ice that was cut from the Cedar River for use through the warm months each year. As a museum, the icehouse displays gear that was used to cut and move ice from the river into storage as well as other items related to the history of Cedar Falls, including early cars and horse-powered equipment.

Two blocks to the south is the **George Wyth House and Viking Pump Museum**, 303 Franklin Street, (319) 277-8817; donation appreciated. Designed in the Arts and Crafts style with an art deco influence, the majority of the house reflects the period it was occupied by the Wyth family, while the third floor holds examples of the rotary pumps made by Wyth's Viking Pump Company, including wooden prototypes of the pumps.

A block to the east is the **Victorian House and Carriage House Museum**, 308 W. 3rd Street, (319) 266-5149; donation appreciated. An Italianate home built at the beginning of the Civil War, this house with a cupola in the middle of its roof has 18-inch walls, and shutters on the inside of the windows with vertical louvers. Servants' quarters are upstairs and another part of the house holds the 13-by-26-foot O-scale model train layout made by William J. Lenoir, who was internationally known for the fine detail he put into crafting his trains and hand-built steam locomotives. Out back, the carriage house hosts various exhibits and contains the local historical society's library and archives.

On Saturday mornings from late May through October, the section of 3rd Street between the museum and Overman Park to the north is blocked off and used as a Farmers Market, (319) 277-1745.

Main Street

From here it's a pleasant walk to Main Street where a left turn puts you between 3rd and 1st Streets, an interesting area with decorative street lights, trees, and baskets of flowers amid restaurants, unique shops, and a coffee bar. A city project downtown calls for works of public art to be on display throughout the area, as well as in the Hearst Center for the Arts, and changed every year. There's also a place to rent bikes downtown, **Bike Tech**, 112 Main Street, (319) 266-5979, so you can pedal on the more than 30 miles of trails within Cedar Falls, which connect to more in Waterloo as well.

One of the places you might visit while downtown is the **Iowa Band Museum**, 203 ½ Main Street, (319) 266-4308; donation appreciated; open 2–4 p.m. Wednesday and Sunday, June–July. Called one of the finest band halls in the nation by John Philip Sousa, this 1870s structure is the last band hall in Iowa and serves as the offices and practice hall for the state's oldest municipal band, the Cedar Falls Municipal Band. It also houses the James A. Melichar Exhibit of band instruments, including tenor, bass, and baritone saxophones, trom-

The Victorian House Museum, Cedar Falls

bones, "rain catcher" Sousaphones, and the gigantic sarrusophone. Uniforms on display include those worn throughout the years by the band's members. There's even a sign listing rules of dress and conduct that were used years ago. The 45-piece band gives free open-air concerts at 7:30 p.m. each Tuesday, June-August, in the band shell at **Overman Park**, which is near the Victorian House Museum.

On the next block is the **Black Hawk Hotel**, 115 Main Street, which was the Burr Hotel when it was built in the 1870s. Still a hotel, the Black Hawk has a restaurant on its first floor and, unusual for a hotel, it also rents canoes. Inquire at the main desk and you can find yourself paddling down a stretch of the nearby Cedar River.

Just north of the hotel is the Northeast Iowa Weavers and Spinners Guild, located in the **Fiber Arts Studio**, 111 Main Street, (319) 266-7815. Here, the crafts of spinning, weaving, dyeing, and making rugs, baskets, and paper are shared with others.

And just north of there is the **Oster Regent Theater**, 103 Main Street, (319) 277-5283, home of the Cedar Falls Community Theater and productions ranging from drama to comedies to musicals.

South Side

Drive south about two dozen blocks to W. Seerley Boulevard, on which you will find the **James and Meryl Hearst Center for the Arts**, 304 W. Seerley Boulevard, (319) 273-8641; free. Concentrating on works by regional artists such as Grant Wood, Marjorie Nuhn, Mauricio Lasansky, John Page, and Gary Kelley in its permanent collection, the center sponsors a variety of workshops and lectures on various forms of art for adults and children. Outside, a number of sculptures contrast and complement the trees, bushes, and flowers of the **Woodland Sculpture Garden**.

Continue west on W. Seerley to a T intersection and turn left (south) on College Street. Then turn right (west) on University Avenue. Take that to Hudson Road where you turn right (north) and watch for the University of Northern Iowa's **University Museum**, 3219 Hudson Road, (319) 273-2188; free, which features exhibits about biology, geology, anthropology, and history with approximately 100,000 artifacts, specimens, and other items.

Also on campus is the **UNI Gallery of Art**, W. 27th Street and Hudson Road, (319) 273-6134; free, located in the Kamerick Art Building. Besides hosting temporary exhibits of all forms of art, the gallery's permanent collection has works from John Buck, George Grosz, Berenice Abbott, Jerry Uelsmann, and more. The gallery is also responsible for placing more than 30 sculptures throughout the campus by such artists as Fletcher Benton, Janet Loftquist, and Cork Marcheschi.

Before you leave the building, and if you're in town on a Monday evening, you might want to visit the studios of **KUNI-FM, 90.9 radio**, (319) 273-6400; (800) 772-2440; admission. The facility is in the Communications Arts Center, an adjacent part of the Kamerick Art Building. Perhaps the best public radio station in Iowa, KUNI hosts *Live From Studio One* with live entertainment that you can observe as it's broadcast from 7 to 8 p.m. every Monday.

*B*eyond the Cities

To visit some outlying attractions, return to University Avenue and head east until you reach Highway 58 where you will go south. If you want to visit another John Deere plant, leave the highway at Ridgeway Avenue and go east. In a short drive you will find the **Engine Works**, 3801 Ridgeway Avenue, (319) 292-5347; free. Be sure to make reservations; only kids 12 and older are allowed.

After visiting either plant, continue east on Ridgeway until you reach Sergeant Road (also Highway 63) and go south to Highway 20 to head east. If you didn't visit the plants but remained on Highway 58, go east when you reach Highway 20.

From Highway 20, exit at Hawkeye Road and go south until you reach Orange Road where you turn to the left (east). In a few moments you'll arrive at **Cedar Valley Arboretum**, 1927 E. Orange Road, (319) 226-4966; free. With more than 400 types of trees, the 74-acre arboretum has 10 picture-perfect gardens. Among them is the Community Gardens where residents and groups of the region tend 10-by-10-foot display beds to show their creativity. In the Enabling Garden, people with physical limitations find tools and designs of gardens that allow them to enjoy working with plants. There are also trial gardens (where a particular type of eggplant really looks like an egg!), a forest of Iowa's native trees and a wheel garden where plants representing various ethnic groups form the spokes. A Children's Pond is another of the features at the arboretum.

For wet and wild times, visit **Lost Island Theme Park**, 2225 E. Shaulis Road, (319) 234-3210; admission, a short distance away from the arboretum. Among the ways to get you wet are five waterslides, a wave pool, and a lazy river, while on the wild side are go-carts and a "goofy-golf" golf course. Getting here from the arboretum is simple: continue east on E. Orange Road to Hess Road and turn left (north). The water park is at the next major intersection.

Fans of long-distance bicycling will be interested in this next opportunity. Continue north on Hess to its junction with Highway 218/I-380 and head toward Cedar Rapids (that's right, Cedar Rapids this time, not Cedar Falls). Stop far short of Cedar Rapids by taking the first exit on the other side of the Cedar River. That will put you into Evansdale where you will take River Road to the head of the **Cedar Valley Nature Trail**, one of Iowa's longer hike-bike trails. It will take you toward the Cedar Rapids metro area 52 miles away.

SIDE TRIPS

To the North

A bit more than four miles north of Cedar Falls on County Highway V14 is **Antique Acres**, 7610 Waverly Road, (319) 987-2380, which has a museum displaying farm machinery that's more than a century old. Among the items in the collection are a 140-horsepower Reeves steam plow, which is one of the larger traction engines built anywhere, a 1918 Moline Universal Tractor, the small 4-horsepower Litchfield six-cycle, gas-powered engine, and a mighty 400-horsepower steam engine. On the weekend before each Labor Day, the grounds become the site of the **"Old Time Power Show,"** which features live demonstrations of threshing, plowing, and other work done by antique tractors and stationary engines. There's also a tractor pull featuring antique and classic tractors.

Farther north is Waverly, which each spring and fall hosts the **Midwest Draft Horse Sale**, 2212 5th Avenue NW, (319) 352-2804. This event is big in several ways: the record-setting numbers of horses sold; the fact that the auction lasts several days; and the size of the critters—huge, 2,000-pound equines that make everything else called horses look like ponies. Even if you're not buying or selling anything, it's still fascinating to visit here during the sales, which move the huge but gentle Percherons, Belgians, Clydesdales, Fjords, and Haflingers as well as contemporary and vintage wagons, carriages, and all types of gear. Buyers and sellers range from Budweiser and Disney to Amish farmers and tourism buggy drivers. It is quite a show.

About another 20 minutes drive up Highway 218 is Nashua, home of the **Little Brown Church** (described in the "Side Trip" in chapter 7).

To the East

Going east on Highway 20 from the Waterloo/Cedar Falls area and leave the four-lane highway at Highway 282 to visit Quasqueton, home of **Cedar Rock** and some great fossil hunting grounds on the Wapsipinicon River (discussed in the "Side Trip" for chapter 15).

LODGING

Cedar Falls

Black Hawk Motor Inn, 122 Washington Street, (319) 277-1161; (888) 577-1161. Downtown, behind and connected to the Black Hawk Hotel at 115 Main Street. Restaurant, continental breakfast. Canoe rentals. $

Country Inn & Suites, 2910 S. Main Street, (319) 268-1800; (800) 456-4000. South side of city near UNI. Indoor pool, continental breakfast. $$-$$$$

Holiday Inn-University Plaza, 5826 University Avenue, (319) 277-2230; (800) HOLIDAY. Southeast side of city. Restaurant, indoor and outdoor pools. $$

University Inn, 4711 University Avenue, (319) 277-1412; (800) 962-7784. Southeast side of city, midway between Cedar Falls and Waterloo. Continental breakfast. $-$$$$

Waterloo

Best Western Starlite Village, 214 Washington Street, (319) 235-0321; (800) 903-0009. Downtown near Grout Museums and Waterloo Center for the Arts. Restaurant, indoor pool. $$

Comfort Inn, 1945 La Porte Road, (319) 234-7411; (800) 228-5150. South side of city off Highway 218. Near restaurants. Indoor pool, continental breakfast. $-$$

The Grand Hotel, 300 W. Mullin Road, (319) 234-7791; (877) WATERLOO. Downtown. Outdoor pool, continental breakfast. $-$$$$

Quality Inn & Suites, 226 W. 5th Street, (319) 235-0301; (800) 480-6422. Downtown near Grout Museums. Continental breakfast. $$-$$$$

Heartland Inn, I-380/Highway 218, Exit 72, (319) 235-4461; (800) 334-3277. South side of city. Near restaurants. Indoor pool, continental breakfast. $$-$$$$

Waverly

Best Western Red Fox Inn, 1900 Heritage Way SW, (319) 352-5330; (800) 397-5330. On west edge of city near Waverly Horse Sale Barns. Restaurant, indoor pool, continental breakfast. $$-$$$$

BED AND BREAKFASTS

Cedar Falls

Carriage House Inn B&B, 3030 Grand Boulevard, (319) 277-6724. East of downtown near Hartman Reserve Nature Center. Two rooms. $$$$

House by the Side of the Road, 6804 Ranchero Road, (319) 988-3691. South side of metro area in the country. Two rooms. $$

La Porte City

Brandt's B&B, 1279 53rd Street, (319) 342-2912. About 20 minutes southeast of Waterloo. Near Cedar Valley Nature Trail. Private sunroom suites. Three rooms. $$

Waterloo

Wellington Place B&B, 800 W. 4th Street, (319) 234-2993. Near downtown and Grout Museums. Four rooms. $$-$$$$

DINING

Cedar Falls

Biemann's Black Hawk Restaurant, 119 Main Street, (319) 277-4050. Downtown in Black Hawk Hotel. Home-style with daily specials.

Blue Moon Café, 2223 College Street. (319) 266-6512. Lunch and dinner; vegetarian items.

The Broom Factory, 125 W. First Street, (319) 268-0877. In historic building near downtown. Upscale American and Cajun dining. Entertainment Friday evenings.

The Brown Bottle, 1111 Center Street, (319) 266-2616. Upscale Italian cuisine.

Cup of Joe, 102 Main Street, (319) 277-1596. Downtown coffee shop with sandwiches, desserts, pastries.

Montage, 222 Main Street, (319) 268-7222. Downtown. Upscale dining with American and international dishes.

Nicker's Grille, 205 E. 18th Street, (319) 277-3426. South of downtown. Home-style cooking.

Waterloo

Broadway Diner, 504 Riehl, (319) 234-5712. East side of river near downtown. Casual dining.

Cedar Valley Fish Market, 218 Division Street, (319) 236-2965. Downtown on east side of river. Casual dining.

The Cellar, 320 E. 4th Street, (319) 274-8889. A downtown pub with its entrance on the alley. Local and visiting musicians play blues and jazz on Saturday evenings, and UNI students play jazz every other Thursday.

Garfield's Café, 2820 Falls Avenue, (319) 291-6742. West of downtown. Casual dining.

Mama Nick's Circle Pizzeria, 1934 Washington Street, (319) 233-3323. Good reputation for pizza.

Steamboat Gardens, 1740 Falls Avenue, (319) 232-0344. North of downtown on east side of river. Bar and grill.

Waverly

Abe Downing Steakhouse, 1900 Heritage Way, (319) 352-5050. On west side of town in Red Fox Inn. Upscale dining, evenings.

Martin's Brandenburg Restaurant, 215 E. Bremer Avenue, (319) 352-9170. Downtown.

INFORMATION

Cedar Falls Tourism and Visitors Bureau, 10 Main Street, PO Box 367, Cedar Falls, IA 50613, (319) 268-4266; (800) 845-1955; www.cedarfalls tourism.org

Waterloo Convention and Visitors Bureau, 215 E. 4th Street, Waterloo, IA 50703, (319) 233-8350; (800) 728-8431; www.waterloocvb.org

Chapter 13

Cedar Rapids:
Home of American Gothic

The metropolitan area that's known as Cedar Rapids, including the separate communities of Marion and Hiawatha, began like most others in Iowa—with a simple log cabin. This one was erected in 1837 near the rapids of what was then called the Red Cedar River. Forty years later, Cedar Rapids had grown into a major grain-milling center, and it remains so today. The city is home to the Quaker Oats mill, the largest cereal mill under one roof in the world (unfortunately, no tours are given); the structure dominates the downtown skyline along the Cedar River. However, this is much more than a mill town, as you will see.

Most of the attractions in Cedar Rapids are located in the downtown area, but there are some very interesting places to see before you get there. As you approach the metro area on I-380 from the south, leave the interstate at Exit 17 and at the end of the ramp, turn right onto 33rd Avenue SW. Go to the first intersection and turn left (north) onto J Street SW, where in a short distance on the left is **Duffy's Collectible Cars**, 250 Classic Car Court SW, (319) 364-7000; admission. With a host of fantastic classics of the automotive industry, Duffy's is no ordinary car museum. Here, if you find yourself wishing you could own one of these beauties, you can! That's right, this is a combination museum and showroom and because cars are always coming and going, the vehicles are different each time you visit. On nice days, expect to see some gleaming classics such as early Ford Mustangs and GTOs sitting outside.

Czech Village

From Duffy's, get back on J Street SW and go north to 16th Avenue SW and turn right (east). In a few blocks the street will veer to the left and you'll be in the **Czech Village**, 16th Avenue SW, (319) 362-2846. A part of Cedar Rapids settled predominantly by Czechs and Slovaks (about one-quarter of all of the city residents are their descendants), the village is no glitzed-up tourist attraction but an authentic neighborhood. There are *obchody* (stores), a *pekarna* (bakery), a *restaurace* (restaurant) and more—even a business started in 1885 that still makes feather-and-down pillows and comforters—all reflecting the Old World atmosphere. This is most evident at the 16th Avenue Bridge, which is guarded by stone lions, and the massive clock tower near the foot of the bridge. In case you were wondering, English is usually the language spoken here although *Jak se mas?* (How are you?) and other Czech and Slovak phrases are heard now and then.

Just down the way from the clock tower is the **National Czech and Slovak Museum and Library**, 30 16th Avenue SW, (319) 362-8500; admission, with the flags of the Czech and Slovak Republics flying next to the American red, white, and blue outside the front door. A very modern building with a European flair, the museum has exhibits related to kroj (ethnic costumes), the homeland, politics, language, and folk arts such as batik eggs. Some artifacts date back 400 years, and one exhibit features a restored immigrant home with furnishings. A unique item that the museum is proud to have is a full-size bronze statue of the first president of Czechoslovakia, Tomas Masaryk. Exhibited here for the first time ever, it had been buried several times in its homeland to hide it from Nazi troops and then the Soviets, who wanted to destroy it. Although you might expect the museum to be local in scope, it is in fact a national museum and its exhibits and library represent all the Czechs and Slovaks who came to America. The gift shop features items made in the republics, including glassware, dolls, Modra ceramicware, and music.

For those who like to buy fresh produce, across the street from the museum is the **Round House,** which hosts a farmers market during the summer on Wednesday evenings and Saturday mornings.

Now you could cross the Cedar River at this point on 16th Avenue SW (which, for some unknown reason, becomes 14th Avenue SE on the other side). Or, for this tour, return down 16th or 15th Avenue SW to C Street SW and take a right turn. That street will merge with 1st Street SW, with the river appearing on your right. There are a few places along the way to pull over and walk along the river; the walk goes for a few miles to the north if you want to really stretch your legs and get the best view of the Cedar Rapids skyline.

*D*owntown

To get a closer look at downtown Cedar Rapids, continue up 1st Street SW to 1st Avenue and take a right to cross the Cedar River as well as the island in the middle of it. When you get to the first street on the other side of the river, appropriately named 1st Street SE, you should see the **Cedar Rapids Convention and Visitors Bureau**, 119 1st Avenue SE, (319) 398-5009; (800) 735-5557, about a half-block beyond the intersection on the right side of 1st Avenue. Pick up brochures, booklets, and maps to help you get around. Two brochures in

Veterans Memorial and City Hall, Cedar Rapids

particular that are nice to have are *Grant Wood Neighborhood Self-Guided Tour* and *Cedar Rapids Historic Downtown Walking Tour and Art Map*, the latter a guide to about 20 public sculptures located in the downtown area.

Just west of the CVB is a riverfront plaza featuring the 60-foot-tall, stainless steel sculpture called *Tree of Five Seasons*. Located where the first log cabin was built in 1837, the tree has a base with an audio kiosk that tells some of the history of the region.

To go to the next stop on this tour, you might choose to simply walk along Riverfront Park or 1st Street SE. Go to 2nd Avenue SE (a one-way street going west) and turn to the right toward the island in the middle of the Cedar River. The large building rising high on your right is **Veterans Memorial and City Hall**, 2nd Avenue on Municipal Island. Just inside its main doors is a magnificent stained glass window, called "Veterans of All Wars," designed by Grant Wood in 1928. There also is a 1960 bronze sculpture by Felix de Weldon that honors the men who fought at Iwo Jima.

If you walked here, after visiting the memorial and city hall simply walk back to 1st Street SE and turn to the right. Stay on the side of the street that's close to the river.

If you drove, you have a little more driving to do: go across the island and the other channel of the Cedar River to 1st Street SW, turn left for a block and come back into downtown on 3rd Avenue. Then turn right onto 1st Street SE.

Now that everyone's on the right street and pointed in the right direction, go less than two blocks and you'll come to the **Science Station and McLeod Busse IMAX Dome Theatre**, 427 1st Street SE, (319) 366-0968; admission. The Science Station, which was the first element to open its doors, is located in the former central fire station—the firepole is still in the lobby—and has three floors of hands-on exhibits, many of which concentrate on electricity, light, and optical illusions. Live demonstrations about various science projects are held six to eight times a day in the museum. The IMAX theater opened in the spring of 2001 and features screenings of large 70mm format movies that change throughout the year.

𝒜 Grant Wood Tour

For the next attraction, you can either drive or walk. If you walk, keep those brochures about the downtown's historic buildings and public sculptures handy. And note that it's six blocks to the next stop. From the Science Museum, turn onto 5th Avenue SE (a one-way going east) and go to 5th Street SE, where you head left for two blocks. At the intersection of 5th Street SE and 3rd Avenue SE, you will see the **Cedar Rapids Museum of Art**, 410 3rd Avenue SE, (319) 366-7503; admission. Part of the museum is located in the former Carnegie Library that was built in 1904. The rest is in the spacious modern gallery alongside the Carnegie and connected to it by a large glass atrium that serves as the main entrance.

The art museum houses the largest collection of works—at least 16 pieces— by Grant Wood, who lived in Cedar Rapids for most of his life. Unfortunately, his most famous work, *American Gothic*, which is the second-most recognized painting in the world after Leonardo da Vinci's *Mona Lisa*, hangs in the Chicago Art Institute where it won a competitive prize in 1930 and was originally purchased for $300. Still, Cedar Rapids is the place to see Wood's

Getting around Cedar Rapids

Unlike most other communities in Iowa where the majority of streets run north-south and east-west, much of Cedar Rapids was laid out to relate to a stretch in the Cedar River that runs northwest to southeast. So think of the river as being a dividing line between east and west in Cedar Rapids.

Now, think of 1st Avenue as being the dividing line between north and south.

So, if you see that an attraction is located on 5th Avenue SE, that street is south of 1st Avenue and east of the river, while 10th Street NW is north of 1st Avenue and west of the river.

And just to make getting around a bit more challenging, 1st Avenue is sometimes called, simply, 1st Avenue. Other times, however, it is known as 1st Avenue SE (on the east side of the river) and 1st Avenue SW (on the west side of the river).

"Woman With Plant," "December Afternoon," and "The Hired Girl," among others. The museum also owns Wood's studio, in another part of town, and eventually hopes to make it accessible to the public on guided tours.

Another artist represented at the museum is Wood's friend, Marvin Cone, who helped Wood form the Stone City Colony and Art School in the 1930s. Works painted by Cone from the age of 29 through 70 are here. Also in the permanent collection are works by sculptor Malvina Hoffman, who studied with Rodin, and by Mauricio Lasansky, whose renowned prints span 50 years of his life.

A Bit of History

About four blocks from the art museum is **The History Center**, 615 1st Avenue SE (319) 362-1501, admission. The facility has been around for years but recently moved into new quarters that have allowed it to display its exhibits better than before. Chief among the exhibits is Time Quest, a 3-D time-tripping experience that takes you on a virtual tour of 25 blocks of downtown Cedar Rapids as they were a century ago. As you go through town, you can

The Brucemore mansion, Cedar Rapids

even enter certain buildings like theaters, a depot, and schools to visit the people of that era. The one and only adventure of this type in the nation, Time Quest will have additional scenarios in the future, including some set in the 1920s and war years. Besides Time Quest, the center features 35,000 other items, ranging from hat pins to electric cars, to grab your interest.

For a more tangible way to experience history, it's time to head into the country for a while. Leave the History Center on First Avenue SE going east, one block later turn left on 8th Street NE and then go north on I-380. About three miles later, leave the interstate at 42nd Street and at the bottom of the ramp, go left (west) for another three or so miles to Seminole Valley Road where you turn left (south). At the end of this road you will find two historical settings.

The first is **Seminole Valley Farm**, Seminole Valley Park, (319) 378-9240; admission, a 1900-era farm that is maintained as it was then. On the grounds are the farmhouse and various outbuildings plus a number of exhibits related to farming a century ago.

A bit past there is **Ushers Ferry Historic Village**, 5925 Seminole Valley Trail, (319) 286-5763; admission, a re-creation of a small town of yesteryear where, indeed, there are signs telling you to put "hands on" different exhibits. Among the buildings are the 1855 house built by early Cedar Rapids settler Henry Usher, a livery stable, telephone house, blacksmith, general store, hotel, depot, school, and Grange Hall. Besides being open every day from mid-May through October, the village hosts special events throughout the summer such as a buckskinners rendezvous, Civil War re-enactments, and antique engine shows.

From Ushers Ferry, return to downtown, right to where you got on I-380 at 8th Street NE. Turn left onto 1st Avenue SE to go to 19th Street SE where you turn to the right; after going two blocks, turn left on Linden Avenue. Follow the signs to **Brucemore**, 2160 Linden Drive SE, (319) 362-7375; admission. A 21-room Queen Anne mansion that is one of 20 properties owned by the National Trust for Historic Preservation, Brucemore was built in 1886 by Caroline Sinclair, the young widow of a wealthy packing plant owner. The house subsequently underwent extensive renovation by the next owner in 1907 and in 1925 Grant Wood fashioned a cement plaster mural for a second-floor sleeping porch.

In the Great Hall, a mural runs around the top of the paneled walls and the square design of the Grand Staircase makes you feel like you're in a tower. While the rooms on the main and upper floors show the lifestyle of yesteryear's upper class, two co-joined rooms in the basement transport you far away courtesy of the last of the three families that lived in Brucemore. Called the Tahitian Room and Grizzly Bar, the rooms resemble a getaway on a South Pacific island. Palm fronds hang from the supports of the sheet metal ceiling, Polynesian furniture decorates the rooms and at the flip of a switch, a tropical storm unleashes falling rain on the metal roof. No, that's no recording, it's real water pounding down on the metal and falling down alongside the inside walls of the room! Guided tours start on the hour.

Marion

Granger House, 970 10th Street, (319) 377-6672; admission, is another historic home but one of more modest means and located in Marion, the city braced against Cedar Rapids's east side. Even though it's a middle-class home of the late 19th century, Granger House nevertheless has a touch of class in the form of a brick carriage house out back.

The last stop is out in the country. Leave Granger House by going south on 10th Street, cross Main Street to go one more block alongside a park, turn left (east) on 6th Avenue to go to 11th Street, turn right (south) and just keep going. This will turn into East Post Road and a couple miles later, after some twists and turns, you will arrive at a T intersection with Mt. Vernon Road SE. Turn left (east) for a mile or so and you'll see Bertram Road on the right (south) and signs showing the way to **Indian Creek Nature Center**, 6605 Otis Road SE, (319) 362-0664; admission. Near the Cedar River, this preserve has savanna, prairie, and forested grounds, covering more than 200 acres and featuring lots of trails. A visitors center located in a barn explains the flora and fauna of the preserve which is adjacent to a couple recreational trails that run along picturesque Indian Creek and the Cedar River.

Besides those trails, the 52-mile **Cedar Valley Nature Trail**, (319) 266-0328; user fee, begins north of the Cedar Rapids area in Hiawatha and ends at Evansdale on the east side of the Waterloo metro area.

$\mathcal{E}$vening Time

Cedar Rapids has three historic theaters in town, and another one that requires a drive in the countryside, but is well worth the trip.

Paramount Theater, 123 3rd Avenue SE, (319) 398-5211; admission, hosts speeches by prominent individuals, fine art performances, concerts, and plays. A few blocks away, **Theater Cedar Rapids**, 102 3rd Street SE, (319) 366-8591; 366-8592; admission, is the home of the region's largest community theater, which presents comedies, musicals, classics, and dramas from September through July.

Ten blocks down 3rd Street SE is **CSPS**, 1103 3rd Street SE, (319) 364-1580; admission, a smaller theater that was originally a social hall for Czech and Slovak residents. Known for cutting-edge live entertainment in the form of music and theater, CSPS also is an art museum open from 11 a.m.-7 p.m. Wednesday to Sunday.

For that drive out in the country, there are two ways to go. If you're in Cedar Rapids, get onto I-380, go north to Exit 28, head east on County Highway E34 until you turn north on Highway 13. If you're in Marion, continue east out of town until you turn north on Highway 13.

Continue through Central City to Coggon, about five miles farther north. In the downtown of this small community, you'll find the **Opera House Theater**, where the **Faye Dudley Show**, (319) 435-2004; admission, is presented from fall through spring on one weekend a month. Born and raised near here, Dudley, who has performed in Branson, Missouri, puts on one-woman musical shows as well as productions with other entertainers who play bluegrass, country, and other types of music and perform comedy shows in this 1915 vaudeville theater. Sometimes the American Legion hosts steak suppers before the shows.

SIDE TRIPS

To the South

For the first tour, head south from Cedar Rapids on I-380, then head east on Highway151/30. At the second exit go south onto C Street SW and turn to the left (east) within a quarter-mile onto Ely Road, which is also County Highway W6E. In less than eight miles is a T intersection with Highway 382. Turn right and you will go to **Lake Macbride State Park** or, if you turn left, you will go into Solon and can continue to the south part of **Coralville Lake** (see chapter 20 for details on Lake Macbride and Coralville).

Another place to visit in the countryside south of Cedar Rapids is **Curtis Hill Indian Museum**, 1612 NE Curtis Bridge Road, (319) 848-4323; donations appreciated; call for appointment. It houses the state's largest private collection of Native American artifacts. Of the tens of thousands of artifacts from every state in the nation, about 10,000 were collected in 40 states by the owners of the museum themselves during the last 50 years. The majority of the items are points, used as arrowheads and spear points, but there also are about 500 axes, 100 pieces of pottery, and numerous pipes. Beside the artifacts themselves, the stories of how they were acquired are very interesting.

To reach the museum, head south on I-380 to Exit 10, where you leave the interstate to go east to Schueyville. At the stop sign in town, turn right (south) and go a mile to another stop sign, where you go onto the road marked Dead End. A sign marks the house/museum down the hill on the left side of the road.

St. Joseph's Church on the way into Stone City, northeast of Cedar Rapids

To the East

Grant Wood didn't spend all of his time in Cedar Rapids. He also frequented the little town of **Stone City**, appropriately named because of the stone quarries that began operating there in the 1860s. Actually, it's hard to find any building made totally out of wood there. Although there are no buildings open to the public, it's still an interesting place to drive through. It's easy to see the prevalence of the cream-colored stone—it's even in the gravel alongside the road.

The best way into Stone City is to leave Marion heading east on Highway 151; in about 12 miles, you will reach the junction of Highway 1 (on your right, south) and County Highway E34 on your left (north). Turn to the left and at the immediate junction beyond that, turn to the left (west) again. In just over a mile you will see County Highway X28, the turnoff to Stone City. After driving up and down this hilly stretch, you'll come to a crest that reveals what may be a familiar scene to those who know Wood's 1930 painting, "Stone City," especially with Saint Joseph's Church along the road. When you reach the bottom of the hill, turn to the right and proceed into Stone City. Just across the Wapsipinicon River is the Old General Store, which is private property now

Anamosa State Penitentiary

but still a building to admire from the outside. Other stone buildings in the area as well as the still-active quarry are worth driving by for a look.

The best time to visit Stone City is on the second Sunday of each June when the village hosts the **Grant Wood Art Festival**, (319) 462-4267. The event honors Wood's Stone City Colony and Art School, where he taught in the summers of 1932 and 1933. During the festival, some of the impressive stone buildings are open, artists sell their works, and a replica of the famous American Gothic house is available for a backdrop for anyone wishing to paint or photograph it (the actual house is discussed in chapter 11).

Leaving Stone City, you will come to a T intersection; turn right (east) on County Highway E28 to head to Anamosa a few miles away. The birthplace of Grant Wood, Anamosa is also where he was laid to rest at the age of 50 in 1942. A lion tops his gravestone in Riverside Cemetery.

As you continue into town on County Highway E28, which becomes Main Street, you will see the Jones County Courthouse up the hill on your left (north). If you turn up the very next street, N. High Street, you cannot help but notice the large walled compound immediately behind the courthouse that looks like a 19th century castle. That's Iowa's second-oldest state prison, the Anamosa State Penitentiary, which first opened in 1873 and was built almost entirely by prisoners who quarried and cut its stone and made the bars in a blacksmith shop. In late 2001 the **Anamosa State Penitentiary Museum**, N. High Street, (319) 462-4101; admission, opened on the north side of the complex. The museum is set *outside* the walls in what had been the prison's cheese factory (some cheeses the prisoners made were rated as high as second-best in the nation during the 1930s). The only prison museum at an active prison in Iowa, this facility also helps to dispel many of the myths generated by movies and television about prison life.

On the main floor of the museum are displays of prisoner clothing, utensils, cell keys, shackles that were made here, nightsticks, photographs, and a replica of one of the early 4-by-8-foot cells that were only 7 feet high. Exhibits detail when the all-male prison once had a women's reformatory and housed the criminally insane for about 100 years. A souvenir shop is in the museum.

Another attraction that opened in 2001 and is helping to put Anamosa on the map is the **National Motorcycle Museum and Hall of Fame**, 200 E. Main Street, (319) 462-3925; admission, which moved from Sturgis, South Dakota, to a beautiful wood-front building in downtown Anamosa. Among the popular, rare, and vintage motorcycles shown in the collection are those made by Indian, Ariel, Royal Enfield, Harley-Davidson, Armac, Yankee, BSA, Triumph, and Lambretta. In the Hall of Fame, individuals connected with racing or the industry are honored, such as Linda "Jo" Giovannoni, who started the first motorcycle publication for women; Gary Nixon, who began his racing career in 1958 at the age of 17; and actor-director Peter Fonda, who brought recognition to motorcycle riders with his movie *Easy Rider*.

LODGING

Cedar Rapids
Cedar Rapids Inn and Conference Center, 2501 Williams Boulevard SW, (319) 365-9441. On Highway 151 in western Cedar Rapids. Near malls. Restaurant, indoor pool. $$-$$$

Collins Plaza Hotel and Convention Center, 1200 Collins Road NE, (319) 393-6600; (800) 541-1067. North side of metro area off I-380. Near Ushers Village. Restaurant, indoor pool. $$$-$$$$

Crowne Plaza Five Seasons Hotel, 350 1st Avenue NE, (319) 363-8161; (888) 363-3550. Downtown. Near The History Center and theaters. Restaurant, indoor pool. $$$-$$$$

Holiday Inn Express Hotel and Suites, 3320 Southgate Court SW, (319) 399-5025; (800) HOLIDAY. Near I-380 on south side. Close to Czech Village and Duffy's Collectible Cars. Near restaurants. Indoor pool, continental breakfast. $$-$$$$

Howard Johnson Airport Express Inn & Suites, 9100 Atlantic Drive SW, (319) 363-3789; (800) 446-4656. Near airport on southwest side of metro area. Indoor and outdoor pools, continental breakfast. $$-$$$$

Marion

Best Western Long Branch Hotel, 90 Twixt Town Road NE, (319) 377-6386; (800) 443-7660. Near boundary of Cedar Rapids and Marion at junction of Highways 151 and 100. Close to Granger House and Brucemore. Restaurant, indoor pool. $-$$$$

BED AND BREAKFASTS

Cedar Rapids

Belmont Hill Victorian B&B, 1525 Cherokee Drive, (319) 366-1343. An 1880 Victorian home that's west of Cedar River near downtown. Private guest house. Three rooms. $$$$

Joy in the Morning B&B, 1809 Second Avenue SE, (319)363-9731; (800) 363-5093. Just east of downtown near Brucemore. A 1920 colonial villa. Three rooms. $$-$$$

Marion

Victorian Lace B&B, 300 E. Main Street, (319) 377-5138. On north side of metro area. Two rooms. $$$$

Hiawatha

Prairiewoods, 120 E. Boyson Road, (319) 395-6700. A Franciscan spiritual retreat that's near a pond amid 70 acres of prairie and woods on the metro area's north side. Courses on religious subjects available. Holistic meals. Spiritual guidance, counseling, massage therapy available. Private and semi-private rooms.

DINING

Cedar Rapids

Café de Klos', 821 3rd Avenue SE, (319) 362-9340. Near downtown in 1870s Victorian home. Fine dining with European cuisine.

Pei's Mandarin, 5131 Council Street NE, (319) 362-6165. Northern metro area. Chinese cuisine.

The Spring House Family Restaurant, 3980 Center Point Road NE, (319) 393-4994. Off I-380 at Exit 23. Home-cooked, family-style restaurant.

Sykora Bakery, 73 16th Avenue SW, (319) 364-5271. Czech bakery in the Czech Village since 1903. Rye bread and kolaches among other baked items.

TD's Market, 401 1st Street SE, (319) 362-4638. Downtown riverside cafe in a historic building. Lunch specials with homemade sandwiches, breads, desserts.

Vernon Inn, 2663 Mt. Vernon Road SE, (319) 366-7817. East of downtown. Greek/American cuisine includes gyros, moussaka, baklava, kabobs. Patio dining.

Vino's & R.G. Books, 3600 First Avenue SE, (319) 363-7550. In Town and County Shopping Center between Marion and Cedar Rapids. Italian cuisine and setting.

Zindricks Czech Restaurant, 86 16th Avenue SW, (319) 365-5257. Czech food in the Czech Village.

Marion

Longbranch Restaurant, 90 Twixt Town Road NE, (319) 377-6386. At Best Western Longbranch Hotel. Barbecue.

Yen Ching Restaurant, 3211 Armar Drive, (319) 373-1513. On east side of metro area. Mandarin cuisine and seafood.

INFORMATION

Cedar Rapids Area Convention and Visitors Bureau, 119 1st Avenue SE, Cedar Rapids, IA 52406, (319) 398-5009; (800) 735-5557; www.cedarrapids.com

Eastern Iowa Tourism Region, PO Box 485, Vinton, IA 52349, (319) 472-5135; (800) 891-3482; www.easterniowatourism.org

Chapter 14

Amana Colonies: A Touch of the Old World

In a world where flashing lights, bullhorn-equipped tour guides, and much razzmatazz are what usually pull in visitors, it may seem surprising that a clutch of seven quiet villages surrounded by farmland would be Iowa's top tourist attraction. Well, perhaps that's why people visit the Amana Colonies, where Old World charm envelops everything, including the visitors. Barns may be old and weathered but they're well-kept. Grape vines grow up trellises that almost serve as shutters around many of the houses. Craftsmen shave away curls of wood before fitting together pieces of furniture. Home-cooked meals look heavy enough to break plank tables.

During the day, there's a fair amount of hustle in the colonies, but at 5 o'clock every afternoon, the shops and stores close and, three hours later, the restaurants stop admitting guests. If you want communities that are truly quiet at night, here they are.

Some people mistakenly believe the residents of the Amana Colonies are related to the Amish, perhaps due to the similarities in their names. But you won't see numerous horses and buggies trotting about the colonies; you will enjoy electricity; and you are allowed to shoot pictures.

Here's a brief background: The Community of True Inspiration was founded in Germany in 1714. Members of that group immigrated to Buffalo, New York, in 1842 and then to Iowa, where 1,200 of them purchased 26,000 acres of land in 1855. The new settlers created the villages, each about two miles (or an hour by ox cart) from each other, where they practiced communalism. People had personal possessions but they worked together in businesses, including farming the nearby fields, and met in the communal kitchen and church in each town. In 1932, residents voted to separate the Amana Church from the economic side of their lives; and that's the way things remain, with 1,700 people still residing in these communities. The largest industries are Amana Refrigeration, a furniture factory, and a woolen mill.

A typical rustic scene in the Amana Colonies

By the way, the word *amana* comes from the "Song of Solomon" and means "remain true."

Amana, the Largest Colony

A good way to tour the colonies is to start at the largest colony, Amana, which is located at the junction of Highways 151 and 220. The best way to begin there is to visit the **Amana Colonies Welcome Center**, 39 38th Avenue, (319) 622-7622; (800) 579-2294, which is accessed by drives both west and north of the highway intersection. As is typical with welcome centers, you will find almost anything you need there. Its building also houses the theater used by the **Old Creamery Theatre Company**, (800) 352-6262, which stages productions between March and December.

From here, drive back into Amana, park, and just start walking around—you're bound to bump into something you like among the 19th-century brick and wood buildings. Stores along the main drag, called 220 Trail, carry just about everything you'd expect in a setting like this: candles, homemade candies, art prints, quilts, lace, wind chimes, books, dolls, glassware, antiques, and on and on.

However, consider the shops to be the sideshow because the real reputation of the Amana Colonies is based on food and Amana has the largest concentration of places to eat among the villages. While in most other restaurants outside the colonies, each person's meal is served on a separate plate, here you're served your entree on a plate and everything else comes family-style in large bowls that are refilled as long as you keep eating. Not only is the quantity of the food good but so is the quality, with emphasis on foods reflecting the Amanas' German heritage such as schnitzel, sauerbraten, knackwurst, kassler rippchen, and bratwurst.

Visiting the Amanas means returning home with lots of baggage—in the form of items from the shops and a few extra pounds around your waist. But you feel good in the process!

Besides the food in restaurants, you can pick up meats, cheeses, pastries, breads, and, last but definitely not least, wine, another item that has put the Amanas on the map. Remember those grape vines on the trellises? Well, they aren't for decoration. Along with a number of other fruits and berries, the grapes get turned into nearly two-dozen specialty wines that are sold, along with table wines and sherries, throughout the colonies. Among them are cranberry, blackberry, piestengel (rhubarb), grape, dandelion, and plum wines. All are made at the colonies' wineries.

If you enjoy homemade beer and root beer, then visit the **Millstream Brewing Company**, (319) 622-3672, the state's oldest microbrewery, which recalls a time when the Amanas had three breweries. Located at the east end of Amana, it's near the old mill race leading to the mill across the street. If you need to work off those calories gained in the local restaurants, note that the paved **Kolonieweg (Colony Way) Recreational Trail** has a trailhead at the nearby depot and heads west from there for more than three miles where it encircles Lily Lake.

Also on the east end of town is the **Amana Woolen Mill**, (319) 622-3432, which sells blankets, apparel, and other items fresh off the looms. Various craft items are also made and sold here. A walk behind the mill takes you to **Roger's Anvil and Industrial Machine Shop Museum**, (319) 622-3482, where the blacksmith isn't just putting on a show at the forge but hammering out wind vanes, fireplace tools, candle holders, and more that you can buy to take home.

Walking a short ways to the north from the blacksmith leads you to the **Amana Furniture Shop**, (319) 622-3291, where you can either browse around through finely crafted furniture in the showrooms or take a tour through the workshops to see the craftsmen at work. The shop also boasts of having the most complete clock shop in the state.

Back on the west end of town are two places you really should visit. One is the **Amana General Store**, (319) 622-7650, which is the original general store built here in 1858. And it's still selling products made by the Amana Society, including wines and food.

The other place to visit on the west end is the **Museum of Amana History**, (319) 622-3567; admission. If you want to learn more about the Amanas, there's no better place than here to do it. Operated by the Amana Heritage Society which has three other museums in the colonies (all covered by the same admission), the museum in Amana is located in what had been a communal kitchen built in 1864. An audio-visual production in the old schoolhouse on the museum grounds presents a good story about the Amana Colonies history and the main building has displays showing the other crafts that once existed in town. There are also wine-making and gardening displays.

If you've walked around Amana enough, it's time to hit the 220 Trail, as they call the various highways that link the colonies, and head west. (We won't be discussing East Amana because it has no commercial establishments.)

A bit past the turnoff to the Welcome Center is **Lily Lake** on the left (south) side of the highway. Developed as a millpond when the woolen mill was powered by water, the 160-acre lake is now more picturesque than functional, but it's still a nice place to pull over and enjoy the scenery, especially when the lotus lilies are in bloom.

Middle Amana

Just past the pond is the plant entrance to Amana Refrigeration, Inc., which is known worldwide for creating and manufacturing fine home appliances, including refrigerators and microwave ovens. And then just past that but on the right side of the road are the turnoffs into the older portion of **Middle Amana**. Obviously smaller than Amana, Middle Amana is also quieter (not that Amana was like New York City by any means).

Here you will find another element of the Amana Heritage Society, the **Communal Kitchen and Coopershop Museum**, J Street, (319) 622-3567; ad-

Hahn's Hearth Oven Bakery in Middle Amana

mission. Built in 1863, the kitchen is the last of the society's communal kitchens to retain its original look—all of the others have been remodeled for other purposes. Most of the women of the village worked at its brick hearth and dry sink to prepare meals that were enjoyed by the residents, who sat at long tables in the dining room. Guides describe the early Amanas and also explain the cooper shop, where barrels and other containers were made.

A short stroll to the west of the communal kitchen leads you to the only hearth oven that's still working in the colonies, **Hahn's Hearth Oven Bakery**, J Street, (319) 622-3439. If you want some of the breads, coffeecakes, and streusels that are baked in its brick oven, get there early in the morning. The doors open at 7:30 a.m. and close when the last items are sold.

High Amana

Back on Highway 220, keep heading west; in about two minutes you'll arrive at **High Amana**, which is even smaller than Amana or Middle Amana. Here, you'll find the **Amana Arts Guild Center**, 1210 G. Street, (319) 622-3678, where residents and visitors come to create art objects in the studio or admire them in the shop. The center also hosts weeklong art classes in various media during the summer.

About a block east of the center, the **Old Fashioned High Amana Store**, G Street, was once a popular attraction. It closed in 2001 when its owner died, but it may re-open; so check it out while you're in town. If it's open, you'll pinch yourself to make sure that you haven't crossed some time warp because, with the exception of the electric lights, the store looks much like it did in the late 19th century.

West Amana

After you've visited High Amana, continue on Highway 220 to the west and in no time you're at **West Amana**, the second oldest of the colonies. Here, the main attraction is the **Broom and Basket Shop**, Highway 220, (319) 622-3315, where you can watch the broom-maker use a century-old machine to make tall brooms, hand brooms, side brooms, and more. All of them are for sale, as are woven baskets. An outlet for Schanz Furniture is right here too, and it has the state's largest rocking chair. Made of solid walnut, it can easily hold two adults.

South Amana

At West Amana, Highway 220 turns to the south to lead to (where else?) **South Amana**. Fairly close to each other are this town's two main attractions. The first is the **South Amana Barn Museum**, Highway 220, (319) 622-3058, which has an impressive collection of 175 handmade 1/12th-scale miniatures created by master craftsman Henry Moore and his son, John, who now carries on the family tradition. Many of the miniature buildings are of the Amanas, but there are plenty of others representing buildings Henry Moore encountered across the state.

A short walk away is the Amana Heritage Society's **Communal Agriculture Museum**, (319) 622-3567; admission. Constructed about 1860 to shelter livestock, the barn was built of native timber and now houses exhibits of farm implements used during the colonies' early years. At the south end of town, where Highway 220 meets Highway 6, it's said that the bank that was there (now Fern Hill Gifts & Quilts) was robbed by Jesse James and company in 1877.

For a great view of the area, continue south of South Amana for a short way and head up the hill. You'll soon be in **Upper South Amana**, which has no commercial establishments. When you turn around, however, you'll realize you have a good vantage point to see the valley of the Iowa River and all the colonies at one time from the highest place in the area.

Return to Highway 6 and take a right (east). Just outside of South Amana, you'll find the factories and showrooms of both Schanz Furniture and Krauss Furniture Shop, which also makes wonderful clocks.

Homestead

Five miles east of South Amana on Highway 6, you'll enter **Homestead**, the only colony that doesn't have the name Amana in it somewhere. That came about in 1861 when the Inspirationalists (as Amana residents called themselves back then) realized they needed a stop on a proposed rail line and Homestead

Interior of the Amana Community Church, Homestead

155

looked like the best place. So they bought the whole place, lock, stock, and barrel and now, despite its name, Homestead is just as Amana-ish as the other colonies. That's most evident when you visit the **Amana Community Church**, V Street, (319) 622-3567; admission, another part of the Amana Heritage Society. In this spartan hall, residents of Homestead worshipped for more than 60 years, sitting on the long benches during the services. On the other side of the street is the **Amana Meat Shop and Smokehouse**, (319) 622-3931, one of the original meat markets in the colonies.

For another side of the colonies, return to Highway 151 on the west edge of Homestead and start toward Amana, two miles to the north, but almost as soon as you start up the highway, turn at the only turnout on the left side. Here begins the Amana Colonies Nature Trail, a 3.2-mile route through the woodlands down to the Iowa River. It's a nice way to wind up a trip to the Amanas.

LODGING

Amana
Guest House Motor Inn, 4712 220 Trail, (319) 622-3599; (877) 331-0828. In the heart of Amana. Within walking distance to anything there. Restaurants nearby. $-$$

Little Amana
(Note: Little Amana is the name that's applied to the area near Exit 225 on I-80, which is about five miles south of the Amana Colonies. Little Amana is not a formal member of the Amana Colonies. Another welcome center, (319) 668-9545, is located there.)

Amana Colonies Holiday Inn, Exit 225 on I-80, (319) 668-1175; (800) 633-9244. Indoor pools, restaurant. $$-$$$

Comfort Inn, Exit 225 on I-80, (319) 668-2700; (800) 228-5150. Indoor pool, continental breakfast. $$-$$$

Days Inn, Exit 225 on I-80, (319) 668-2097; (800) DAYSINN. Continental breakfast. $-$$

My Little Inn, Exit 225 on I-80, (319) 668-9667. $-$$

BED AND BREAKFASTS

Amana
Judy's Guest Haus, 716 46th Avenue, (319) 622-6064. Near Farmers Market about midpoint in Amana. Three rooms. $$

Homestead

Die Heimat Country Inn, 4430 V Street, (319) 622-3937; (888) 613-5463. Once a stagecoach stop. 19 rooms. $-$$$

Rawson's B&B, 4424 V Street, (319) 622-6035; (800) 637-6035. In a historic brick home. Six rooms. $$-$$$

Middle Amana

Cloister Haus B&B, 1117 26th Avenue, (319) 622-6091; (800) 996-6964. A former communal kitchen built in 1893. Five rooms. $-$$

Dusk to Dawn B&B, 2616 K Street, (319) 622-3029; (800) 669-5773. Sunroom and deck. Seven rooms. $$

Rose's Place, 1007 26th Avenue, (319) 622-6097; (877) 767-3233. Renovated 1870s Sunday school. Three rooms. $$-$$$

South Amana

Babi's B&B, 2788 Highway 6, (319) 662-4381. Country retreat in woods with brooks. Eight rooms. $$-$$$$

Baeckerei B&B, 507 Q Street, (319) 622-3597; (800) 391-8650. Former communal bakery. Three rooms $$

DINING

Amana

Colony Inn Restaurant, (319) 622-6270; (800) 227-3471. First opened in 1935.

Ox Yoke Inn, (319) 622-3441; (800) 233-3441. Family-owned restaurant.

Ronneburg Restaurant, (319) 622-3641; (888) 348-4686. Entertainment on weekends.

Homestead

Zuber's Restaurant, V Street, (319) 622-3911; (800) 522-8883. Established in 1948 by former baseball star Bill Zuber.

Little Amana

Ox Yoke Interstate Restaurant, Exit 225 on I-80, (319) 668-1443; (877) 668-1443. Related to the Ox Yoke in Amana.

INFORMATION

Colonies Convention and Visitors Bureau, 39 38th Ave., Amana, IA 52203, (319) 622-7622; (800) 579-2294; www.AmanaColonies.com

Chapter 15

Iowa City:
Iowa Spoken Here

If you're looking for a place where the name "Iowa" is popular, this is the spot: Iowa City, home of the campus of the University of Iowa and bisected by the Iowa River. The capitol of Iowa was here for a while, but that slipped away to Des Moines more than a century ago.

However, not all is Iowa here, not with the smaller community of Coralville showing a lot of economic muscle on Iowa City's west side. All in all, both communities blend their personalities to create a nice place to visit.

Start by picking up brochures and information at the **Iowa City/Coralville Area Convention and Visitors Bureau**, 408 First Avenue, (319) 337-6592; (800) 283-6592; free. The easiest way to get there is to leave I-80 at Exit 242 (First Avenue) in Coralville, and go south to where the center is located in a small strip mall, on the right (west) side less than a mile away.

The first major attraction you might want to visit, especially if you're traveling with kids, is the **Iowa Children's Museum**, 1451 Coral Ridge Avenue, (319) 625-6255; admission. Signs lead to it in the southeast corner of the Coral Ridge Mall, near the food court and ice rink. You can get there by continuing down First Avenue to Highway 6 and turning right (west). You'll reach the mall in two miles. And no, the museum will not watch your children while you play in the shops; an adult must accompany each group of children.

To get to Iowa City from the mall, go east on Highway 6. But first we're going to visit the University of Iowa. Right after you enter the city limits of Iowa City, turn left onto Rocky Shore Drive. That will become West Park Road, and upon seeing a large, silvery, multistory building, you've reached the university campus. Turn right there onto North Riverside Drive, and you'll find yourself driving along the university art complex, which includes **Hancher Auditorium**, site of large performances and concerts, (319) 335-1160; (800)

HANCHER; admission; the performing arts theater; and the **Museum of Art**, 150 N. Riverside Drive, (319) 335-1727; free, which overlooks the Iowa River. The museum has Iowa's best collection of African art and offers several visiting art exhibits each year. Parking meters are near the auditorium and across North Riverside Drive from the museum.

*D*owntown

You can do two things to get to downtown Iowa City from here. One is to walk across the river on a nearby pedestrian bridge. The other is to drive up North Riverside Drive to Highway 6, turn left, and go to the first intersection, which is Iowa Avenue, where you again turn left (east). That will bring you right up to the west face of the **Old Iowa Capitol**, bounded by Washington, Clinton, Jefferson, and Madison Streets, (319) 335-0548; free.

A word of warning to those driving tall vehicles: Iowa Avenue runs through an underpass with a 10.5-foot clearance. Taller vehicles should continue on Highway 6 to the next intersection, Burlington Street, and turn left there to enter the downtown.

Before you get ready to see the sights in this part of Iowa City, be alert that parking is at a premium here due to the university and downtown businesses. The best approach might be to explore on foot, so find the best parking space

The Old Iowa Capitol in downtown Iowa City

159

you can—there are well-marked parking garages in the area, especially along Burlington Street—and plan to hoof it for awhile.

The **Old Iowa Capitol** has been restored to its heyday when the governor, legislature, and supreme court met here to govern, first, a territory and then a young state. One thing that is sure to catch your interest is the simple but elegant wooden spiral staircase that connects the upper and lower floors. The rest of the building, which served as the capitol from 1842 to 1857, reflects a similar understated style. On the main floor are offices for the governor, treasurer and auditor, the chamber of the supreme court, and a reception room. Upstairs are the chambers for the house and senate. That's all that was needed in those days to govern Iowa.

Leaving the Old Iowa Capitol by its main entrance, go directly to your left and enter **Macbride Hall**, which houses the **Museum of Natural History**, (319) 335-0480; free. There are three major galleries: Mammal Hall, Iowa Hall, and the newly renovated Bird Hall, which includes a renowned diorama of the feathered residents of Laysan Island, a remote part of the Hawaiian Islands. In another area of the museum, you can walk through 500 million years of natural history beginning when this region was an ocean harboring strange-looking fish, including a carnivorous beast called a *Dunkleosteus* that had a mouth twice as wide as a great white shark. A few steps away—and about 200 million years later—you can visit a swamp rich with peat that, given time, will become seams of coal far under the Iowa soil. And then you come upon the arrival of Europeans in Iowa in June 1673, as seen from the vantage point of Indians atop a cliff in the northeast part of the state. These exhibits and more make the museum a very worthwhile stop for visitors of all ages.

Returning to the busy world outside Macbride may jar you a bit, but a good way to relax is to cross Clinton Street and go one block east to Dubuque Street, then turn south. About mid-block, you'll see **Prairie Lights Books**, 15 S. Dubuque Street, (319) 337-2681. A large, independent bookstore, Prairie Lights has been a mainstay of downtown Iowa City since 1978 and now fills more than three floors with books ranging from light children's reading to heavy scholarly tomes. Its 1,100-square-foot coffeehouse is located where the city's literary society once hosted famous authors and poets, including Carl Sandburg, Robert Frost, and e. e. cummings. The tradition continues with the bookstore now hosting readings by contemporary writers.

Just south of the bookstore is the **Pedestrian Plaza**, a pleasant space sprinkled with trees, benches, sculpture, and food vendors featuring everything from expresso and gyros to grilled-cheese sandwiches and hot dogs. At its south end are a children's playground and playful arches of water. At times live performances are staged in front of the hotel there, most often on weekend evenings in the summer and sometimes on Fridays at noon.

Also in the area, and being renovated, is the **Englert Theater**, 221 E. Washington Street, (319) 688-2653; admission. Originally a vaudeville-style theater that was later a movie house, the Englert will once again host live perform-ances beginning in 2002. Three blocks east of the mall is one of the larger and more innovative food cooperatives you'll find, **New Pioneer Co-op**, 22 S. Van Buren, (319) 338-9441, which opened in 1970. You don't have to be a member to purchase from its wide array of foods—non-chemical fruits, vegetables, meats, cheeses, chocolates, wine, beer, and home-baked breads. (The co-op also has a retail outlet/bakery featuring an eight-ton brick oven at City Center Square, 1102 2nd Street in Coralville, along Highway 6, (319) 358-5513.)

For a bit of early Iowa history, go east from the co-op until you meet South Dodge Street, turn right (south), and drive until you reach Kirkwood Avenue. Turn right (east) and watch immediately for signs leading to **Plum Grove**, 1030 Carroll Street, (319) 351-5738; free. Built in 1844 as the retirement home for Iowa's first territorial governor, Robert Lucas, Plum Grove remains a quiet set-ting and its furnishings show what life was like in Iowa City's early years.

The Great Outdoors

Now it's time to get back to nature, specifically **Coralville Lake**, 2850 Prairie du Chien Road NE, (319) 338-3543. There are several ways to drive to this 5,430-acre lake, created behind a dam on the Iowa River by the U. S. Army Corps of Engineers.

The easiest is to head north from downtown Iowa City on Dubuque Street and continue on after passing I-80. Almost three miles past I-80, West Overlook Road appears on the right (east) and serves as the entrance to a complex of campgrounds, nature trails, a visitors center, boat ramps, administrative offices, a beach, a nine-hole Frisbee golf course, picnic shelters, and more, all near the dam at the lower end of the lake. Fees are charged for boating, camping, and swimming.

Also here is the **Devonian Fossil Gorge**, free. In 1993, heavy rains caused the lake to flood and the tremendous overflow gouged a 15-foot-deep gorge through the emergency spillway. After the gorge dried, visitors began to find fossils, in-cluding coral, brachiopods, and crinoids that last saw the light of day about 365 million years ago during the Devonian Age. Displays in the visitor center explain the fossils, but you can explore the fossil beds by using a self-guided trail that be-gins at an easily seen plaza alongside the gorge. The easiest fossils to find are those in the big boulders flanking the sidewalk between the plaza and another over-look a short distance to the north. The best time to spot fossils in the gorge is when the sun is low, creating good contrast. No collecting is allowed.

For another look back in time, although not as far back as the Devonian Age, return to Dubuque Street, which is also County Highway W66 here, and resume going north to North Liberty. There, take a right on Front Street, which becomes County Road F28 when it leaves town to the north. Just outside of town it turns to the northeast. Watch for Rice Ridge Lane NE on the right. Turn

161

there, stay on the lane, and park on the pavement when it reaches the end. A short hike takes you into **Old State Quarry State Preserve**, one of several quarries that began operating here in the 1830s. Stone from the quarries was used to build the Old Capitol in Iowa City and as the base of the present capitol in Des Moines. On some faces of the quarry, it's still possible to see hand-drilled holes made to put in spikes to pry away blocks of stone. Considering the abundance of hardwood trees here, think about visiting during the fall when the leaves are at their most colorful.

Continuing on County Road F28, you'll cross Coralville Lake and, immediately after the bridge, see a road going off to the right (south). That leads to **Sugar Bottom Campground**, which has campsites with and without electricity, a day-use area, boat ramp, trails (including an equestrian trail), and a beach. One thing that Sugar Bottom has that many other sites run by the Corps don't is an off-road mountain bike trail with sections ranging from novice to expert.

Back on County Highway F28 is the **Merrill A. Stainbrook Geological Preserve**, another place with bedrock from the Devonian Age, plus, on the hill southeast of the roadcut, visible furrows left in the bedrock by glaciers about half a million years ago.

Just beyond that preserve is the **Macbride Nature Recreation Area**, home of the **Macbride Raptor Project**, (319) 398-5495, which shelters birds of prey such as hawks, eagles, and owls that were injured and are being rehabilitated for release back to the wild. Among the project's permanent residents, which must remain captive due to their injuries, are bald and golden eagles and all of the hawk and owl species that one would expect to see in Iowa. There's also a bird blind where you can watch songbirds. For a fee, tours can be arranged; this is the major way the project earns money to care for these birds.

Continuing up County Highway F28 brings you through a portion of **Lake Macbride State Park**, (319) 624-2200; camping fee. If you keep going, you'll end up in the town of Solon. Go a few blocks north on Highway 1 and then take a left (west) turn onto Highway 382, which takes you to the main part of the state park. Like many other state parks, Macbride has hike/bike trails, camping, picnic facilities, boat ramps, and a beach. It also has a concessionaire, (319) 624-2315, that rents pontoons, motorboats, water bikes, pedal boats, and canoes, which can be reserved ahead of your arrival.

To return to Iowa City from here, go back to Solon and take Highway 1 south.

SIDE TRIPS

To the East

A lot of people associate Herbert Hoover, our nation's 31st president, with the onset of the Great Depression. But if you make a short trip outside of Iowa

The cottage in which President Herbert Hoover was born, West Branch

City, you'll learn that the only president from Iowa was a great humanitarian whose work touched people all over the world, both before and after he was in the White House.

To reach Hoover's hometown, less than 10 miles from Iowa City, go east on I-80 until you reach the turnoff to West Branch, Exit 254. Coming into town, you can take either the first left, which brings you to the **Herbert H. Hoover Presidential Library**, (319) 643-5301, or the second left, which leads to the visitors center of the **Herbert H. Hoover National Historic Site**, (319) 643-2541. Either one will do because most of the sights you'll want to see are within walking distance of each other.

If you start at the library, you'll get a good overview of Hoover, the first president born west of the Mississippi. Permanent exhibits present a broad assessment of him as a man who helped feed 300 million people in 21 European countries after World War I, who dealt with the expanding roles of radio and aviation as secretary of commerce and, after his presidency, who dealt with famine again during the 1940s. Similarly his wife, Lou, is accorded recognition for her work with the Girl Scouts and creation of the first White House history. The library also hosts a number of traveling exhibits.

A short walk from the library is the two-room cottage where Hoover was born in 1874, the visitors center, a blacksmith shop that's similar to the one run by Hoover's father, a one-room school, and a Quaker meeting house. In the other direction from the library are the simple gravesites of President and Mrs. Hoover, which overlook his birthplace.

163

A number of stores, including those selling antiques, and places to eat are in the business district of West Branch, adjacent to the grounds of the Hoover site.

For a look at one of the more unusual and larger octagonal barns anywhere, you should visit the **Secrest Barn**, 5750 Osage, Downey, (319) 643-2260; admission, reservations required. Constructed in 1883, this wooden octagon could hold 200 tons of hay in the loft and 32 horses and 16 head of cattle on the lower floor. The cupola on top is 75 feet above the ground. To see the barn, drive south to Downey, a few miles from West Branch on County Highway X30. In Downey, take the third street on your right (west) and go to where that T's into another road. Turn left and that gravel road will quickly veer west and you will see the barn on the north side of that road within a couple miles.

To return to Iowa City from the barn, continue west down the gravel road to a T intersection, turn left (south), and in a few moments you'll be at Highway 6, which leads into Iowa City's southeast side.

To the South

Located 18 miles southwest of Iowa City and Coralville is a world that's much slower paced than those cities. Buttons are gone, replaced by pins or hooks and eyes. Women wear white prayer caps and black bonnets and men never wear neckties or mustaches. German-accented English is heard in the stores and horses pulling carriages replace horsepower-rated engines.

This is the land around Kalona, the largest Amish-Mennonite community west of the Mississippi. Not everyone here is Amish or Mennonite but if you want to learn about the lifestyle of these gentle people, Kalona is one of the better places to do it. To get there, take Highway 1 southwest from Iowa City. On the way you might want to stop at the **Kalona Cheese Factory**, 2206 540th Avenue SW, (319) 656-2776. About four miles north of Kalona, it makes its own white cheddar cheese, which it sells with other cheeses, sausages, crackers, and bread.

Once you arrive in Kalona, the best way to learn about this region is to turn left (east) at Highway 22 and visit the **Kalona Historical Village**, Highway 22 E and 9th Street, (319) 656-3232; admission, which is on the far end of the business district. Recently joining the historical buildings, which include a country church, schoolhouse, depot, post office, Amish house, and country store, is a modern visitors center. Inside are the Kalona Quilt and Textile Museum, comprising quilts from the 1840s to 1950, and the Reif Mineral Collection, featuring gems from as far away as Germany. Also on the grounds are the **Mennonite Museum and Archives**, 411 9th Street, (319) 656-3271, which tell the history of the Amish and Mennonite communities and serve as a genealogical repository as well.

Another good way to learn about the Amish and Mennonites is to take the **Kalona By-Ways Tour**, 514 B Street, (319) 656-2660; fare, which is run by the local chamber of commerce. Visitors board a minibus for a 90-minute ride through the region narrated by a guide who describes the lifestyles of the Mennonites and different orders of Amish who live here. Stops on the tour, which starts at 11 a.m. and 1:30 p.m., Monday-Saturday, may include the Cheese Factory, Amish stores, and an Amish farmers market.

Later, you can stroll among the shops in the business district where you'll find a variety of items from handmade furniture, quilts, and original glass decorations to books, baked goods, and horse harnesses.

Remember that many of the Amish prefer not to be photographed, so please respect their views. Also, be cautious while driving in this area of horse-drawn, slow-moving vehicles.

On the way back to Iowa City, you could complete a loop, first going east on Highway 22. As you pass through Riverside, note that (according to Star Trek lore) the town someday will be the birthplace of James T. Kirk, captain of the future starship USS Enterprise.

Once you're at Highway 218, turn left (north) and go straight up to Iowa City. First, though, you may want to stop a bit beyond the intersection at **Bock's Berry Farm**, (319) 629-5553, where, from about late May through October, you can pick your own produce ranging from strawberries to pumpkins.

LODGING

Coralville

Best Western Cantebury Inn and Suites, 704 1st Avenue, (319) 351-0400; (800) 798-0400. Off Exit 242 of I-80. Restaurant, indoor pool, continental breakfast. $$-$$$

Clarion Hotel and Conference Center, 1220 1st Avenue, (319) 351-5049; (800) CLARION. Off Exit 242 of I-80. Restaurant, indoor pool, continental breakfast. $$-$$$.

Comfort Inn, 209 W. 9th Street, (319) 351-8144; (800) 228-5150. Indoor pool, continental breakfast. $$-$$$$

Heartland Inn, 87 2nd Street, (319) 351-8132; (800) 334-3277, ext. 19. Near Exit 242 of I-80. Indoor pool, continental breakfast. $$-$$$$

Iowa City

Iowa House Hotel, University of Iowa Memorial Union, (319) 335-3513; (800) 553-IOWA. On campus and near downtown. $$

Sheraton Iowa City Plaza Hotel, 210 S. Dubuque Street, (319) 337-4058; (800) 848-1335. On the Pedestrian Mall downtown. Near campus. Restaurant, indoor pool. $$-$$$$

Kalona

Pull'r Inn Motel, junction of Highways 1 and 22, (319) 656-3611. Continental breakfast. $

BED AND BREAKFASTS

Iowa City

The Golden Haug, 517 E. Washington Street, (319) 354-4284. Near downtown and University of Iowa campus. Five rooms. $$$-$$$$

Bella Vista B&B, 2 Bella Vista Place, (319) 338-4129. Near campus and downtown. Overlooks Iowa River. Six rooms. $$-$$$$

Haverkamp's Linn Street Homestay, 619 N. Linn Street, (319) 337-4363. Near campus and downtown. Three rooms. $

Historic Phillips House, 721 N. Linn Street, (319) 337-3223. Near campus and downtown. Overlooks Iowa River. Three rooms. $$

Kalona

The Carriage House, 1140 Larch Avenue, (319) 656-3824. Countryside setting less than two miles from Kalona. Four rooms. $$

Columns and Chocolate, 212 4th Street, (319) 656-2992. In town. Four rooms. $$-$$$$

Home on the Hill, 1208 J Avenue, (319) 656-5300. In town. Three rooms and a cabin. $$-$$$

RESTAURANTS

Coralville

Cancun Restaurant #3, 708 1st Avenue, (319) 339-8500. Mexican food prepared from scratch.

Iowa River Power Company, 501 1st Avenue, (319) 351-1904. Steak and seafood in an old power plant with views of the Iowa River.

Three Samurai Japanese Restaurant, 1801 2nd Street, (319) 337-3340. Guests sit around grills where chefs prepare stir-fry meals. Japanese beers.

Iowa City

A & A Pagliai's Pizza, 302 E. Bloomington Street, (319) 351-5073. Long-time establishment whose followers say it has the best pizza.

Aoeshe Japanese Restaurant, 624 S. Gilbert Street, (319) 351-7000. Near downtown. Japanese cuisine.

Bread Garden Bakery and Café, 224 S. Clinton Street, (319) 354-4246. Downtown.

The Brewery, 525 S. Gilbert Street, (319) 356-6900. Near downtown. Up-scale restaurant connected to college-style pub.

Devotay, Inc., 117 N. Linn Street, (319) 354-1001. Cooking store/culinary school specializing in tapas from the Mediterranean. Lunch and dinner.

Givannis Café, 109 E. College Street, (319) 338-5967. Downtown. Italian food in art deco setting.

Hamburg Inn No. 2, 214 N. Linn Street, (319) 337-5512. Just north of downtown. A neighborhood café that's a local legend. Ronald Reagan ate here. Good breakfasts too.

Linn Street Café, 121 N. Linn Street, (319) 337-7370. North end of downtown. High-end dining with well-rounded menu and cuisine. Small, intimate, and worth it.

Masala Indian Vegetarian Cuisine, 9 S. Dubuque Street, (319) 338-6199. Downtown. Indian cuisine. Some say it's the best ethnic restaurant in the cities.

Panchero's Authentic Mexican Food, 32 S. Clinton Street, (319) 338-6311. Downtown.

Sanctuary Restaurant and Pub, 405 S. Gilbert Street, (319) 351-5692. Great pizza and a large selection of beer.

Kalona

Kalona Bakery, 209 5th Street, (319) 656-2013; (800) 213-4531. Downtown. Breads, soups, sandwiches, desserts, coffee bar.

Kalonial Townhouse Restaurant, Highway 1 S, (319) 656-2514. South end of town. Friday night catfish and chicken buffet. Saturday night shrimp, chicken, and roast beef buffet.

Yotty's Ice Cream Shop, 501 B Avenue, (319) 656-2512. Ice cream desserts.

INFORMATION

Iowa City/Coralville Convention and Visitors Bureau, 408 First Avenue, Coralville, IA 52241, (319) 337-6592; (800) 283-6592; www.icccvb.org

Eastern Iowa Tourism Region, PO Box 189, Dyersville, IA 52040, (563) 875-7269; (800) 891-3482; www.easterniowatourism.org

Section IV

Northeast Iowa
Towns and Countryside

Chapter 16

Decorah: A Bit of Norway in Mid-America

Most people think of Iowa as a state with an open landscape that rolls on forever. The northeast corner of the state, however, presents a contrast. Here, rumpled hills look like they're almost pushed up against each other. Creeks, streams, and rivers—not to mention roads—ramble where they can. Trees cover the hills, rugged faces of limestone poke out here and there, and farm fields are small, showing how little humans have disturbed this area.

Welcome to the Driftless Region—a large oval-shaped area encompassing northeast Iowa, southeast Minnesota, southwest Wisconsin, and a bit of northwest Illinois. Over thousands of years, one glacier after another pushed down into the Midwest, pretty much flattening everything in the way. Yet somehow, all of those glaciers drifted around one region, leaving quite a hilly area even though the Mississippi River managed to cut a path right through it. This is the Driftless Region, and Decorah is in the heart of Iowa's portion.

Decorah

The largest community in northeast Iowa, Decorah is a good place to start a tour of the Driftless Region. Although settled by both English and Norwegian immigrants, it's the Norwegian influence that is still most evident here—a Norwegian flag here, a sign with Norwegian words there, and statues of Nisse (a Norwegian imp) in someone's garden over yonder.

Probably the best place to learn about Norwegian culture in the United States is the **Vesterheim Norwegian-American Museum**, 523 W. Water Street, (563) 382-9681; admission. The nation's largest and oldest museum that's dedicated to telling the story of immigrants from one nation, Vesterheim is located in a historic, three-story brick hotel that looks original on its exterior but on the inside has been changed into a top-notch museum. Besides displays that one might expect here—traditional clothing, folk arts, and equipment used by

Vesterheim Norwegian-American Museum in Decorah

the early Norwegians—there's a display about boats that includes a 25-foot-tall sailboat. Out back is one of the nation's earliest collections of historical buildings, including a 19th-century farmhouse and gristmill from Valdres, Norway, pioneer homes, and a four-story limestone mill.

Between June and September, the museum's staff teaches traditional crafts such as rosemaling, wood carving, dyeing fabrics, ship carving, spoon carving, and Danish needlework. Some classes for beginners take place over weekends while others last up to five days. Prices begin at $120 for those who aren't members of the museum. One-day Norwegian cooking classes cost $35-$45.

If you don't want to make your own Norwegian foods, then visit the museum's **Norwegian Café**, which serves *lapskaus* (a thick meaty stew), *lefse* (a flat potato bread cooked on a griddle), *rømmegrøt* (hot cream pudding that's as rich as can be), and a number of other traditional Norwegian and American selections.

About four blocks away is the **Porter House Museum**, 401 W. Broadway, (563) 382-8465; admission. An Italianate mansion that was once the home of Adelbert Field Porter, a nationally known collector, the museum displays his three major collections: butterflies, moths, and insects; stamps and first-day covers; and rocks and minerals. Porter's knowledge of the last items is evident by the rock wall surrounding the mansion that took six years to fashion out of agate, jasper, onyx, petrified wood, crystal, rose quartz, and amethyst.

Decorah is a town full of pleasant surprises. And one of the most spectacular is a hotel built in 1905, the **Hotel Winneshiek**, 104 E. Water, (563) 382-4164; (800) 998-4164, that will knock your socks off the moment you walk into its octagonal, wood-paneled, three-story lobby with its cherry grand staircase to the third floor. There's more—a marble fireplace, brass chandelier, and a 19-foot-wide skylight. Now that's an entry few buildings anywhere can match.

Standing in the entry, you'll probably have two reactions: "Wow," followed by "What's all this doing in a town of 8,500 people?" Everyone who visits would agree with the first reaction. As to the second, one could ask, "Should elegant surroundings be reserved only for big cities?" Obviously not.

To immerse yourself in more of the hotel's ambience, you might want to eat in its **Victorian Rose** restaurant or have tea when it's served from 3:30 to 5:00 p.m., Thursday through Saturday.

Outdoor Activities

Decorah has a 15-mile system of trails excellent for hiking, skating, and biking, along with cross-country skiing in the winter. You can rent bicycles from **Decorah Bicycles**, 101 College Drive, (563) 382-8902, which also rents tandem bikes, child carriers, skates, cross-country skis, and tubes for those who want to take the lazy way down the Upper Iowa River.

About 300 yards from the western head of the **Oneota Trail** (which is accessed off Highway 52 just north of the intersection with Highway 9), you'll see something that's very rare—an algific cave. Fortunately it's marked by a sign, since many of these caves, also called cold air seeps, are hard to spot unless you're really searching for them. What's an algific cave? It's a very small opening in the ground—usually on the north slope of a hill—that leads to underground chambers where the air remains cool in the summertime. As the cave air leaves the small opening, it cools everything within a short distance of the opening, creating a micro-ecosystem of plants that couldn't survive in the warmer air just a few inches away. Feel free to look at these tiny, rare plants, but please leave them because they won't survive anywhere else.

Northeast Iowa is full of caves, but there are no commercial caves to visit in this area. The few that can be explored require true spelunking ability, so they aren't mentioned here. However, there are some near **McGregor, Dubuque**, and **Maquoketa** that the public can access, so check chapters 17, 19, and 20.

Since you're outdoors, head to **Dunning's Spring**, (563) 382-4158; free, which is less than a mile out of town and is reached by taking College Drive to Quarry Street and heading east to the clearly marked entry to the spring. Here, in a very picturesque setting, the cold waters of a spring tumble through jumbled limestone rocks. On a warm day, it's a pleasure to walk through the waters barefoot but do take care not to slip. Similarly, don't even think about climbing the rocky escarpments along the spring—they can be deadly. However, you can safely cross the stream and go up a trail on the other side where you'll find a boardwalk that overlooks the upper end of the spring.

You can go farther into the country but you need to backtrack a bit to do so. At College Drive, take a right, go one block and take another right onto Locust Road. Now go 10 miles out into the country. At the four-way stop with Big Canoe Road, you'll see **Locust School**. Built in 1854 and in use until 1960, this country school is open for tours on summer weekends from 1-4 p.m. Another country school, **Highlandville School**, is but a few miles to the east down Big Canoe Road and then up Highlandville Road on the left to the tiny community of Highlandville. On some summer evenings the Footnotes, a local group of musicians, perform traditional Norwegian-American folk songs at dances. The best way to learn if dances or performances are scheduled at Highlandville School is to watch for notices posted around Decorah or check with the Decorah Area Chamber of Commerce.

SIDE TRIPS

To the North

You will head north of Decorah again but in a slightly different way this time. Go five miles north of the Highways 52 and 9 intersection on Highway 52. Watch for the signs to **Seed Savers Heritage Farm**, 3076 N. Winn Road (563) 382-5990; admission, and turn where indicated. The farm is about a mile to the east. Not a farm in the usual sense of having livestock and crops, this is the headquarters of Seed Savers Exchange which produces a variety of heirloom vegetable, fruit, flower, and herb seeds. These seeds represent strains that are no longer commonly grown and predate plant hybridization. Here, you can find Bird Egg bean, Moon and Stars watermelon, Brandywine tomatoes, and at least a thousand more varieties. In the apple orchard alone are 700 types of apples.

From Seed Savers, return to Highway 52 and go farther north still, to **Burr Oak** to the **Laura Ingalls Wilder Park and Museum**, 3603 2346th Avenue, (563) 735-5916; admission. When Wilder was 9, she came here with her family when her father agreed to manage the 11-room Burr Oak House Hotel, today restored to its 1876 appearance. For part of the year the Ingalls family lived in Burr Oak, they resided in this small, white, wooden one-and-a-half-story hotel. The only Iowa site linked to Wilder, it is the only one of her childhood homes still on its original site. For some of the author's fans, this is the "missing link" in Wilder's writings; although she wrote about every place she lived, her publisher never printed her writings about her family's time here at the Little Hotel in the Hills.

At Burr Oak, take County Highway A18 to the west for about two-and-a-half miles until you reach County Highway W20, where you will turn left (south). About four-and-a-half miles later you'll reach the small community of Bluffton, perched atop the tall buff-colored bluffs along the Upper Iowa River and one of the prettiest sights in Iowa. You can rest at **Bluffton Fir Stand**

The Bily Clocks Museum in Spillville, south of Decorah

State Preserve, a stand of rare balsam fir. On the last full weekend of each July, Bluffton hosts an outdoor concert featuring top country music entertainers.

After driving a bit more than five miles south of the Bluffton bridge on County Highway W20, you'll see a sign for **Malanaphy Springs State Preserve**, (563) 534-7145, a shady place to rest and watch the waters of the springs ramble down to the Upper Iowa River. To return to Decorah, just continue down W20, which leads to Highway 52 at the north edge of town a few miles away.

To the South

From Decorah, take Highway 52 south for about seven miles to Highway 325 which leads to Spillville a few miles to the west. Just to the right of where the highway T's into the town, you'll see the **Bily Clocks Museum**, 323 Main Street, (563) 562-3569; admission, with its huge outdoor clock. Inside is the entire collection of 40 wooden clocks and two model churches carved by brothers Frank and Joseph Bily between 1913 and 1958 between their chores on the farm nearby. Ranging from a tabletop blacksmith shop clock to a 10-foot-tall timepiece featuring the 12 Apostles parading every hour, the clocks are made of butternut, maple, oak, and walnut. The Bilys never sought to sell any of the clocks they made, despite an offer of $1 million from Henry Ford in 1928 for their American Pioneer Clock.

The building housing the museum is also where composer Antonin Dvorak stayed during the summer of 1893 while he worked on scores, including "American Quartette" and "New World Symphony." Dvorak said he was inspired to write "Humoresque" by walking along the Turkey River that flows nearby.

The library in the Montauk mansion, Clermont

Before leaving town, go north a couple blocks, turn onto Church Street and park at the base of the hill below the magnificent red-roofed, limestone **St. Wenceslaus Church**, completed in 1870 for a Czech congregation. You can walk around its grounds and visit inside the unusual church, which has no central aisle. On the far side of the church, the cemetery is loaded with cast-iron grave markers made by a local craftsman a century ago.

Return to Main Street and head south. The road will become County Highway W14, which leads to the town of Fort Atkinson about five miles away. On the way there, you'll see its namesake, **Fort Atkinson**, (563) 425-4161; free. Built in 1840, it was the only fort built to protect one group of Indians, the Winnebago, from another, the combined Sauk and Fox tribes. Remains of some of the limestone buildings and some reconstructions are at the site, which is now a state preserve open from 9 a.m. to 5 p.m. daily.

From there, take County Highway B32 to the east where it connects with Highway 150 about three miles away. Just as you turn right (south) onto Highway 150, watch for signs on the right (west) side of the road announcing the turnoff to the **Chapel of St. Anthony of Padua** (open daylight hours), often called the world's smallest cathedral. Built in 1886 by Johann Gaertner, a former French soldier who survived Napolean's retreat from Moscow, the limestone church measures just 14 by 20 feet.

As you go south, you'll descend into the valley of the Turkey River at Eldorado and as you pass the town, the road climbs a long hill where a turnout lets you look back north for a wonderful panorama of northeast Iowa. Five miles south of there is West Union, where you'll take a left (east) onto Highway 18. About two miles out of town, a country road heads to the left (north) to take you to **Dutton's Cave Park**, (563) 422-5146, a Fayette County Conservation

Board recreation area. Not as big as it once was due to siltation, the cave can still be easily explored. It's less than a mile from Highway 18.

On Highway 18 again, keep heading east to Clermont. On the east side of town is **Montauk**, (563) 423-7173; free, the home of William Larrabee, Iowa's 12th governor, who built the brick and limestone mansion in 1874. The beauty of this place, owned by the State Historical Society, is that it was turned directly over to the state by the family in 1960, complete with furnishings. The artwork was purchased by the family, including a rare life mask of Abraham Lincoln. The grounds are sprinkled with statues of the legendary men of Larrabee's day.

On Highway 18 once more, keep going east to Highway 52 where you'll take a left (west) turn to go to Castalia, following the signs to **Molineland**, (563) 567-8344; 567-8143, home to several restored Minneapolis Moline Tractors and antique Dodge cars and trucks. From Castalia, it's about 21 miles back to Decorah.

Canoeing

Northeast Iowa has the best canoeing in the state, especially the **Upper Iowa River**, which draws canoeists from across the Upper Midwest. It's not so much the river that attracts people—it's rather gentle, although one must avoid the old power dams below Decorah—but the surrounding scenery, particularly the portion between Kendallville and Decorah. If you want a pleasant paddle on the river during a weekend visit that allows time to see other places too, put in at Bluffton and get out at one of the river access points in Decorah, about 16 miles downriver or six hours by canoe. Along the way you can visit Malanaphy Springs.

Tips: Canoeing is best in the spring and early summer when the water is high, and the best fishing is generally thought to be below the lower power dam, about 10 miles northeast of Decorah.

The best information about canoeing in Iowa is in the free guidebooks about each of its rivers available from the Iowa Department of Natural Resources, 900 E. Grand Avenue, Des Moines, IA 50319-0034. You can call (515) 281-9361, wait for the state phone mail operator, press 4-5421 and the # sign, and, after listening to the taped message, leave your name, address, and the specific river guides you would like sent to you.

To rent canoes and equipment, contact one of the following firms:
Chimney Rock Campground and Canoe Rental, Bluffton, 3312 Chimney Rock Road, (563) 735-5786; (877) 787-CAMP. Canoes, camping, fishing. Shuttle.

Hruska's Canoe Rental and Campground, Kendallville, 3233 347th Street, (563) 547-4566. Canoes, kayaks, tubes, camping. Shuttle.

Johnson Canoe Rental and Campground, Bluffton, 2643 W. Ravine Road, (563) 735-5577. Shuttle.

Randy's Bluffton Store, Campground, and Canoe Livery, Bluffton, 2619 W. Ravine Road, (563) 735-5738. Canoes, kayaks, camping, lunches. Shuttle.

Upper Iowa Canoe Rental, Decorah, Pulpit Rock Road (563) 382-2332. Shuttle.

LODGING
Decorah
Country Inn & Suites, 1202 Highway 9, (563) 382-9646; (800) 456-4000. On southern edge of town. Indoor pool, continental breakfast. $$-$$$$

Hotel Winneshiek, 104 E. Water Street, (563) 382-4164; (800) 998-4164. In downtown area, near Vesterheim. Rooms and suites. Restaurant, lounge, afternoon tea. Connected to Royal Opera House. $$-$$$$

Villager Lodge, junction of Highways 52 and 9, (563) 382-4241; (800) 632-5980. South edge of town. Rooms and suites. Indoor pool, restaurant with Norwegian selections. $-$$

West Union
Elm Motel, 705 Highway 150 S, (563) 422-3841; (800) 422-3843. About 7 miles from Montauk. $-$$

Super 8 Motel, Highways 18/150 (563) 422-3464; (800) 800-8000. About 7 miles from Montauk Indoor pool, continental breakfast. $-$$

BED AND BREAKFAST
Burr Oak
Elmhurst Cottage, 3618 258th Avenue, (563) 735-5310; (888) 413-5600. Ten miles north of Decorah. Private kitchen, living, dining areas in cottage plus patio. Farm environment. Nine rooms. $-$$

Clermont
Mill Street B&B, 505 Mill Street, (563) 423-5531. Near restaurants, shops, and Montauk historic site. Two rooms. $

Decorah
Dee Dee's B&B, 201 Riverside Avenue, (563) 382-2778. Victorian cottage on east end of downtown. Two rooms. $$

Montgomery Mansion B&B, 812 Maple Avenue, (563) 382-5088; (800) 892-4955. Close to Vesterheim, Porter House, and a historic neighborhood. $$

Spillville
Taylor Made B&B, Main Street, (563) 562-3958. Across the street from Bily Clock Museum. Four rooms and private cabin. $$-$$$

DINING

Decorah

Back Home Bakery/Coffee Shop, 202 W. Water Street, (563) 382-8696. In downtown. Fresh-baked goods including lefse. Lunch counter and breakfast specials.

Burl's, 1101½ Montgomery Street, (563) 387-0167. East end of town. Homemade breads, pies, and desserts in a country dining atmosphere. Breakfast and lunch.

Cho Sun Chinese Restaurant, 802 Commerce Drive, (563) 382-8309. Chinese cuisine. Seating and take-out.

Dayton House Norwegian Café, 520 W. Water Street. (563) 382-9683. At Vesterheim. Norwegian-American items on the menu.

Family Table Restaurant, 817 Mechanic Street, (563) 382-2964. Family atmosphere with home-cooked food.

Mabe's Pizza, 110 E. Water Street, (563) 382-4297. Downtown. Pizza, salads, pasta, and sandwiches. Local delivery.

Stone Hearth Inn, (563) 382-4614. South edge of town near motels. Steaks, seafood, pasta, sandwiches.

T-bocks Sports Bar & Grill, 508 W. Water Street, (563) 382-5970. Downtown. Ostrich is on the menu at times.

Victorian Rose, 104 E. Water Street, (563) 382-4164. In the Hotel Winneshiek in downtown area. Dining room with palm trees.

Villager Lodge, 101 Highway 9 (563) 382-4241. Norwegian and American items on the menu. Buffet on Tuesday, Friday, and Saturday evenings.

INFORMATION

Decorah Chamber of Commerce, 300 W. Water, Decorah, IA 52101, (563) 382-3990; (800) 463-4692; www.decorah-iowa.com.

Eastern Iowa Tourism Region, PO Box 189, Dyersville, IA 52040, (563) 875-7269; (800) 891-3482; www.easterniowatourism.org.

Chapter 17

Marquette and McGregor: Rolling on the River

There are so many great places in northeast Iowa that you're faced with a dilemma, albeit a fun one—selecting one place to serve as a base of operations for your weekend.

$\mathcal{M}$cGregor

For this trip, how about starting along the Mississippi River at the small town of McGregor? When you enter it on Business Highway 18 from the west, there's only one way through town and that's on Main Street. After a slight jog in the road, you pass from a housing area into the small business district where many of the brick storefronts go back a century ago and those on the left appear to be built partially into the hill behind them. Suddenly you're at the Mississippi River and if you don't make the turn where the highway does you could find yourself in the water.

Try walking along the business portion of Main Street. It won't take long and the stores might interest you. One place you shouldn't miss is **River Junction Trading Company**, 312 Main Street, (563) 873-2387. Founded in 1973, the store produces goods associated with the Old West and what you see for sale here is as good as you can get without stealing the real McCoys out of a museum. Hey, if movie and television companies making Westerns see fit to order their gear from here, you know it's good enough for you. Want a flashy vest used by riverboat gamblers? It's here. Ditto with shirts tailored from patterns used by General Armstrong Custer and sporting pearl and tin buttons. And there's much more: cartridge belts, saddlebags, chaps, spurs, tepees, pocket watches, revolvers that fire only blanks, ladies high-top shoes, longjohns, and longhorns (the horns that is, not the cattle).

Other businesses along Main Street sell collectibles, antiques, books, and gifts including homemade items. **The McGregor Historical Museum**, 254

Main Street, McGregor

Main Street, will inform you that this is the birthplace of the Ringling brothers, who started the famous circus that bears their name. If your interest leans more toward tractors, visit the **Froelich Foundation Tractor History Museum**, 24297 Froelich Road, (563) 536-2841, which is about nine miles west of town on Highway 18. This is where John Froelich built the world's first gas-powered tractor in 1892, creating the Waterloo Gasoline Tractor Engine Company, which was later absorbed by John Deere. Also at the site are an 1891 "iron clad" mercantile store and a one-room schoolhouse.

Outside of McGregor is the region's main draw—**Pikes Peak State Park**, (563) 873-2341; free. Pikes Peak? In Iowa? Yes. Lieutenant Zebulon Pike, the same fellow after whom the Colorado peak is named, came here in 1805 before he went west and recommended that a fort be built on the bluff where the lookout of this state park is now located.

The lookout is the first place that most people visit when they come here and the view of the Mississippi River valley 500 feet below is impressive. To the east, the river braids its way though countless islands and to the south is the Wisconsin River, the waterway down which French explorers Jacques Marquette and Louis Joliet paddled on June 17, 1673, to become the first whites to see the Mississippi River.

If you can tear yourself away from the overlook, take the foot trail to the north and visit Bridal Veil Falls, a thin but nice waterfall and one of the few in the state. A number of ups and downs exist along the way with helpful stairs in many places, but take your time. The park has some other trails that lead

A view of the Mississippi River from Pikes Peak State Park

into these beautiful tree-filled hills. One begins just north of the entrance to the park and is a loop trail to an old quarry and effigy mounds. Another trail comes south from Front Street in McGregor and runs along the base of the bluffs to a parking area where you can continue hiking to more lookouts and see more effigy mounds along the way.

If you're interested in going on the river, you can rent houseboats that carry from eight to 12 passengers each from **Boatels**, 400 Business Highway 18 N., (563) 873-3718; (800) 747-2628, the second-oldest houseboat rental company in the nation. You can also view the Mississippi from the decks of the *Isle of Capri* Casino riverboat, 101 Anti-Monopoly Street, (563) 873-3531; (800) 496-8238), which docks just north of McGregor on Highway 340. Going on the river daily during the summer, this large riverboat has blackjack, poker, craps, roulette, slots, and a snack bar. At the riverboat's onshore pavilion is a full buffet and showroom with Las Vegas-style entertainment.

$\mathcal{M}$arquette

Just north of here is the small town of Marquette, nestled close to the big bridge that carries Highway 18 to Prairie du Chien, Wisconsin, across the Mississippi. Keep going north though and the road you're on becomes Highway 76. Three miles north of Marquette you'll cross the mouth of the Yellow River and arrive at **Effigy Mounds National Monument**, 151 Highway 76, (563) 873-3491; admission. A 2,526-acre site, the monument encompasses 195 mounds built between 450 B.C. and A.D.1250. Some are burial mounds, some ceremonial. Most are conical, a few are linear, but what makes this place special are 31 mounds that are shaped like bears and birds.

The mounds easiest to see are some conical ones just outside the new visitor center, which does a fine job of explaining how it is thought the mounds came to be. Outside the center, a handicapped-accessible boardwalk provides access to four linear and conical mounds near the Yellow River while, in the other direction, a trail leads north to more mounds atop the bluffs. That trail is a bit of a hike, so pace yourself on the switchbacks, but once you're on top, you'll find the terrain is fairly level. Most of the mounds up there are conicals but there are two bear mounds. Besides the mounds—some singly, some in groups—you'll find fantastic overlooks of the river valley below.

The best group of effigy mounds, though, is on a bluff south of the visitors center, requiring about a 45-minute hike to reach them at the end of a rough, 2-mile service road (no private vehicles permitted). Once atop the bluff, you'll see the marching bears, a line of 10 bear-shaped mounds that look like they're following one another across the hilltop. Two well-defined swallow mounds are near the bears.

Occasionally, rangers give guided mound tours during summer months, and in July there's a moonlight hike that requires reservations. Check with the visitor center for more information on these hikes.

There are no amenities in the southern part of the monument where the marching bears are. Be sure to pack water, and think about bringing insect repellent on warm, humid days.

From Effigy Mounds, take Highway 76 north 10 miles to the entrance of **Yellow River State Forest**, Highway 76, (563) 586-2254; free. Comprising 7,068 acres of heavily wooded hills with what some say are two great trout streams, the forest is a popular place for hiking, fishing, horseback riding, camping, snowmobiling, and cross-country skiing. You can easily spend a weekend traipsing through this forest and having a good time.

SIDE TRIPS

To the North

North of Marquette, a series of roads ramble up and down the hills, flatten out on ancient floodplains and run along the mighty Mississippi in places. Don't expect to make time here—just drive to enjoy seeing the countryside.

To start, go north on Highway 76 but turn onto Highway 364 before you get to Yellow River State Forest. In a few miles you'll be alongside the Mississippi on your way into **Harpers Ferry**, a quiet riverside community. At this point, the state highway designation on your road ends but the pavement keeps going on as County Highway X52, which, you'll see, is marked with Great River Road signs. It goes along the river for a mile or so and then runs inland for awhile before reaching **Lansing**, about 14 miles away, which sits picture-perfect at the bottom of a tree-heavy hill next to the river.

You could go through town but think about visiting the business district on Main Street (also Highway 9) for three reasons:

1. To visit the Model Bakery, 288 Main Street, (563) 538-4009, a longtime family-owned bakery that itself makes a trip here worthwhile.
2. To get, via Main Street and Sixth Street, to the top of **Mount Hosmer**, a 25-acre city park that has one of the best views across the Mississippi River as well as of the town below.
3. To take in the view of the river at the foot of this small town's business district as you return down Main to your chief riverside route. There may be few other places like this in Iowa.

At the bottom of Main Street, you'll find the **Museum of River History**, 61 S. Front Street, (563) 538-4641; free, which gives a good history of this part of the Mississippi, especially that of clamming and buttons. You can experience more of the river by leasing a houseboat from **S & S Rentals, Inc.**, 990 Front Street, (563) 538-4454; (800) 728-0131; fee.

You might think about crossing the river on the Highway 82 bridge, but, to be truthful, there's not much on the Wisconsin side at this point other than more scenery along the river. However, once across the main channel, the roadway dips down to near water level and you can find several turnouts that are good places to launch canoes.

All along this riverside journey you've been in the **Upper Mississippi National Wildlife and Fish Refuge**, whose office is located at Business Highway 18 N, north of McGregor, (563) 873-3423. A canoe is a great way to see wildlife around here, and with 228 species of birds, 57 kinds of mammals, 35 types of amphibians and reptiles, and 118 species of fish, the refuge provides you with plenty to see! Early morning and evening twilight are good times to see beaver and muskrat in the backwaters. Raccoon, fox, and opossum frequent the area, along with deer and some harder-to-spot coyote and otter.

The big birds soaring along the bluffs on wide wings in the summer are often turkey vultures, although you might spot red-tailed and rough-legged hawks at times. In shallow waters, great blue heron and egrets practice patience as they stalk fish, and ducks of all types use the backwaters as well as the deeper main channel.

Most reptiles you'll see here are turtles and frogs, although you might spot a water snake at times; not to worry, they're nonvenomous. A bit of advice from one who has canoed part of the Mississippi: if you're canoeing on the big river for the first time, the still backwaters are far easier to paddle and usually have more to see than the main channel. If you do go in the main channel, definitely

The burial mounds at Fish Farm Mounds, north of Lansing

stay away from the tows—they're dangerous from any angle and at any speed—and be wary of the wakes generated by fast powerboats.

Now, back in Lansing, take Highway 26 north for about six miles. Watch for a sign directing you to **Fish Farm Mounds** on your left (west) side and pull off for a short visit. A number of prehistoric conical burial mounds sit on a small plateau that is easily reached by walking up a gentle slope, making this place much more accessible than the longer, steeper walks at Effigy Mounds. If you're wondering about the name, Fish Farm, it's the name of the family whose farm encompassed the mounds before they became state property.

You can continue north to **New Albin** for the chance to say you've been at the state's northeasternmost community, on the Minnesota border. Or you can backtrack to Lansing, where you have three choices of how to return to Marquette and McGregor:

1. The Great River Road (County Highway X52), which is the way you came.
2. County Highway X42, which splits off from County Highway X52 just south of Lansing (it's another way to Harpers Ferry and passes through some pretty hills and open areas).
3. Highway 9, which, if you take it west for 17 miles, will bring you to Waukon and the **Allamakee County Historical Museum**, 107 Allamakee Street, (563) 568-2954; admission. Housed in the striking old county courthouse, the museum has maintained the original courtroom and has collections that include Indian artifacts and antique clocks. Outside are a log cabin built by Norwegian immigrants and a red, one-room schoolhouse.

If you have been seeking a way to put adventure in your life and see the world from a different vantage point, then, believe it or not, this quiet little town has some pretty good offerings. **Driftaway Tours**, 106 E. Main Street, (563) 568-2051; (800) 643-9229; admission (call for reservations) will take you on 45-60 minute hot-air balloon flights across northeast Iowa, 80-minute airboat rides on the Upper Iowa River, day-long fishing trips on the Mississippi, and, if you're around in the winter, ice fishing and eagle watching excursions. Similarly, **Paint Creek Riding Stables**, 1048 Sand Hill Road, (563) 535-7253; admission, offers supervised trail rides and hay rides on weekend evenings.

South of Waukon is Highway 76, which will take you south to Marquette and McGregor.

To the West

About 10 miles west of McGregor on Highway 18, a sign points the way to **Spook Cave**, 13299 Spook Cave Road, (563) 873-2144, admission. You don't walk through this cave, you motor through it on a guided 35-minute tour via boat. Camping is available on the site.

To the East

By now you've noticed a city on the other side of the Mississippi while you've been going up and down the Iowa side of the river. That's Prairie du Chien, Wisconsin, the largest community around these parts.

Obviously the best way to get there is to cross the big bridge from Marquette. That's Highway 18 and it will bring you right into Prairie du Chien (pronounced "prairie doo sheen," in case you're not up on your Anglicized French). Meaning "prairie of the Dog," the name was given to the area by French trappers and traders in honor of a prairie where an Indian chief named Dog lived.

At the bottom of the bridge in Prairie du Chien, you're at Main Street. You'll immediately see a triangular-shaped building with five flags in front of it, which is the **Prairie du Chien Chamber of Commerce**, 211 S. Main, (608) 326-8555; (800) PDC-1673. After you get all the information you want there, drive two blocks to the east to Beaumont Road and go south there seven blocks to the **Fort Crawford Museum**, 717 S. Beaumont Road, (608) 326-6960; admission. Originally a museum related to the history of medicine on the frontier, the museum has added other displays to become more general in scope and is a good way to learn about the region.

North of the bridge, on Saint Feriole Island, is **Villa Louis State Historical Site**, at Villa Louis Road and Bolvin Street, (608) 326-2721; admission. Pronounced "villa loo-ee," the Victorian mansion was built in 1870 by H. Louis Dousman, son of a local entrepreneur who made his money in land deals, lumber, and railroads. The villa, which recently underwent an extensive restoration, is furnished with items used by the Dousman family, an unusual bonus for a mansion open to the public.

Upon leaving Villa Louis, you'll see Brisbois Street , which heads east to become Washington Street in just a few blocks. That intersects with N. Marquette where you should easily see **The Cannery**, 300 N. Marquette, (608) 326-6518. Once a pickle factory, The Cannery is now an unusual store that sells antiques, lace, candles, pottery, imported rugs, and curtains. There's even a fudge shop to satisfy your sweet tooth.

Should you be interested in items related to enjoying the great outdoors, then head about a mile north on N. Marquette (also Highway 35) to find **Cabela's**, 1601 N. Wisconsin, (608) 326-5600, a wilderness outfitter so popular that it runs a shuttle to and from the local airport for those who fly and buy. Besides selling almost anything that one could use to fish, camp, hike, snowshoe, hunt, etc., the store has a stunning collection of animals mounted in action poses on the side of a rocky cliff.

Back to the country: Go south of town on Highway 18 and cross the Wisconsin River. Take County Highway C to the right (west) and, 27 miles from town, you'll wind up at **Wyalusing State Park**, 13342 County Highway C, (608) 996-2261, Wisconsin's equivalent of Iowa's Pikes Peak State Park. Perched on 500-foot bluffs overlooking the Wisconsin and Mississippi Rivers, Wyalusing is one of Wisconsin's more popular state parks. Twenty-five miles of trails wander through this 2,700-acre park, which also provides boat access to the Mississippi. A six-mile canoe trail leads through the Mississippi's backwaters as well as on part of the main channel.

To the South

If you take Highway 340 south from McGregor but keep going past Pikes Peak State Park, the road becomes County Highway X56, a part of the Great River Road (with a parallel bike trail). This leads to **Guttenberg**, a pleasant riverside community (there seem to be no other types in this area). The main attraction in this town is Lock and Dam No. 10 where a visitors platform provides an overview of the process it takes to raise and lower all kinds of boats as they pass around the dam spanning the Mississippi.

Immediately behind the viewing area is the **Lockmaster's House Heritage Museum**, (563) 252-1531; free. The last remaining house used by the lockmasters of the Mississippi River dams, the wood-frame museum is furnished as it was in the first half of the 20th century. An extensive collection of photos depicts the history of the river in this region.

Another popular place is the two-mile-long park that fronts the river. Shelters, benches, and shade trees provide spots to sit back and watch the Mississippi. If you want a picnic, the park also has grills. As you stroll through the park, you may notice three stone warehouses; all date to the 1850s. The northernmost was once owned by the family of Ulysses S. Grant when he was a merchant in Galena, Illinois. The middle one holds a number of small businesses now and the southernmost warehouse serves as a B&B.

Another stop is the **State Fish Aquarium and Hatchery**, 331 S. River Park Road, (563) 252-1156; free, where aquariums hold fish found in the Mississippi River and nearby trout streams.

Canoeing

Much shorter than the Upper Iowa, the **Yellow River** has a 19-mile stretch that's pretty good for canoeing, especially in the spring and early summer. Beginning at the town of Volney (which one gets to by taking County Highway X26 south from Rossville, reachable via Highway 76 northwest of Yellow River State Forest), the route finishes where the Yellow empties into the Mississippi near a set of mounds at Effigy Mounds National Monument.

The best information about canoeing in Iowa is in free guidebooks about each state rivers that can be obtained from the Iowa Department of Natural Resources, 900 E. Grand Avenue, Des Moines, IA 50319-0034. You can call (515) 281-9361, wait for the state phone mail operator, press 4-5421 and the # sign, and, after listening to the taped message, leave your name, address, and which guides you would like sent to you.

LODGING

Guttenberg

A.R. Motel, 115 Lorenz Lane, (563) 252-1653. North on Highway 52. On a bluff overlooking the valley. $-$$

Century Lodge Motel, 10 Lorenz Lane, (563) 252-1456. In the country, on a bluff overlooking the Mississippi. $-$$

Guttenberg Motel, 923 Highway 52 S, (563) 252-1433. On Highway 52 in town. $

Lansing

Scenic Valley Motel, 1608 Main Street, (563) 538-4245. $

Marquette

Frontier Motel, 101 S. First Street, (563) 873-3497. Outdoor pool. $-$$$

Isle of Capri Motel, Business Highway 18, (563) 873-3531; (800) 4-YOU-BET. Part of the casino complex. Overlooks the river valley from a rocky perch. $$-$$$

McGregor

Alexander Hotel, Main Street, (563) 873-3838. Brick hotel built in 1899. Café, wood-paneled restaurant, and Ringling's Bar. Limestone cellar bar with live entertainment on weekends. Rooms and suite. $-$$$

Holiday Shores Motel, 101 Front Street, (563) 873-3449. Faces the Mississippi. Indoor pool. $-$$$

Prairie du Chien, Wisconsin

AmericInn Motel, 130 S. Main, (608) 326-7878; (800) 634-3444. In downtown area. Near Villa Louis. Indoor pool, continental breakfast, fitness room. $$-$$$

Hidden Valley Lodge, Highway18/35/60, (608) 326-8476; (800) 349-8476. South edge of town near airport. Outdoor pool. $-$$$$

Holiday Motel, Highway18/35/60, (608) 326-2448; (800) 962-3883. South edge of town near airport. Historical theme rooms. $-$$$

Windsor Place Inn, Highway18/35/60, (608) 326-7799. South edge of town near airport. Indoor pool. $$-$$$

Waukon

Stoney Creek Inn, 407 Rossville Road, (563) 568-2220; (800) 659-2220. Rooms and three theme suites. Continental breakfast. $$-$$$$

BED AND BREAKFASTS

Clayton

Claytonian Inn, 100 S. Front Street, (563) 964-2776. Across the street from the Mississippi. Near restaurants. Bikes available. Six rooms. $$

Guttenberg

Courthouse Inn, 618 S. River Park Drive, (563) 252-1870. The former Clayton County Courthouse is now a renovated inn on the waterfront. Three rooms in this building and four more in another on Schiller Street. $$

Guttenberg River Inn & Café, 308 S. River Park Drive, (563) 252-3706; (877) 521-4790. European styling in 1856 stone building with views of the Mississippi. Walled courtyard. Two suites. $$$-$$$$

The Landing, A River Front Inn, 703 S. River Park Drive, (563) 252-1615. A limestone building that was a button factory, located on the waterfront one block from downtown. No food service. Fourteen rooms and suites with balconies and patios. $-$$$

189

Old Brewery, 402 S. Bluff Street, (563) 252-2094; (800) 353-1307. A former stone brewery built in 1858. Brewing equipment on view, art gallery, cave with wine, and beer room. Three rooms. $$

Harpers Ferry

Cedar Valley Lodge/Cabin, 621 Downing Lane, (563) 586-2200. Surrounded by Yellow River State Forest. Five rooms. $$

The Houlihan House B&B, 617 W. Jefferson Avenue, (563) 586-2639. A block from the Mississippi. Children welcome. Four rooms. $-$$

Lansing

The Captain's House, 160 N. 3rd Street, (563) 538-4872. An 1863 Victorian home on a bluff overlooking the Mississippi. Children welcome. Five rooms. $$-$$$

Suzanne's Inn B&B, 120 N. 3rd Street, (563) 538-3040. Gothic Revival home. Sauna in root cellar. Children welcome. Four rooms. $$

Marquette

Eagles Landing B&B, 82 North Street, (563) 873-2509. With gazebos and verandah overlooking the Mississippi. Family suite. American, Norwegian, or German breakfasts. Children welcome. Three rooms. $$

Eagle's View Carriage House, 523 Fifth Street, (563) 873-3654. B&B with kitchenette, deck. Three rooms. $$-$$$

McGregor

American House Suites, 116 Main Street, (563) 873-3364. Two suites. $$-$$$$

Little Switzerland Inn, 126 Main Street, (563) 873-2057. A 125-year-old building and a 150-year-old cabin at the base of a bluff and facing the Mississippi. Four rooms. $$$-$$$$

Grumpster's Log Cabin Getaway, 535 Ash Street, (563) 873-3767. Cabins in the forests near town. Kitchens, lower and loft BRs. Garden tub and shower.

Hilltop Cottage/Ridgewood Cottage, (563) 873-2600. Five rooms. $$$$

McGregor Manor, 320 4th Street, (563) 873-2600. Victorian home on a side street. Cottages available. Four rooms. $$

River's Edge B&B, 112 Main Street, (563) 873-3501. Upper deck view of the Mississippi. Among shops and restaurants. Three rooms. $$

Prairie du Chien, Wisconsin

Neumann House, 121 N. Michigan, (608) 326-8104. Civil War-era home. Three rooms. $$-$$$

La Maison Ravoux, 316 N. Beaumont, (608) 326-0458. City's oldest privately restored home. Flower and herb gardens. French-Canadian breakfasts. Three rooms. $$

Preachers Inn, 34909 Winegar Lane, (608) 875-6108; (877) 845-0887. Victorian inn on 20 acres outside of city. Three rooms. $$-$$$

DINING

Guttenberg

Guttenberg Bakery & Café, 408 River Park Drive, (563) 252-2225. Fresh baked items. Open 6-10:30 a.m., Monday-Saturday; 6 a.m.-1 p.m. Sunday.

Guttenberg River Inn & Café, 308 S. River Park Drive, (563) 252-3706; (877) 521-4790. Fine dining in the riverfront area. Part of an inn.

Kanndle Restaurant & Lounge, 106 Schiller Street, (563) 252-3494. A block from the waterfront.

Lansing

Milty's, 200 Main Street, (563) 538-4585. Family style, downtown.

T.J. Hunter's Pub and Grill, 367 Main Street, (563) 538-4544. American and Mexican dishes.

Marquette

Calypso, at the Isle of Capri Casino,101 Anti-Monopoly Road, (563) 873-3531; (800) 496-8238. Breakfast, lunch, and evening seafood buffets. Crab legs served each night.

River Country Restaurant & Antique Shop, 214 North Street (563) 873-2304. Homemade soups, salads, breads, and desserts. Sandwiches and ice cream.

McGregor

Alexander Hotel, Main Street, (563) 873-3838. Brick hotel built in 1899 with cafe, wood-paneled dining room, Ringling's Bar, limestone cellar bar with live entertainment on weekend evenings. Italian food on Wednesday, Mexican on Thursday.

White Springs, one mile west of McGregor on Business Highway 18, (563) 873-9642. Steak, seafood, chicken, hickory smoked ribs.

Prairie du Chien, Wisconsin

Fort Mulligans, 214 W. Blackhawk Avenue, (608) 326-0639. Supper club for lunch and dinner.

Huckleberry's Restaurant, 1903 S. Marquette, (608) 326-5488. Family-style eatery with buffet for breakfast, lunch, and dinner.

INFORMATION

Allamakee County Economic Development, 101 W. Main, Waukon, IA 52172, (563) 568-2624; www. allamakeecounty.com

Civic and Commerce Club, 323 S. River Park Drive, Guttenberg, IA 52052, (563) 252-2323; (877) 252-2323; www.guttenberg-iowa.org

Eastern Iowa Tourism Region, PO Box 189, Dyersville, IA 52040, (563) 875-7269; (800) 891-3482; www.easterniowatourism.org

McGregor-Marquette Chamber of Commerce, 146 Main Street, McGregor, IA 52157, (563) 873-2186; (800) 896-0910; www.alpinecom.net/mmcofc

Prairie du Chien Chamber of Commerce, PO Box 326, Prairie du Chien, WI 53821, (608) 326-8555; (800) PDC-1673; www.prairieduchien.org

Chapter 18

Backbone State Park: Forest and Rock on the Prairie

The oldest of Iowa's state parks, **Backbone State Park**, (563) 924-2527 is named after a ridge of exposed rock that looks like a large, lumpy backbone, around which the Maquoketa River flows. The park is located midway between Dubuque and Waterloo and not far from several of Iowa's larger communities. Thus, it has been a popular park since it was dedicated in 1919.

As in many other state parks, you can pitch a tent or park an RV here but, unlike most other parks in Iowa, Backbone also has year-round cabins. Because of the park's popularity in summer, the cabins are leased only for a full week at a time between Memorial Day and Labor Day. However, if a cabin has not been rented by the Wednesday of an open week, the park will lease it for two-night stays, though that happens infrequently.

Why, then, am I suggesting trying to stay here? Simple: just being at the park is worth it no matter how you stay. If you're after a cabin, don't dally about reserving one. By January 2 of one year, almost all the cabins had been reserved for the summer, although there were still plenty of opportunities to rent them during the off-season. Also note that the cabins must be rented for at least two nights, perfect for weekend travelers.

Once you've arrived for a stay at Backbone, then what? Well, some will say all they need is a place to spend a quiet weekend, perhaps curled up with a book.

But if you want to do something, you have many choices. Hike the many trails in the park. Swim at the beach at Backbone Lake. Rent a paddleboat, boat, canoe, kayak, or surf-bike. Cast a line in the trout stream. Rappel the cliffs. Have a picnic. Visit the park's museum, which explains how the Civilian Conservation Corps constructed many of the buildings in the park in the 1930s (by the way, the National Park Service was so impressed with how Iowa designed its park buildings that it incorporated similar designs into the buildings constructed in the national parks for years thereafter).

The Maquoketa River flowing through Backbone State Park

For hiking, the best place is the backbone itself, which is fairly heavy with trees but not an arduous hike. It's a great place for the kids to scamper although they should be cautioned not to run flat out because a fall here could be painful. At some places, the trail affords a nice view of the Maquoketa River far below.

Besides the backbone, which is in the southern part of the park, the northern end has picturesque features for hikers, although not as dramatic as the backbone. Up north are Balanced Rock, a small cave, and Richmond Springs, which feed cool water into a small trout stream. And, of course, you can walk anywhere else in the 1,750-acre park you want.

Another way of walking here is to remove your shoes and wade the Maquoketa River, more like a stream than a river at this point in its route down to the Mississippi miles from here. You couldn't ask for a better river to wade in—we're talking ankle deep most of the time—and you couldn't ask for better scenery in which to do it.

There are a ton of things to do in the park that make for a fun-filled and relaxing weekend. But if you're up for more activities, you can use Backbone as a base while visiting surrounding areas.

SIDE TRIPS

To the North

Two miles north of Backbone is **Strawberry Point**, the town to visit if you need food (at Strawberry Food, the local grocery). Another reason to stop is the **Wilder Memorial Museum**, 123 W. Mission Street, (563) 933-4615; admission; with its more than 800 heirloom dolls.

Continue north up Highway 13 to Elkader, 14 miles away. But first you'll want to pull over about 10 miles north of Strawberry Point to visit the **Osborne Conservation and Nature Center**, (563) 245-1516. Like all Iowa Welcome Centers, it's more than just a place with brochures, especially with three miles of trails lacing through 300 acres of wooded property. You also can take a self-guided tour through its pioneer village, which includes a false-front hotel, an 1840s log cabin, general store, depot, and more. Continue on to the live animal exhibit, with species ranging from the common to those that no longer inhabit Iowa—black bear, coyote, wolf, wild turkey, white-tailed deer, cougar, bobcat, and more. There also are colorful flower gardens and prairie exhibits. Inside, a gift shop and nature center complement the Welcome Center.

As you leave the center and approach Elkader, you'll see the 142-foot spire of **Saint Joseph's Catholic Church**, 330 1st Street, rising above all else in this picturesque community tucked into the Turkey River valley. Pause on your journey into town, though, to take Grape Road, which leads off to your right (east).

Follow this gravel road three miles to Galaxy Road, another stretch of gravel that runs off to your right (south). Don't worry about the Dead End sign. In three more miles you'll pull up to that dead end, where the village of Motor existed at one time alongside the Turkey River. Everything is in ruins except for the **Motor Mill**, (563) 245-1516, an impressive six-story limestone mill that was built in 1867 on the north riverbank. It's said to be the largest mill in Iowa. Unfortunately it isn't open, but the property, which belongs to the Osborne Center, is free to hike and picnic.

After visiting Motor Mill, retrace your route to Elkader. When you reach the highway, just go right into town on Bridge Street. You'll see the **Carter House Museum**, at the corner of Bridge and High Streets (563) 278-2770; admission; open 2-4 p.m., Saturday and Sunday, or by appointment. A Greek Revival mansion built in 1850, the museum is operated by the Historical Society and houses collections of 19th century clothing, military artifacts, pharmacy items, and more.

You could drive around Elkader, but it may be best to leave your car at the museum and walk around the downtown. You can cross the Turkey River on the **Keystone Bridge**, the longest bridge of its type (436 feet) west of the Mississippi. For a good view of the bridge, take a left when you get across it and go in to the Keystone Restaurant for a meal on the deck. It's a pleasant place to have lunch.

Beyond the restaurant, the **Elkader River Walk**, a 6-foot-wide walkway, leads along the Turkey River to the city park on the south side of town where it connects to **Pony Hollow Trail**. That trail follows the path of the old Chicago-Milwaukee-Saint Paul Railroad through some magnificent scenery for about four miles.

If you haven't taken to the walkways or trails, check out the three-story **Opera House**, 207 Main Street NW, that was built in 1903 and restored in the 1970s. Although the city hall occupies a portion of it now, it's still an active

The Motor Mill, on the Turkey River, southeast of Elkader

playhouse. Its horseshoe balcony alone is worth a visit and someone in the city office should be able to let you in for a look.

After visiting Elkader, leave town via High Street to the north. It will turn to the right and in a moment you'll see County Highway X16 on your left (north). Start following the brown signs that lead the way to **Big Spring Trout Hatchery**, 16212 Big Spring Road, (563) 245-2446; free, where rainbow, brook, and brown trout are raised. You can walk around on your own or take a guided tour of the largest spring in Iowa. If you want to fish in the Turkey River, which is on the property, you can buy a fishing license right here. Ask about the hatchery's acid rain gauge (you don't see many of those) and inquire about the minute particles that were found in it following a tornado years ago that hit Oklahoma City hundreds of miles away. You might be amazed to learn how far things travel in our atmosphere.

To return to Backbone, go south on County Highway X16 until you get to High Street, take a left (east) to Highway 13 and go south on that to pass through Strawberry Point on the way to the park.

To the South and West

For a tour of the area southwest of Backbone, leave the park by its west entrance, which is County Highway C57. At Highway 187, turn south and, in Lamont, take County Highway C64 to the west, which leads to County Highway

W45. Turn right (north) toward Aurora, where you'll find the **Richardson-Jakway House**, 2791 136th Street, (319) 636-2617; free. Built in 1851 as a relay station for stagecoaches, this house also served as a post office and an overnight inn. Call at least three days in advance to arrange a tour here.

Next, go west on County Highway C57 to Hazelton and turn south on Highway 150. Outside of town is **Fontana Park**, a nice place to camp and tour a nature center. As you continue south toward Independence, you may encounter some Amish. So be careful of their slow-moving, horse-drawn wagons and carriages. Some may permit photographs of their horses, buggies, and related items, but please be respectful and do not photograph the Amish themselves.

If you want to visit Amish businesses in the area, check with the **Buchanan County Tourism Bureau**, 115 1st Street East, (319) 334-3439, in **Independence** for Amish maps or check with the shops in town for quilts, furniture, and other handmade items. On Fridays and Saturdays, Amish baked goods are available in town.

While in Independence, you can visit the **Wapsipinicon Mill**, 115 1st Street West, (319) 334-4182; free. One of the largest mills in the state, it was built in 1867 alongside the Wapsipinicon River to process wool. Later it was used to grind feed and generate electricity. Now the picturesque structure houses a museum on its second floor, complete with burr stones, grain bins, pulley systems, and mill machinery.

From Independence, go east on Highway 20 to Highway 282, which leads down to Quasqueton, the first community established in this county in 1847. Follow the highway through town and, immediately after you pass over the Wapsipinicon River (called the "Wapsi" by many in eastern Iowa), hang a right into the city park. If you meander along the riverbank below the dam and pick through the rocks you'll quickly start finding fossils of creatures that lived here millions of years ago when this was a seashore. If you don't find any, you aren't looking closely enough.

Once you finish your visit below the dam, go back up the highway and on the north edge of town you'll see a sign pointing the way to **Cedar Rock State Park**, 2611 Quasqueton Diagonal Boulevard, (319) 934-3572; free. Follow County Highway W35 for a few miles, which will bring you to a house that architect Frank Lloyd Wright considered to be among his best designs. Built for Lowell and Agnes Walter as a summer residence in 1950, the house has a specially fired tile bearing Wright's initials, something he did for only 19 of his designs across the world and the only one in Iowa.

Now a historic site, Cedar Rock is one of Wright's most complete creations. He not only designed the house but its furniture, drapery, upholstery, carpet, china, silver, crystal, glass knickknacks, and more. He even altered the baby grand piano. Outside, he designed the grounds, a barbecue pit, path lights, and the two-story boathouse/guesthouse.

*A*rea Canoeing

The **Turkey River** is a favorite of canoeists and you might consider putting in at Big Springs Trout Hatchery and getting out at the Motor Mill southeast of Elkader, although longer stretches above and below this section are also navigable, including portions of the Little Turkey River north of Eldorado.

The **Volga River** is another that some like to canoe, starting at the Volga River Recreation Area and going to the Garber Bridge. Along the way, canoeists can visit the Osborne Conservation and Nature Center and the site of an old sawmill in Mederville. At Elkport, the Volga joins the Turkey River.

Next, the **Wapsipinicon River**, which runs through the area you're visiting in this chapter, can be nice to canoe when its waters are high. Above Independence, one can explore its backwaters, while below that city, canoeists pass through heavily timbered areas. Along the way, it passes Cedar Rock and then the dam at Quasqueton. Canoeists can continue as far downstream as Anamosa, more than 37 miles away.

Finally, there's the **Maquoketa River**. If you've been in Backbone State Park, you know there's no canoeing there except in Backbone Lake, a dammed portion of the river. The real canoeing starts below the park's dam and many like to paddle the stretch from there to Manchester, 13 miles away. You could, however, continue all the way to the Mississippi, 106 miles downstream.

One of the many bends in the twisting Maquoketa River

The best information about canoeing in Iowa can be found in the free guidebooks about each river. They can be obtained from the Iowa Department of Natural Resources, 900 E. Grand Avenue, Des Moines, IA 50319-0034. You can call (515) 281-9361, wait for the state phone mail operator, press 4-5421 and the # sign and, after listening to the taped message, leave your name, address, and which river guidebooks you would like sent to you.

LODGING

Elkader

Elkader Inn, 24886 Highway 13 N, (563) 245-2020. Motel with separate cottage among the trees. Near hiking and cross-country ski trails. $

Independence

Rush Park Motel, 1810 1st Street W, (319) 334-2577; (800) 429-2577. On west edge of town. Continental breakfast. $-$$

Super 8 Motel, 2000 1st Street W, (319) 334-7041; (800) 800-8000. On west edge of town. Continental breakfast. $-$$$

Strawberry Point

Franklin Hotel, 102 Elkader Street, (563) 933-4788. Historic inn in downtown area. Restaurant. $

BED AND BREAKFASTS

Elkader

Goshawk Farm B&B, 27596 Iron Wood Road, (319) 964-9321; (319) 964-9321. A 19th-century farm among the timber and fields. Three rooms. $-$$

Little House in the Woods, 16153 Big Spring Road, (319) 783-7774. An 1891 farmhouse in the country that sleeps seven. Children welcome. Two rooms. $$$$

Independence

The Purdy House B&B, 215 3rd Avenue SW, (319) 334-7336. A Victorian home on a quarter-block lot a few blocks from main highway. About 20 flower gardens. Freestanding 22-foot-tall staircase with a mural painted on it. Gift shop. Breakfast on weekends only. Two rooms. $$

Riverside B&B, 506 2nd Avenue SW, (319) 334-4100. A 1915 home in the downtown area near historic mill and shops. Children welcome. Two rooms. $

Strawberry Point

Ivy Rose Inn, 624 Commercial, (563) 933-4485. Close to Wilder Museum and Backbone State Park. Four rooms. $$

CABINS

Backbone State Park, (563) 933-4225. Eight two-bedroom, year-round cabins, $$$-$$$$. Eight one-bedroom summer cabins, $. The concessionaire has firewood. The park prefers to rent cabins by the week from Memorial Day to Labor Day; two-night minimum otherwise.

DINING

Elkader

Al's Steak & Stein, 104 W. Bridge Street, (563) 245-2541. Tavern atmosphere and food. Lunch specials. Carryout available.

Johnson's Supper Club & Reception Hall, 916 High Street, (563) 245-2371. Family atmosphere. Breakfast, lunch, supper. Buffet on Friday and Sunday noon.

Julie's Deli, 105 N. Main, (563) 245-3313. Sandwich shop with homemade soups and sandwiches.

Keystone Restaurant, Saloon, & Patio, 107 S. Main, (563) 245-1992. Patio seating overlooking the Turkey River and Keystone Bridge.

Marcia's Sweet Shop, 133 S. Main, (563) 245-2886. Coffee, homemade chocolates, pastries, ice cream, and ice cream treats.

Pedretti's Bakery, 101 N. Main, (563) 245-1280. Bagels, muffins, croissants, breads, rolls, cookies, pastries, and doughnuts.

The Pizza Well, 127 N. Main, (563) 245-2414. Sandwich bar with soup, salad, pizza, and ice cream.

Two-Mit Burgers, at the junction of Highways 13 and 56. This is a small business in a trailer but the lines can cause you to wait several minutes to place an order for old-time steamed hamburgers "mit" or "mit out" (German for "with" or "without") grilled onions, quarter-pound hot dogs, and bratwurst with kraut. Open mid-April to mid-October.

Independence

Bill's Pizza & Smokehouse, 201 1st Street W, (319) 334-2455. In downtown area.

Old Mill Pizza Company, 416 1st Street W, (319) 334-3385. Pizza in the downtown area.

Paradise Donut & Fountain Shop, 1826 1st Street W, (319) 334-4225. Donuts and soda fountain on west edge of town.

Two Brothers Restaurant, 220 1st Street E, (319) 334-3312. In downtown area.

INFORMATION

Buchanan County Tourism Bureau, 115 1st Street E, Independence, IA 50644, (319) 334-3439.

Eastern Iowa Tourism Region, PO Box 189, Dyersville, IA 52040, (563) 875-7269; (800) 891-3482; www.easterniowatourism.org

Elkader Area Chamber of Commerce, PO Box 559, Elkader, IA 52043, (563) 245-2857; www.elkader-iowa.com

Osborne Conservation and Nature Center, Highway 13, 29862 Osborne Road, Elkader, IA 52043, (563) 245-1516.

Strawberry Point Economic Development and Information Center, 104 Commercial, Strawberry Point, IA 52076, (563) 933-4417.

Chapter 19

Dubuque: Jewel on the Mississippi

Dubuque is like a diamond on the Mississippi. Even though it's old—the oldest city in the state—it continues to sparkle so brightly that it never ceases to attract visitors who are not only charmed by the city's rich history but also pleasantly surprised by its revitalized riverfront.

To begin your trip to Dubuque, start where its earliest white residents began, at the **Mines of Spain Recreation Area**, 8899 Bellevue Heights, (563) 556-0620; free. The best way to go there is to head east on Highway 52 from the intersection of 52 and Highway 151/61. In a moment you'll be at the **E.B. Lyons Nature Center**, which provides a good overview of the mines' early years as well as the natural history of the region. Outside the center are an old lead mine, a farm site, and bird and butterfly gardens.

The Mines of Spain, despite their rich-sounding name, are indeed lead mines. But the stuff was important enough to attract the interest of Julien Dubuque, a French-Canadian fur trader who settled here in the 1780s when the Spanish controlled the territory. Learning of the lead's presence from his Meskwakie friends, Dubuque applied to the Spanish governor in New Orleans for permission to dig, and soon the mines were operating. By 1829, more than 4,000 miners held permits to dig here, creating one of the nation's first mineral rushes.

Originally part of a 189-square-mile tract awarded to Julien Dubuque, the Mines of Spain are now a state-owned 1,380-acre preserve encompassing riverside bluffs, prairie, forest, streams, and a host of resident animals including bobcat, flying squirrel, bald eagle, white-tailed deer, and various songbirds.

From the nature center, go east on Highway 52 again until, less than a mile away, you see Old Massey Road on the left (east). Take that until you see the next left and turn there. You're in the heart of the preserve now as you wind your way through prairie areas. Small parking lots serve as starting points for 14 miles of trails if you want to venture around on foot. When you decide to

The Julien Dubuque Monument overlooking the Mississippi River

continue driving, keep going in the same direction and in less than two miles from where you left Old Massey Road you'll see Monument Road on the right. By going up that road, you'll end up at a parking area atop a bluff with a pretty view of the Mississippi River and Dubuque to the north.

Down a path from the parking lot is the **Julien Dubuque Monument**, a stone tower marking where he was buried in 1810 by his relatives and Indian friends. The area around the tower is another good observation point, this time with a southern view of a portion of the Mississippi River valley that's relatively untouched by humans.

Return to the main road through the preserve and continue in the same direction as before. The road will lead across some railroad tracks and to a T intersection with Julien Dubuque Drive, where you take a left. That leads you up a hill to an intersection with Grandview Drive. Turn to the left for about a car length and then to the right to go down an entrance ramp to Highway 52/151/61, a four-lane road that leads into Dubuque.

Downtown

Follow the signs directing you to the **Ice Harbor/Casino/Museums**—they're all at the same place. As you drive toward the Ice Harbor, you will see ahead of you what looks like a chimney that's standing all alone. That's the **Shot Tower**, one of the oldest structures in Dubuque. Built in 1856 to produce ammunition, it may be getting a facelift soon, so keep your eyes on it in the years to come—it could be a worthwhile visit.

When you arrive at the Ice Harbor, you should enter the Mississippi River Museum's large main building. In there you'll find the **National Rivers Hall of Fame** (tickets purchased there are good for admission to the Woodward River-boat Museum, which is in another building a short walk away). The hall's popular film, *River of Dreams*, gives you a good start to visit the rest of the facility, which honors people whose names are forever tied to the Mississippi and other U.S. rivers, such as Black Hawk, Mark Twain, John J. Audubon, Robert Fulton, Louis Joliet, and Jacques Marquette

The building is also the place to catch a ride on the **Trolleys of Dubuque**, (563) 552-2896; (800) 408-0077; fare. Leaving most days at 12:30 p.m., the trolleys take you on a one-hour narrated tour of Dubuque's historic downtown areas.

Among the other businesses in the building is the ticket office for the *Spirit of Dubuque*, (563) 583-8093; (800) 747-8093; fare. This is the state's only paddle-powered boat, which offers narrated cruises on the river as well as luncheon and dinner cruises with live entertainment.

Similarly, **Celebration River Cruises**, (309) 764-1952; (800) 297-0034; fare, operates its *Celebration Belle*, a four-deck boat, out of the Ice Harbor each Tuesday for a 100-mile cruise to the Quad Cities (see chapter 21). Passengers return to the Ice Harbor by bus the same day.

Dubuque's revitalized riverfront, with the *William M. Black* in the foreground

Another boat in the Ice Harbor is the *Diamond Jo Casino*, (563) 583-7005; (800) LUCKY-JO, which has video and slot machines and gaming tables. The boat cruises the Mississippi each morning, Monday–Friday, from May through mid-October. A portside facility provides dining and live entertainment.

Down the way from those boats alongside the Ice Harbor is the **Woodward Riverboat Museum**, (563) 557-9545; (800) 226-3369; admission. Quite hard to miss because a huge paddle wheel stands outside its entrance, the museum is a great family place. You can walk through an exhibit of what life is like under the surface of the Mississippi, visit an old lead mine, and examine artifacts from the Indians and fur traders who lived here.

In a smaller, nearby building, you can watch small wooden boats being made. Close to that is a boat shed that looks like the fishermen just stepped away for a few moments. And at this end of the Ice Harbor is still another large boat, the *William M. Black.* Built in 1934 to dredge the navigation channel on the Missouri River (yes, the *Missouri* River), the steam-powered *Black* is open for visitors to walk through the pilot house, crew quarters, dining room, and more, giving an intimate look at what life was like for those who kept the river open for commercial traffic.

Upon leaving the Ice Harbor, proceed west on 3rd Street; at its intersection with Main Street is the new **Iowa Welcome Center**, (563) 556-4372; (800) 798-8844. Parking is available on the street and in a nearby ramp. With lots of printed information, displays, and excellent guides, the center is a good place to acquaint yourself with almost anything in the area you'd want to know about. Once you're finished, take 3rd to the next intersection, which is Locust, a one-way street going north. There you'll turn right and immediately shift to the left lane so you can turn left at the very next intersection, which is 4th Street.

As you can see, 4th Street dead-ends in two blocks at a small white building that sits at the bottom of what looks like a small railroad track misplaced on a very steep hill. That's the **Fenelon Place Elevator**, 4th and Bluff Streets, (563) 582-6496; fare, which was built in 1882 by a banker who wanted a shortcut home and is billed as the world's shortest and steepest scenic railway. A round trip to the top of the 189-foot bluff in one of the little green and white cars is one of the area's better bargains, only $1.50. For that you get unlimited time at the building atop the tramway, which provides a magnificent view across Dubuque and neighboring Wisconsin and Illinois.

Because the elevator is such a draw for visitors, it's only natural that a cluster of shops occupies the older buildings near the elevator's lower station on 4th Street. You're also a few blocks away from the **Dubuque Museum of Art**, 701 Locust Street, (563) 557-1851; donation appreciated.

For more works of art, head up Locust again to 12th Street, turn left one block to Main, and you'll find **St. Luke's United Methodist Church**, the corner of 12th and Main, (563) 582-4543; free but a fee for guided tours. After checking in at the church office on the second floor, you'll find yourself amid one of the largest and best collections of stained-glass windows made by Louis B. Tiffany. Most of the windows in the church were made by Tiffany and the most colorful are the six large ones in the sanctuary.

On the North Side

From St. Luke's, go east on 12th Street as far as you can go; here 12th turns into Kerper Boulevard, which goes north. Take that to 16th Street, go right and, on the other side of a small channel of the Mississippi River, you turn left onto Greyhound Park Drive. That leads you to the **Dubuque Greyhound Park and Casino**, 1855 Greyhound Park Drive, (563) 582-3647; (800) 373-3647, which has slots and features live and simulcast greyhound races.

Farther north are more sights. Back on the mainland, turn right (north) onto Kerper again, proceed to Fengler Street where you turn left to drive a few blocks to Rhomberg Avenue, where you turn right. Ten blocks later, turn left on Shiras Avenue and in two blocks you'll see the **Mathias Ham House Museum Historic Site**, 2241 Lincoln Avenue, (563) 557-9545; admission. Not only do you get to experience the high life of the 19th century by touring the 23-room limestone Victorian mansion but also you'll get a taste of the rugged life, depicted in the 1833 log cabin on the grounds.

Dubuque Arboretum and Botanical Gardens

From the mansion, continue up Shiras Avenue to reach **Eagle Point Park**, (563) 589-4263, in a few moments. Besides the usual items one might expect in a park—picnic facilities, playground equipment, a wading pool, and a band shell—trails lead to overlooks of the Mississippi River valley and Lock and Dam No. 11 far below.

Your last stop in Dubuque takes a bit of doing to get to but it's worth visiting. Go back on Rhomberg and continue retracing the route you came but continue about a mile past Fengler until you reach White (Highway 52), where you'll turn right on this one-way, north-bound street. After 11 blocks, turn left onto 32nd Street, which winds around a bit. After about two-and-a-half miles you'll reach the **Dubuque Arboretum and Botanical Gardens**, 3800 Arboretum, (563) 556-2100; donations appreciated. This is the home of the nation's largest planting of hostas: more than 13,000 of them, representing 700 varieties. On its 52 acres, the arboretum also has rose, herb, and Japanese gardens plus a beautiful memorial to military veterans made of stainless steel arches.

To return downtown, take 32nd Street a bit farther to the west, where at the intersection with John F. Kennedy Road, it will turn into the Northwest Arterial, which will lead you back to Highway 20 on Dubuque's west side. Turning left (east) there takes you back to the downtown.

SIDE TRIPS

To the North

This side trip takes you into the country but a word of caution is needed. The route twists and turns so much that passengers, at least those with strong stomachs, will enjoy this ride far more than the driver who must keep eyes glued to the curves. And, although you will be rolling through some of the prettiest parts of Iowa, there are few places to pull over to enjoy the scenery while parked.

This trip begins by going north on Highway 52. As a side note, off to the left about three miles out of the city is the Dubuque trailhead of the **Heritage Bike Trail**, (563) 556-6745; fee, a hike-bike trail that leads to Dyersville 26 miles to the east.

A short distance beyond the trailhead is County Highway C9Y, heading off to the right. Sometimes it's called Sherrill Road, but more often it's known as the Balltown Road. Whatever its name, the road leads you up, down, and around the hills while, off to the side, farm fields roll on forever, crops twist and turn with the terrain, and dark trees crown distant hills. Because the road hugs the hillsides, is full of curves and narrow, paying attention to driving is a must. You can find yourself sharing the road with tractors, pickup trucks towing farm wagons, combines, and other slow-moving vehicles at times (possibly including other tourists checking out the scenery). In short, enjoy this drive but be careful and don't go too fast.

About seven miles from where you left Highway 52, you'll enter the south side of the very small community of **Balltown** (population 74), where a large number of vehicles may be parked near a rather large and somewhat rambling building that houses **Breitbach's Country Dining**, (563) 552-2220. Operated by the same family for more than a century, Breitbach's has such fine meals that countless people have driven the Balltown Road just to reach this establishment, which serves three meals a day.

At the north end of town, a short walk from Breitbach's, is one of the few wide spots in the road which gives one of the broadest panoramas of the hills of northeast Iowa.

Here, you have at least four choices of what to do:

1. Return to Dubuque by the way you came.
2. Make a loop by continuing up County Highway C9Y past another small community, North Buena Vista, to where you'll see a sign on the right pointing toward the **Mississippi River Car Ferry**, (608) 725-5180; fare. By going out that road, you'll come to the landing of the only ferry that touches Iowa soil, crossing the Mississippi to Cassville, Wisconsin. Carrying everything from walk-on passengers to semi-truck trailers, the ferry operates from 9 a.m.-9 p.m. daily, with the last run at 8:20 p.m. in the summer months.

If you do go to Cassville, there are two nice places to visit. One is **Nelson Dewey State Park**, (608) 725-5374; admission, most of which is set atop wooded bluffs overlooking the Mississippi valley. The other is **Stonefield**, (608) 725-5210; admission, a state historic site that consists of buildings gathered to form a living history exhibit resembling a 1900-era village.

From Cassville, take Highway 133 to Potosi, where you can take Highway 61 south directly to Dubuque.

3. Make another loop by continuing to go up County Highway C9Y to just west of Balltown, where County Highway C63 leads off to the southwest. In another few minutes that road meets County Highway Y13, which you then take south to Highway 52. Take that to Dubuque, about 20 miles to the southeast.
4. Make the loop described above, except that at Highway 52, turn west to Luxemburg, four miles away. There, you turn left (south) onto Highway 136, which leads to Dyersville (see the next side trip), and from there loop back to Dubuque on Highway 20.

To the West

This is a tour for those with eclectic tastes because it covers baseball, religion, toys, and wood carving. Leave Dubuque on Highway 20 going west until you reach the Dyersville exit in about 25 miles. Go north on Highway 136 to the first stoplight and turn right there to go to the **National Farm Toy Museum**, 1110 16th Avenue Court SE, (563) 875-2727; admission. If there's been a farm toy made somewhere in the world at one time or another, chances are pretty good that a copy of it is among the 30,000 toy tractors, farm implements, trucks, and pedal tractors here. The museum also has miniature farm scenes of different eras, a small theater featuring a movie on how toys become collectibles, and an exhibit on how real farming practices have changed over the years. Besides farm toys, the museum also has toy banks, fire engines, construction equipment and more, all of which can make grown men cry when they realize the value of the toys they gave up long ago.

If you want to see still more farm toys, in the immediate area is the **Toy Farmer Country Store**, 1161 16th Avenue Court SE, (563) 875-8850, and the **Toy Collector Club of America**, 1235 16th Avenue Court SE, (563) 875-9263, which is basically an outlet store for SpecCast, a Dyersville toy manufacturer.

Back on Highway 136, you'll see the outlet store for **Racing Champions ERTL**, (563) 875-5613, where you can pick up items made by that company, whose main factory is nearby. A short distance up the highway is **H&W Motorsports**, 1314 9th Street SE, (563) 875-7656, another toy store specializing in cast metal items.

If you haven't had your fill of toys, follow the highway signs to the business district, where you'll find **Evers Toy Store**, 204 1st Avenue E, (563) 875-2438. It carries a range of toys from different manufacturers and also does a mail-order business. The final toy stop is at **Scale Models**, 502 5th Street NW, (563) 875-2436. This outlet shop also offers free 30-minute tours of the adjacent factory every half-hour from 9 a.m.-2 p.m. Small wonder that Dyersville bills itself as the Toy Capital of the World. But now it's time for some things completely different.

Even when you were a few miles outside of town, you couldn't miss the big church with twin black-capped spires, the **Basilica of St. Francis Xavier**, (563) 875-7325. Since you're now in downtown Dyersville, you should stop in. One of 37 minor basilicas in the U.S., this is the only one set on what was prairie when it was dedicated in 1889. Guided tours can be arranged on weekdays by calling the church office.

Now, grab your bat, ball, and glove 'cause it's baseball time. Head out of downtown to Highway 136 again and take a left (north). Just across the railroad tracks you'll see the west end of the **Heritage Bike Trail**, (563) 556-6745, which leads back to Dubuque. Just beyond that are signs directing you to the **Field of Dreams Movie Site**, 28963 Lansing Road, (563) 875-8404; (888) 875-8404; free.

When the producers of the 1989 movie *Field of Dreams* were searching for a cornfield to turn into a baseball diamond, this is the place they picked. After the filming was over, Don Lansing, who owns most of the site, decided to leave his portion of the ballfield as the film crew had left it and people started to visit, playing pickup games of baseball and lending credence to the phrase used in the movie: "If you build it, they will come." And come they have ever since.

The ball field straddles a property line and the other portion is owned by **Left and Center Field of Dreams**, 29001 Lansing Road, (563) 875-7985; (800) 443-8981; free. The facility occasionally hosts performances by the Ghost Players—baseball enthusiasts who dress in old-style baseball uniforms.

The picture-postcard village of St. Donatus, southeast of Dubuque

If nothing formal is happening, you're certainly welcome to take to the field to shag flies, pitch, bat, and walk through the corn. Who knows who you might end up playing with?

While you're out this way, you should visit the **Becker Woodcarving Museum**, 15426 Becker Lane, (563) 875-2087, admission; reservations required, to view figures, clocks, decoys, and more, including Iowa's largest clock, all made from local woods by artist-in-residence Jack Becker who, at times, works while you visit with him.

To get back to Dubuque, just return to Highway 20 through Dyersville and head east.

To the Southeast

About five miles southeast of Dubuque on Highway 52 is the entrance to **Crystal Lake Cave**, (563) 556-6451, the largest show cave in Iowa. Discovered in 1868 by miners drilling for lead, this natural cave has a variety of formations including one that's found at only one other cave in the U.S. Called anthodites, or cave flowers, this formation was formed when the cave was filled with water years ago; today a small lake still exists. A light sweater or coat is advisable even during the summer as the cave's interior always stays at about 50 degrees.

Six miles beyond the cave on Highway 52 is the village of **Saint Donatus**. If the place looks familiar, you may not be imagining things—these pastoral scenes, particularly of Saint Donatus Catholic Church, which was dedicated in 1860, have appeared frequently in print and television ads. This whole area is a favorite for many photographers. Besides the church, two other historic structures, the **Way of the Cross**, (563) 773-2480; (800) 342-1837, with 14 brick alcoves, and a chapel, make this a very picturesque setting.

LODGING

Dubuque

Best Western Dubuque Inn, 3434 Dodge Street, (563) 556-7760; (800) 747-7760. West edge of town near malls on Highway 20. Indoor pool, restaurant, continental breakfast. $$-$$$

Heartland Inn-South, 2090 S. Park Court, (563) 556-6555; (800) 334-3277, ext. 13. South of downtown near junction of Highways 52 and 61/151. Continental breakfast. $$-$$$$.

Holiday Inn Dubuque Five Flags, 450 Main Street, (563) 556-2000; (800) HOLIDAY. Downtown near Ice Harbor, Fenelon Place Elevator, and next to Five Flags Theater for the performing arts. Restaurant, indoor pool. $$-$$$

Julien Inn, 200 Main Street, (563) 556-4200; (800) 798-7098. Downtown near Ice Harbor and Fenelon Place Elevator. Two blocks from Five Flags Theater for the performing arts. Restaurant. $-$$$$

Dyersville

Colonial Inn, 1110 9th Street SE, (563) 875-7194. On Highway 136. Near downtown and Family Aquatic Center. $-$$

Comfort Inn, 527 16th Avenue SE, (563) 875-7700; (800) 228-5150. South edge of town near Highway 20. Restaurant nearby. Indoor pool, continental breakfast. $-$$$

BED AND BREAKFASTS

Balltown

Hvnlee Bed & Breakfast, 478 Balltown Road, (563) 552-1433. A former rectory on C9Y in Balltown. Walking distance to Breitbach's restaurant. Four rooms. $-$$$

Dubuque

Another World–Paradise Valley Inn, (563) 552-1034; (800) 388-0942. Log inn secluded in the country, about eight miles west of Dubuque. Near bike trail, downhill skiing. Five rooms. $$$-$$$$

Four Mounds Inn B&B, 4900 Peru Road, (563) 556-1908. A 1908 Mission-style mansion in the countryside overlooking the Mississippi. Hiking trails. Five rooms. $$-$$$

The Hancock House B&B, 1105 Grove Terrace, (563) 557-8989. In a historic district on a bluff overlooking downtown. Nine rooms. $$$-$$$$

Lighthouse Valleyview B&B, 15937 Lore Mound Road, (563) 583-7327; (800) 407-7023. Dubuque's only lighthouse. Near trails, downhill skiing, and golf. Four rooms. $$-$$$$

The Mandolin Inn, 199 Loras Boulevard, (391) 556-0069; (800) 524-7996. A 1908 Edwardian mansion near downtown. Seven rooms. $$-$$$$

The Redstone Inn, 504 Bluff Street, (563) 582-1894. Brick Victorian mansion downtown near Five Flags Theater and Fenelon Place Elevator. Fifteen rooms. $$-S$$$

Saint Donatus
Gehlen House Inn, 101 N. Main Street, (391) 773-8200; (800) 280-1177. An 1848 inn in a historic village southeast of Dubuque. Seven rooms. $$-$$$

DINING

Balltown
Breitbach's Country Dining, 563 Balltown Road, (563) 552-2220. Home-style cooking in 100-year-old location.

Dubuque
Athenian Grill, 1091 University Avenue, (563) 556-9046. Greek cuisine.

Choo Choo Charlie's Pizza and Ice Cream, 1895 John F. Kennedy Road, (563) 557-2466. West edge of city. The name says it all.

Dubuque Mining Company, 555 John F. Kennedy Road, (563) 557-1729. West edge of city. A wide range of dishes, featuring hamburgers.

Elizabeth's Tollbridge, 2800 Rhomberg Avenue, (563) 556-5566. Good food and best view of the Mississippi River valley; overlooks Lock and Dam No. 11.

Great Dragon, 3500 Dodge Street, Warren Plaza, (563) 583-8860. West end of city. Mandarin.

Mario's Italian Restaurant & Lounge, 1298 Main Street, (563) 582-0904. Near downtown.

Yen Ching Restaurant, 926 Main Street, (563) 556-2574. Downtown. Chinese.

Dyersville
Country Junction, junction of Highways 20 and 136, (563) 875-7055. Home-style cooking.

The Dyersville Family Restaurant, 226 1st Avenue SE, (563) 875-2181. Downtown.

The Palace, 149 1st Avenue E, (563) 875-2284. Downtown. Home-style cooking.

Ritz Restaurant, 232 1st Ave E, (563) 875-2268. Downtown. Home-style dining, pizza.

St. Donatus

Kalmes Restaurant, 100 N. Main Street, (563) 872-3378.

INFORMATION

Dubuque Convention and Tourism Bureau, 300 Main Street, Dubuque, IA 52001, (563) 557-9200; (800) 798-4748; www.traveldubuque.com

Dyersville Chamber of Commerce, 1100 16th Avenue Court SE, Dyersville, IA 52040, (563) 875-2311; www.dyersville.org

Eastern Iowa Tourism Region, PO Box 189, Dyersville, IA 52040, (563) 875-7269; (800) 891-3482; www.easterniowatourism.org

Chapter 20

Clinton:
Town on the Big River

If things had gone differently in the middle of the 19th century, this tour would be about New York, the name Clinton was given originally. Then it was renamed for DeWitt Clinton, a governor of New York. An old river town on the Mississippi, Clinton is a fine place to visit.

To tour Clinton, approach it from the west on Highway 30. Just as the highway rounds to the north to enter the downtown area, take 8th Avenue S to the left, go one block and turn left again onto S. 4th Street, a one-way thoroughfare. Near the end of the block on the right (west) is **Smith Brothers Hardware Store**, 1016 S. 4th Street, (563) 242-0327. Truthfully, this is not a listed tourist attraction, but because the building dates to 1874 and the business started in 1933, it is more authentic than a re-created store in a historical village. It's a treat to visit.

To get to your next stop, get on Highway 30 again, this time going west but for just one block to S. 5th Street and go north to 5th Avenue S. where you'll take a right to find the **Curtis Mansion**, 420 5th Avenue S., (563) 242-8556; admission. The Victorian home of a lumber baron who spared little expense in decorating it, the mansion now houses Clinton's Women's Club, which offers tours on Wednesday afternoons and by appointment.

Head east on 5th Avenue S. into the downtown business district with its plethora of historic structures. Preeminent among the buildings is the **Van Allen Department Store**, 200 5th Avenue S., which was designed by famed architect Louis Sullivan. Currently empty but possibly being utilized again soon, the store is nevertheless a delight to the eye, especially its ornate detail work.

Across the street is the **River Arts Center**, 229 5th Avenue S, (563) 243-3300, located in a renovated building and featuring the works of regional and local artists. Visitors also will find homemade candy for sale in the gift shop along with pieces of art.

From the arts center, go east and turn south onto S. 1st Street where, in less than a block, you'll see the **Clinton County Historical Society Museum**, 601 S. 1st Street, (563) 242-1201; donations appreciated. Built in 1858, this structure served as a commission house that outfitted riverboats with supplies. Now, visitors walk its original wood floors as they look at displays related to the history of the region. A rare, human-powered fire engine is among the historical items.

Along the Mississippi

After visiting the museum, turn left (east) onto 6th Avenue S. At the top of the hill ahead of you the road veers left suddenly onto a levee, with the Mississippi River just beyond. You might want to park alongside the road on top of the levee for a stroll. The three lighthouses along the levee were built in the 1930s more for aesthetics than function. As you stroll, you'll see a small park on the left where children can play and down the levee is a pair of paddle wheelers, one actually atop the levee. No, it wasn't left there high and dry by a flood but placed there on purpose to serve as the **Clinton Area Showboat Theater**, Showboat Landing, (563) 242-6760. Originally called the *Oscar*, it was a coal-fired towboat that worked the Ohio River but now sports a 250-seat theater offering summer stock productions.

Along the Mississippi at Clinton

215

The other boat is the *Mississippi Belle II*, Showboat Landing, (563) 243-9000; (800) 457-9975. It's a riverboat casino with slots and gaming tables. Public cruises are offered from 1-3 p.m. Monday-Friday, mid-May to mid-October.

Further up the levee is **Riverview Stadium**, a 1930s-era baseball stadium of art deco design that is the home of the Clinton Lumberkings, (563) 242-0727, a farm team of the Montreal Expos.

At this point, hop back in your car to drive around the river side of Riverview Park, where the roadway becomes 6th Avenue N. This takes you to N. 2nd Street (also Highway 67), where you'll turn right (north). About two miles from that intersection, you'll arrive at the turnoff to **Eagle Point Park**, N. 3rd Street at Stockwell Lane. Like several other high overlooks along the Mississippi, this park has a beautiful view across the wide valley and an excellent perch from which to watch boats go through Lock and Dam No. 13 far below. The park has places to picnic and trails to hike along the top of the bluff. The park serves as the northern trailhead of the 3.8-mile **Riverview Park Recreational Trail** for walkers, joggers, in-line skaters, and bicyclists to use between Eagle Point and Riverview Parks.

Return to Clinton on Highway 67 until you reach 2nd Avenue S, where you turn right (west) and proceed to 14th Street, where you turn left (south). Immediately you'll come to **Bickelhaupt Arboretum**, 340 S. 14th Street, (563) 242-4771; free. Located on the grounds are displays of medicinal plants, a rose garden, perennial beds, herb gardens, wildflower gardens, and rare conifers—just part of the more than 1,500 trees, shrubs, and flowers that provide beauty year-round. An education center is near Rock Creek, which flows through the property.

Now it's time to visit Clinton's sister city so return to 2nd Avenue S and go east until you reach Highway 67. Then it's north to 19th Avenue N, where you turn right (east) to cross the Mississippi River on Highway 136.

*F*ulton, Illinois

One of the first things you see as you enter Fulton from Clinton is the 90-foot-tall, red **Dutch Windmill**, 10th Avenue and 1st Street, (815) 589-3371; donations appreciated. It's located just north of the bridge. Manufactured in Holland especially for Fulton, the windmill has a welcome center and gift shops at its base. Efforts are under way to raise money to buy grindstones to make the mill fully functional for visitors.

From the windmill, it's a simple trip up 4th Street to **Heritage Canyon**, 515 N. 4th Street, (815) 589-2838; donations appreciated. Built where a limestone quarry operated near the Mississippi River, this site has more than 20 restorations and reproductions of 19th-century businesses, homes, and other buildings. Tours are self-guided.

Then it's up 4th Street once more to Highway 84, where you take a left (north). Turn left again at Lock Road in about half a mile and go to the end to

Lock and Dam No. 13, 4999 Lock Road, (815) 589-3313; free. Sidewalks along-side the lock and an observation platform give visitors good views of the mechanism by which boats pass through the locks, which relies only on gravity to raise and lower the water. Tours can be arranged by calling ahead.

SIDE TRIPS

To the South

Going south of Clinton on Highway 67 leads you through miles and miles of farm fields but about 12 miles south of town you'll notice that a particular cornfield looks a bit strange, as though someone has run amok with some farm machinery. Well, someone has—and with a purpose. If you were flying over-head, you would see that the 4.3-acre field is mowed in the form of a maze. In fact, it's called the **Amazing Maize Maze,** 28322 Great River Road, Princeton, (563) 289-9999; admission. If you ever wanted to lose yourself, here's where to do it, but should you need help finding your bearings again, a guide who sits atop a 24-foot-high perch is there to offer hints. There also are mini-mazes and a petting farm.

To the West

This tour leads to Maquoketa, with two choices for your travel route from Clinton.

One is by going northwest through the countryside at a leisurely pace on Highway 136, which brings you to Highway 61 just south of **Maquoketa**. The other route is faster, via the four-lane Highway 30 from Clinton, then north on Highway 61.

Either way, from the 136/61 intersection continue on Highway 61 as it slips around Maquoketa's west side. Soon you'll see Highway 428, where you want to turn left (west). About six miles down that road is **Maquoketa Caves State Park**, 10970 98th Street, Maquoketa, (563) 652-5833; free, one of the best places in Iowa to see a variety of caves, most of which are easily visited. The largest, Dancehall Cave, has about 1,100 feet of lighted concrete paths to guide you through it and out into a beautiful rocky valley shaded by tall trees. An-other dozen caves—with names like Hernando's Hideaway, Barbell Cave, and Rainy Day Cave—are nearby, all created by water trickling down through porous limestone over the millennia. Some require you to crawl through nar-row openings that will leave you plenty dirty. Others are glorified recesses in the rocky cliffs. None require special spelunking skills. There also are a 17-ton balanced rock and a large, beautiful, natural stone arch—geologic formations some might not expect to find in Iowa.

When you return to Highway 61, take a left and go up that highway until you reach the small community of **Hurstville** in about a mile. There, you turn right onto Hurstville Road (locals call it Old 61) and in a moment you'll see

A natural stone arch at Maquoketa Caves State Park, west of Maquoketa

several large structures on your left, the remains of the **Hurstville Lime Kilns**, free, which were a major industry of this area at one time. Interpretative signs are at the site.

Continuing down Hurstville Road, you cross the Maquoketa River to enter Maquoketa from the north on what is now N. Main. In a few blocks you'll be in the downtown business district where you'll take a left (east) onto E. Platt Street (also Highway 64). Just one block later take a right (south) onto S. Olive and at the end of that block you'll see the **Old City Hall Gallery**, 121 S. Olive, (563) 652-3405, one of two private art galleries in town that are located in historic structures. This one was built as a fire station in 1901 and later became a police station and city hall before artist Rose Frantzen turned it into her gallery.

The other gallery is just east of town on Highway 64, and that's **Costello's Old Mill Gallery**, 22095 Highway 64, (563) 652-3351; (800) 652-3351. It's a picturesque water mill that ground grain and then housed cattle before artist Patrick Costello made it his residence, studio, and gallery.

From here, you can return to Clinton by continuing east on Highway 64 to Highway 67 near Sabula and then taking that south to Clinton.

To the North

Going north on Highway 67 puts you on the Great River Road, one of two national scenic byways in Iowa. About 16 miles north of Clinton you'll pass

Sabula, Iowa's only island community. The town is the site of the Jackson County Welcome Center, 60488 Highway 64, (800) 342-1837, a replica of a white, one-room schoolhouse that's chock-full of information. Head north from here on what becomes Highway 52.

In 20 miles you'll reach the entrance to **Bellevue State Park,** (563) 872-4019, which has two units. The first one you see has campgrounds; continue two miles north to the other unit's entrance and just inside that you'll find yourself at a fork in the road.

Go to the right and you'll come upon **South Bluff Nature Center** (open Saturday and Sunday afternoons) that houses dioramas describing the natural history of the region. A bit beyond the center is the **Garden Sanctuary for Butterflies**. A garden with about three dozen plants such as wild aster, goldenrod, lambsquarters, and daisy fleabane, the sanctuary attracts about 60 species of butterflies ranging from the American Painted Lady to the Yellowpatch Skipper. In short, if you like butterflies, this is the place for you.

If you take a left at the fork in the road by the entrance, you'll wind up parking at a great overlook that's above the town of Bellevue and the Mississippi River valley. From the parking lot you can take a short trail that runs along the edge of the tree-lined bluff and passes three conical burial mounds that were built 700 to 1,000 years ago.

When leaving the park, go north on Highway 52 again and as you cross Mill Creek into **Bellevue** a moment later, slow down to look left at one of the prettier scenes in Iowa, the red, six-story **Potter's Mill**, 300 Potter's Drive. Built in

Looking down on Bellevue from Bellevue State Park

219

1843 by E.G. Potter, the mill used water power, then steam power, and finally electricity to grind feed for area farmers until 1969. Some businesses have been in there since then but, at the time of this writing, the building is unoccupied, though you can walk around its grounds.

Continuing north on Highway 52, you'll see the **Young Historical Museum**, 406 N. Riverview, (563) 872-5830. Situated in a century-old limestone house, the museum has period furnishings and is known for its collection of Parian ware.

Another unique limestone house in Bellevue is the **Spring Side Inn**, 300 Ensign Road, (563) 872-5452, which was built in 1850 and well known for having hosted Abraham Lincoln. Now a bed and breakfast, this beautiful example of Gothic Revival architecture is open for tours by non-guests, who will also enjoy the magnificent gardens on the grounds. To reach the inn, drive to Bellevue's northern edge and the intersection with Ensign Road; the inn is easily visible on the side of a hill to the west.

At this point, you might consider making this side trip into a loop by going to Maquoketa from here and then back to Clinton. To do this, leave Bellevue on County Highway Z15, which forms the easternmost leg of the **Grant Wood Scenic Byway**, identifiable by its colorful signs. This beautiful byway rolls up and down through the hilly countryside and is quite a joy to take. From the south end of Bellevue, the byway goes to the tiny community of Springbrook (population 165), where it becomes County Highway E17, which meets Highway 62 at Andrew. There you take a left (southwest) and head directly to Maquoketa.

LODGING

Clinton

Best Western Frontier, 2300 Lincolnway, (563) 242-7112; (800) 728-7112. West end of town near intersection of Highways 30 and 67. Indoor pool, restaurant, continental breakfast. $$-$$$

Country Inn and Suites, 2224 Lincolnway, (563) 244-9922; (800) 456-4000. West end of town at the junction of Highways 30 and 67. Indoor pool, continental breakfast. $$-$$$$

Travel Inn, 302 6th Avenue S, (563) 243-4730; (877) 237-5261. Downtown near Riverview Park. $-$$

Maquoketa

Decker Hotel & Restaurant, 128 N. Main, (563) 652-6654. Downtown in historic building. $$-$$$$

Super 8, 1019 W. Platt, (563) 652-6888; (800) 800-8000. West edge of town. Near restaurant. $-$$

Springbrook

Whispering Meadows Resort, 110 E. Main Street, (563) 872-4430; (563) 357-3784. Two cabins in the countryside. $$$$

BED AND BREAKFASTS

Bellevue

The Bellevue House, 500 N. Riverview, (563) 872-4130; (888) 545-5968. Brick Greek Revival home. Six rooms. $$-$$$$

Green Parrot Inn, 111 N. Riverview, (563) 872-4994. Overlooks Lock and Dam No. 12. Three rooms. $$-$$$

Mont Rest, 300 Spring Street, (563) 872-4220; (877) 872-4220. On a bluff overlooking the Mississippi. Eleven rooms. $$$$

Spring Side Inn, 300 Ensign Road, (563) 872-5452. Historic structure overlooking the Mississippi River. $$$$

Maquoketa

Squiers Manor B&B, 418 W. Pleasant, (563) 652-6961; 652-2359. Within walking distance of downtown. Eight rooms. $$$-$$$$

Sabula

Castle B&B, 616 River Street, (563) 687-2714. Alongside the Mississippi River. Bicycles available. Marina nearby. Three rooms. $$-$$$

DINING

Bellevue

2nd Street Station, 116 S. 2nd Street, (563) 872-5410.

Riverview Hotel and Café, 100 S. Riverview, (563) 872-4142.

Spruce Harbor Inn, 30597 400th Avenue, (563) 872-5637.

Clinton

Rastrelli's, 238 Main Avenue, (563) 242-7441. Downtown. American-Italian.

The Unicorn, 1004 N. 2nd Street, (563) 242-7355. North of downtown. American and French cuisine.

Upper Mississippi Brewing Company, 132 6th Avenue S, (563) 241-1275. Downtown brewpub in historic building.

Yen Ching, 1105 N. 2nd Street, (563) 242-6422. Chinese-American.

Fulton
Fulton Family Restaurant, 1318 17th Street, (815) 589-4499. Near intersection of Highways 136 and 84.

Harbor Café and Pizzeria, 1901 4th Street, (815) 589-4747. Near the Mississippi River.

Maquoketa
Bluff Lake Restaurant, 9369 95th Avenue, (563) 652-3272. In the country.

The Cottage, 111 N. Main, (563) 652-0584. Downtown.

Decker Hotel Restaurant, 128 N. Main, (563) 652-6654. In historic hotel.

Flapjack's Family Restaurant, 101 McKinsey Drive, (563) 652-6779. Family-style restaurant near west end of town.

INFORMATION

Bellevue Area Chamber of Commerce, 210 N. Riverview, Bellevue, IA 52031, (563) 872-5830; (800) 653-2211; www.bellevueia.com/index.htm

Clinton Area Convention and Visitors Bureau, 333 4th Avenue S, Clinton, IA 52733-1024, (563) 242-5702; (800) 828-5702); www.clintonia.com

Eastern Iowa Tourism Region, PO Box 189, Dyersville, IA 52040, (563) 875-7269; (800) 891-3482; www.easterniowatourism.org

Fulton Chamber of Commerce, 415 11th Ave., Fulton, IA 61252, (815) 589-4545; www.cityoffulton.net/chamber.html

Jackson County Welcome Center, 60488 Highway 64, Sabula, IA 52070, (800) 342-1837; www.jacksoncountyiowa.com/visitors.htm

Maquoketa Area Chamber of Commerce, 117 S. Main, Maquoketa, IA 52060, (563) 652-4602; (800) 989-4602; http://chamber.maquoketa.net/

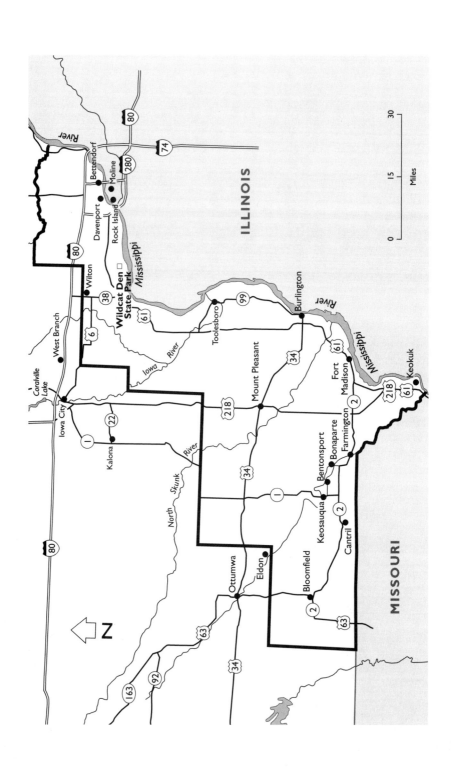

Section V

Southeast Iowa
Clusters of Communities

Chapter 21

The Quad Cities:
Four Times the Fun

When visiting the Quad Cities, you might well assume you'll have four places to visit—Davenport and Bettendorf on the Iowa side of the Mississippi River and Moline and Rock Island over in Illinois. Actually, you have an even bigger selection because a number of other communities are here too, including East Moline, Coal Valley, Milan, Buffalo, Riverdale, and Le Claire. But the region has long been called the Quad Cities, a better alternative than changing the nickname every few years to reflect the number of nearby communities.

Davenport

A good way to enter Davenport, the largest of the Quad Cities, is at Exit 295 on I-80. This brings you to Brady Street where, as you go toward downtown, the southbound lanes you're in shift to the right to become Harrison Street. Along the way you'll see **Vander Veer Botanical Center and Park**, corner of Harrison and W. Central Park Avenue, (563) 326-7818; admission to botanical center; park is free. Just one of many impressive gardens in the cities, Vander Veer has an 1897 glass palm house, a rose garden, shady areas full of hostas, a small lake, and, a favorite of small visitors, a set of three statues of children at play.

From Vander Veer Park, continue south on Harrison and turn right (west) on Locust Street. Go to Division Street and turn left (south) until you reach W. 12th Street, where you'll find three wonderful places starting with the **Putnam Museum of Natural History and Science**, 1717 W. 12th Street, (563) 324-1933; admission. Among the permanent exhibits are those illustrating the ecosystems of the Mississippi River valley and the lives of the early inhabitants of the prairie, displays of animals from near and far, and artifacts from Asia and Africa. A gift shop and new IMAX theater are also part of the complex.

The Centennnial Bridge spanning the Mississippi

Nearby is the **Davenport Museum of Art**, 1737 W. 12th Street, (563) 326-7804; donations appreciated. Its permanent collection contains about 3,500 works of art, including pieces by Alfred Bierstadt, Winslow Homer, and George Eastman. Visiting exhibits enrich the atmosphere throughout the year.

Finally, there's **Fejervery Park**, 1800 W. 12th Street, (563) 326-7812, which has an aquatic center where the entire family can cool off on a warm day. Picnic areas and a small zoo with a Mother Goose theme in one area enhance the park.

From Fejervery, return to Division Street and go south to W. 3rd Street, a one-way going east. Go east to downtown Davenport, where you'll see the **Quad Cities Welcome Center**, 200 W. 3rd Street, (563) 322-3911; (800) 747-7800. One of five welcome centers in the cities, it's a good place for information. From there, head down Harrison Street to the waterfront at **Le Claire Park**, a nicely developed area that brings people right to the magnificent Mississippi, providing a good spot to see the impressive Centennial Bridge connecting Davenport to Rock Island, Illinois.

At the park is the landing of the riverboat of the **Rhythm City Casino**, 212 Brady Street (800) BOAT-711. Offering slots and table games, the boat, the *Treble Clef*, plies the waters of the big river everyday from April through September.

Not far downriver is a sports complex that includes **John O'Donnell Stadium**, 209 S. Gaines, home of the minor league Quad City River Bandits, a farm team of the Minnesota Twins. (For ticket information, call (563) 324-2032.) Close by is the **German American Heritage Center**, 712 W. 2nd Street, (563) 322-8844; admission. In an 1868 hotel that housed German immigrants, the center's artifacts and displays tell how they helped develop this area. A genealogical center is also in the building.

A bit more than a mile downriver on W. River Drive is **Credit Island**, which is linked to the mainland now. A city park with a playground and lots of places to stroll along the river, Credit Island also has a number of sculptures arranged to create a 3-D replica of pointillist Georges Seurat's famous painting, *A Sunday Afternoon on the Island of La Grand Jatte*. Here's a chance to really interact with art.

Going the other way—upriver—from Union Station on River Drive, you'll see the **Village of East Davenport**, Mound Street, and River Drive on the left. Once truly separate from Davenport, this is a quiet area of older buildings housing a variety of shops and eateries. Near the village is **Lindsay Park**, and at the river is a green space sporting a number of geometrical sculptures called **Architectural Park**. There's also a landing for the **Channel Cat Water Taxi**, (309) 788-3360; fare, a summertime boat service that shuttles people across the river with stops near the village and at John Deere Commons, Celebration Landing in Moline, and Bettendorf's Leach Park.

Bettendorf

Getting to Bettendorf is simple on this tour: just keep driving up River Drive from Davenport. Once in town you can pull into **Leach Park**, which is almost under the I-74 bridge, to relax and watch what's happening on the river.

A short distance up the shore is the dock of the *Isle of Capri* **Casino**, 1777 Isle Parkway, (563) 359-7280; (800) 724-5825, another riverboat casino. From here it's a short drive to 18th Street, where you turn left (north) and go less than two miles to the **Family Museum of Arts and Science**, 2900 Learning Campus Drive, (563) 344-4106; admission. In this very hands-on museum, everyone can get a thrill by touching a miniature tornado, creating lightning, "driving" a farm combine, learning what's inside us, operating a camera in a television studio, enjoying a garden made for the under-5 set, and playing outside in Grandpa's Fountain, a waterworks play area.

To continue upriver, and reach the far eastern end of the Quad Cities, you can go various ways but perhaps the simplest thing to do is leave the museum heading south on Spruce Hills Road to Middle Road. Turn (east) and go to Devil's Glen Road, which you will want to take to the right (south) back down to Highway 67. Take a left (east) onto 67, which is also called State Street in this part of the cities.

About a half-mile after you pass under the I-80 bridge on Highway 67, you'll reach Eagle Ridge Road, which leads to the **Mississippi Valley Welcome Center**, 900 Eagle Ridge Road, (563) 289-3009; free, in the small town of Le Claire. Like all welcome centers in Iowa, it has an abundance of travel information, plus this center also houses the **Midcoast Fine Arts Gallery**, featuring works by regional artists.

Back on Highway 67 and a short distance upriver from Eagle Ridge Road is the landing for the *Twilight* (800) 331-1467. A non-gambling, old-fashioned riverboat with a sternwheel, the *Twilight* offers two-day cruises on the Mississippi to Galena, Illinois, from early summer to mid-fall. If cruising isn't to your liking, go further into Le Claire to the **Buffalo Bill Museum**, 200 N. River Drive, (563) 289-5580, where you can walk the decks of the last steam-powered tug on the Mississippi, the *Lone Star*, which is now dry-docked. The museum, as one might guess from its name, also honors one of the town's more famous sons, the legendary William F. "Buffalo Bill" Cody.

When you're finished visiting the museum, get on I-80 heading east and cross the Mississippi to Illinois.

$\mathcal{M}$oline, Illinois

Your journey to Moline begins with a trip through the Illinois countryside on I-80 until you leave the interstate at Exit 9 to take Highway 6 west. After

Deere-Wiman House in Moline

about five or so miles, you'll see the signs to turn to the south to find **Naibi Zoo**, (309) 799-5107; admission, the major zoo of the Quad Cities. Beside lions, tigers, and bears, the zoo has about 100 other species including Kathy Sh-Boom, an elephant that's something of a local celebrity. A scaled-down train drawn by a steam locomotive takes visitors around the grounds, which also have a petting zoo, picnic area, and gift shop.

To enter Moline, return to Highway 6 going west and turn north on I-74 going up to Exit 3. There, you take the frontage road to 12th Avenue, where you turn left (west) to work your way to the first of two gorgeous mansions, the **Butterworth Center**, 1105 8th Street, (309) 765-7970; donations appreciated. Built in 1892, the center, which is actually the 25,000-square-foot home built by Charles Deere for his daughter and son-in-law, is open for guided tours by appointment or on Sunday afternoons in July and August. The grounds are open daily. The same arrangements exist for the **Deere-Wiman House**, 817 11th Avenue, (309) 765-7970; donations appreciated. This is the 15,000-square-foot home of Charles Deere, (the son of John Deere, founder of the farm implement company bearing his name) across the street. Also in the neighborhood is the original home of John Deere, 1217 11th Avenue, which is undergoing restoration.

If you are near the original John Deere home, head north on 12th Street to River Drive (yes, there's a River Drive on this side of the Mississippi too) where you take a right to wind up at **John Deere Commons**. This riverside complex contains a restaurant, travel information center that's also a stop for the MetroLINK Historical Trolley Tours, Channel Cat Water Taxi stop, hotel, and a collection of buildings related to John Deere. Also there is the **Mark**, an impressive arena/exhibit hall/conference center.

Foremost among the buildings related to Deere is the **John Deere Pavilion**, 1400 River Drive, (309) 765-1000; free, a striking, airy, glass and brick version of a long industrial-style building that displays modern and classic John Deere equipment. Right next to that is the **John Deere Store**, (309) 765-1007, a farm toy store for grown-ups. If a toy, print, shirt, cap, or painting has the name John Deere emblazoned anywhere on it, it's more than likely here. In the other direction from the pavilion is the **John Deere Collectors Center**, which opened in 2001. Here, you'll feel like you're entering a 1950s-era Deere dealership but this is no museum. Workers bring in old two-cylinder tractors, disassemble them in front of visitors, and make them look like new again. And if you want to buy one (or parts for the one you want to restore yourself), you can certainly do that. Remember, they come in any color as long as it's green.

Also at the commons is the **Planted Earth Café**, (309) 736-0100, which serves specialty dishes from around the country as a celebration of agriculture. Besides indoor seating, the restaurant has an outdoor patio overlooking the Mississippi.

By the way, grabbing a ride on one of the vintage-looking **MetroLINK Historical Trolley Tours**, 1200 River Drive, (309) 764-4257, ext. 1; fare, is a good way to learn about various sites on the Illinois side of the Quad Cities.

Up River Drive, beyond the I-74 bridge, is the landing for the *Celebration Belle*, 2501 River Drive, (309) 764-1952;(800) 297-0034; fare, a non-gaming riverboat offering local excursions as well as lunch, brunch, supper, and dance cruises. Each Monday, the large riverboat takes passengers on a 100-mile cruise to Dubuque and later that day buses return them to the Quad Cities.

For some military history, turn around at the Celebration Belle's landing and return down River Drive to Rodman Avenue, which lies off to your right, and you're on your way to Rock Island and the arsenal bearing its name.

Rock Island, Illinois

One of the first things you notice on Rock Island are the rows upon rows of white tombstones of the **National Cemetery**, next to a cemetery of Confederate soldiers who died during interment in a prisoner-of-war camp here during the Civil War. A bit farther on is an outdoor display of artillery pieces, tanks, anti-aircraft guns, and more from the U.S. and other nations. There is even equipment captured from Iraqi forces during the Gulf War.

The best look at this island's history is in the **Rock Island Arsenal Museum**, (309) 782-5021; free. It contains an extensive collection of U.S. and foreign weaponry, especially small arms.

Also nearby is the **Colonel Davenport Home**, (309) 786-7336; admission. Built in 1833 by George Davenport, who founded the city bearing his name, the house has been restored to its former glory when it was the place in these parts. By the way, did you notice the huge, light-colored stone mansion with the tall central tower on the way to the Colonel Davenport Home? That's the second-largest single-family dwelling owned by the U.S. government—only the White House is bigger. Unlike the White House, however, this one is not open to the public because it is the official residence of the arsenal's commanding general.

Back on Rodman Avenue, the island's main thoroughfare, you should continue toward the island's far side where you'll see a sign for the **Lock and Dam 15 Visitor Center**, (309) 794-5338; free. Of all the places to see boats pass through the several locks on the Mississippi to skirt around dams, this is the best. On the center's upper level, displays show how the locks work and mention the area's wildlife, including the bald eagles that have been making a comeback. But the real action takes place outside where, on balconies, visitors can watch everything from canoes and pleasure craft to tows and palatial passenger ships pass through the locks. Each time a boat uses the locks, almost seven minutes are needed for nearly one million gallons of water to pour through the locks, raising or lowering the boat 12 feet to the level of the river above or below the adjacent dam. The dam here, by the way, is the world's largest roller dam. It's also neat to watch the nearby combination rail and vehicle bridge pivot to allow the passage of large boats through the locks.

From the locks, continue to the west end of the island where you turn left to enter the city of Rock Island. Once on the mainland, go left (east) on 5th Avenue and note the signs directing you to the impressive **Quad City Botanical Center**, 2525 4th Avenue, (309) 794-0991; admission, a couple of blocks away. Resembling a trio of stackable tables with glass walls and a glass ceiling (literally), the 70-foot-tall center has year-round gardens with plants from throughout the world. The focal point in the center is the tropical Sun Garden, housing a rainforest complete with waterfall. Outside are dwarf conifer and perennial gardens. West of the botanical center is the **Quad Cities Art Cen-**

Quad Cities Trails

In your travels around the Quad Cities, you have obviously noticed a preponderance of bike-hike trails. Well, if you add up all the trails in the cities and parks, they cover about 30 miles. The largest system is part of RiverWay, a 65-mile series of parks, greenbelts, trails, and overlooks along the Mississippi. Rock Island Arsenal also has five miles of trails that are open to the public. Bicyclists must wear helmets on the arsenal's trails.

A unique aspect of biking in the Quad Cities is that the three major transit systems serving the cities have equipped many of their buses with bike racks, as have the Channel Cat Water Taxis, enabling bicyclists to expand their trips.

If you have not brought your own pedal-powered wheels, you can rent some at **Wolfe's Village Bike Shop**, 1018 Mound Street, (563) 326-4686, in the village of East Davenport near Lindsay Park, which is on the trail system.

For more information about bicycling in the Quad Cities, contact **RiverAction, Inc.**, 822 E. River Drive, Davenport, IA 52803, (319) 322-2969.

---

ter, 1715 2nd Avenue, (309) 793-1213; free, the largest center of fine arts in the cities featuring works by local artists. The art center also sits in what's called **"The District,"** an urban neighborhood of nightspots, coffee shops, restaurants, galleries, pubs, and live theaters.

A few blocks from the district at the waterfront is **Jumer's Casino Rock Island,** 18th Street, (309) 793-4200; (800) 477-7747, where visitors can gamble on five floors of the riverside complex.

To wind up your Quad Cities tour, go to its roots by traveling south on 11th Street to Black Hawk Road where you turn left to enter **Black Hawk State Historic Site**, 1510 46th Avenue, (309) 788-0177; free. There, the **John Hauberg Indian Museum**, (309) 788-9536; donations appreciated, describes the early days of this area when the Sauk and Fox Indians once formed North America's largest Indian settlement, called Saukenauk Village. Many artifacts from the family of the great Sauk warrior Black Hawk are here.

SIDE TRIP
To the West

From downtown Davenport, head south on Highway 61 until you're a couple of miles beyond the entrance to Credit Island; where you'll turn left (south) on Highway 22. The highway runs along the river and nine miles later passes through the town of Montpelier. About two miles past, follow the signs leading to **Wildcat Den State Park**, (563) 263-4337; free, a quiet place made even nicer by the presence of a one-room schoolhouse and an 1848 grist mill alongside Pine Creek. Open on summertime Sunday afternoons, the mill is being restored to working condition and may be open longer after that work is done. Camping, trails, and picnic facilities are available at the park. (Although maps show other roads leading to the park from Highway 61, they're not recommended at this time because of their poor condition.)

To continue this side trip, go west out of the park on New Era Road, which winds around a bit in a westerly direction. Ultimately it ends at Highway 61 near Muscatine; when it meets Highway 38, turn to the right (north) to go to Wilton.

At Wilton, turn right (east) on Highway 927 and go slowly through town until you reach Cedar Street where you will turn right (south). Go about a block and a half to the **Wilton Candy Kitchen**, 310 Cedar Street, (563) 732-2278, on the left side of the street. One of the older soda fountains in the nation that's still pumping, the Wilton Candy Kitchen is itself worth a side trip from the Quad Cities. While candy is no longer made there (the sugar shortages in World War II put a stop to that), you can still expect to find homemade ice cream and sauces, and locally picked berries for your cold concoctions.

The restored mill at Wildcat Den State Park, west of Davenport

Well, now that you've had a fun way of gaining some calories that you really didn't need, you need to have a fun way to take them off. So head toward the Quad Cities on I-80 and take Exit 292 on the northwest side of Davenport. Turn left (north) at the bottom of the exit ramp and follow Highway 130 until you just pass under I-80. You'll soon see **Wacky Waters Adventure Park**, 8228 N. Fairmount, (563) 388-9910; admission. The park has a wave pool, water slides, and even a pirate ship and bumper boats. On the dry side, it has go-carts and mini-golf. Granted, it's not quite a place to exercise your muscles but you'll burn some calories having fun here.

LODGING

Bettendorf

The Abbey Hotel, 1401 Central Avenue, (563) 355-0291; (800) 438-7535. Former abbey near downtown. Outdoor pool, continental breakfast. $$-$$$$

Courtyard by Marriott, 895 Golden Valley, (563) 355-3999; (800) 321-2211. Near Family Museum of Arts and Science. Indoor pool, restaurant. $$-$$$

Heartland Inn, Exit 2 on I-74 at Spruce Hills Drive, (563) 355-6336; (800) 334-3277. Near Family Museum of Arts and Science. Indoor pool, continental breakfast. $$-$$$$

Isle of Capri Casino and Hotel, 1777 Isle Parkway, (563) 359-7280; (800) 724-5825. Overlooks the Mississippi. Restaurant, indoor pool. $-$$$$

Davenport

Country Inn and Suites, 140 E. 55th, (563) 388-6444; (800) 456-4000. Near I-80. Indoor pool, continental breakfast. $$-$$$

Rhythm City Casino and Blackhawk Hotel, 200 E. 3rd Street. (563) 328-6000; (800) 553-1173. Downtown near theaters. Restaurant, continental breakfast. $$-$$$$

Le Claire

Comfort Inn Riverview, 902 Mississippi View Court, (563) 278-4747; (800) 227-5150. Near I-80. Close to restaurants. Indoor pool, continental breakfast. $-$$

Moline

Comfort Inn, 2800 52nd Avenue, (309) 762-7000; (800) 228-5150. Near Black Hawk State Site. Indoor pool, continental breakfast. $$-$$$

Hampton Inn, 6920 27th Street, (309) 762-1711; (800) 426-7866. Near Quad Cities Airport and Naibi Zoo. Outdoor pool, continental breakfast. $$-$$$

Radisson on John Deere Commons, 1415 River Drive, (309) 764-1000; (800) 333-3333. Near Mississippi River and historic homes. $$$-$$$$

Rock Island
Four Points by Sheraton, 3rd Avenue and 17th Street, (309) 794-1212; (800) 325-3535. Near The District, Quad Cities Art Center, and Jumer's Casino. Restaurant, indoor pool. $$-$$$$

BED AND BREAKFASTS

Davenport
Beiderbecke Inn, 532 W. 7th Street, (563) 323-0047. Victorian inn near downtown and Mississippi River. Three rooms. $$-$$$

Fulton's Landing, 1206 E. River Drive, (563) 322-4069. Italianate mansion overlooking Mississippi River. Near riverside trails. Five rooms. $$-$$$$

Rock Island
Potter House, 1906 7th Avenue, (309) 788-1906; (800) 747-0339. Near The District and downtown. Four rooms; one suite. $$-$$$

Victorian Inn B&B, 702 20th Street, (309) 788-7068; (800) 728-7068. AAA 3-Diamond rating. An 1876 mansion in Broadway Historic District, second-largest historic district in the nation with 900 homes. Some rooms with fireplaces. Six rooms. $$-$$$.

DINING

Bettendorf
Farraday's, 1777 Isle Parkway, (563) 441-7111. At Isle of Capri Casino. Fortune Garden, 2211 Kimberly Road, (563) 355-7878. Family-style Chinese.

Davenport
Thunder Bay Grille, 6511 N. Brady, (563) 386-2722. Near I-80. North Woods theme.

The Dock, 125 S. Perry Street, (563) 322-5331. At Le Claire Park. Fine dining near the Mississippi.

Duck City Delicatessen and Bistro, 115 E. 3rd Street, (563) 322-3825. Downtown.

Le Claire
Sneaky Petes Cowboy Steaks Inc., 207 Cody Road S, (563) 289-4277. Very casual western atmosphere.

Steventons, 1399 Eagle Ridge Road, (563) 289-3600. Fine dining overlooking the Mississippi.

Moline

Belgian Village Inn, 560 17th Avenue, (309) 764-9222. Said to have the best Reuben sandwiches outside of Belgium.

C'est Michele, 1405 5th Avenue, (309) 762-0585. Fine dining.

Jims Rib Haven, 1600 10th Street, (309) 752-1240. Said to have the best ribs in the area.

Pasteur Restaurant, 2037 16th Street, (309) 797-6336. Vietnamese cuisine.

Rock Island

Blue Cat Brew Pub, 113 18th Street, (309) 788-8247. In The District. Six types of beer made on premises. Full menu and pool hall.

Le Figaro, 1708 2nd Avenue, (309) 786-4944. French gourmet dining in The District.

INFORMATION

Quad Cities Convention and Visitors Bureau, 200 W. 3rd Street, Davenport, IA 52801, (563) 322-3911; (800) 747-7800; www.visitquadcities.com

Chapter 22

Keokuk, Fort Madison, Burlington: A Tale of Three Cities

Tucked into the corner of southeast Iowa are three charming river towns that front the Mississippi: Keokuk, Fort Madison, and Burlington, all within a short drive of each other. They also lie on the Great River Road, Highway 61, which is one of two national scenic byways in Iowa (the other is the Loess Hills National Scenic Byway near the Missouri River; see chapter 2). Along the Great River Road, travelers encounter the history of prehistoric times and early Iowa and see beautiful views of the Mississippi River.

Keokuk

At the south end of the Great River Road in Iowa, Keokuk is nestled against the borders of Illinois and Missouri near the confluence of the Mississippi and Des Moines Rivers.

If you're coming down Highway 218 from the north, you will arrive in downtown Keokuk on Main Street. After you pass 4th Street, find somewhere to park and obtain information from the **Keokuk Area Convention and Tourism Bureau**, 329 Main, (319) 524-5599; (800) 383-1219.

Continuing on Main to the east, just before the bridge that goes to Illinois take a right where signs direct you to Victory Park and the **George M. Verity Museum**, (319) 524-4765; (800) 383-1219; admission. A 1927 paddle wheeler that's now on shore, the *Verity* recalls the days when boats like these were king of our nation's inland waterways. The pilothouse, crew quarters, and engine room appear as if the crew just stepped away for a few minutes, and displays relate to many of the *Verity's* fellow riverboats and their history. If you're wondering about the nearby statue of a soldier on a horse, that's General Samuel Curtis—more on him in a few moments.

After visiting the *Verity*, you can return to Main Street but cross it to the north about one block and turn to the right. In front of you will be an old and very narrow former toll bridge across the Mississippi. When the new one was built, the old bridge was made into an observation platform. You can walk out on the bridge, which has benches every so often. At the end, you can watch tows passing through the 1,200-foot **Lock No. 19**, one of the longest on the Mississippi.

Just upriver is the large **Keokuk Power Plant** and Dam No. 19, sited where a young Army officer named Robert E. Lee once surveyed a set of dangerous rapids that had the respect of every river pilot of the 19th century. Because the dam creates an open pool of water in the winter when much of the rest of the river can freeze over, this site has the largest concentration of bald eagles on the Mississippi from November until about mid-March. The third weekend of each January is celebrated as **Bald Eagle Appreciation Days** in Keokuk and many other places are available for watching the eagles as they swoop down on the river to pluck fish.

Within a few blocks to the west of the overlook is the **Miller House Museum**, 318 N. 5th, (319) 524-5599; (800) 383-1219; admission, home of a U.S. Supreme Court justice appointed by Abraham Lincoln. Owned by the Lee County Historical Society, the house depicts the home of a late 19th-century family and is worth a stop.

If you're feeling up for live performances, just a few blocks from the Miller Home is the **Grand Theater**, 26 N. 6th Street, (319) 524-1026; (800) 383-1219; admission. At the time it was built in the 1920s, movie theaters were in vogue,

One of the many opulent mansions on Grand Avenue in Keokuk.

but the Grand was built as a "hemp house"–a theater for legitimate stage productions where miles and miles of rope, made from hemp, were used to raise
and lower curtains, backdrops, and flies. If you don't want to take in a performance but still want to see the interior, it is possible to arrange a tour by
calling the 800 phone number a day or so ahead of your visit.

A great walking tour past incredible houses is available by going up 6th
Street to Grand Avenue. You'll see plenty to make you "ooh" and "ah." If you
picked up the brochure *On the Avenue* at the tourism office, you'll appreciate
these houses a lot more. Among the past residents was Howard Hughes
Sr.–father of the eccentric billionaire–who built the house at 925 Grand.

For those who are interested in visiting Iowa's only national cemetery, head
west on Main Street to 17th Street and take a left where the sign directs you toward, in about 10 blocks, the **Keokuk National Cemetery**, 1701 J Street, (319)
524-5193. The headstones are identical in shape and size and neatly laid out
as if the soldiers are still in their ranks. During the Civil War, several military
hospitals were in Keokuk and that's partially the reason this cemetery was
started at the same time as the one in Arlington, Virginia, making it one of the
oldest in the nation. Adjacent cemeteries are interesting in their own right, with
a bewildering assortment of headstones, mausoleums, and crypts built into
the hillsides. The site is definitely worth a visit.

From the cemetery, leave toward Main on 17th Street but go across Main
and keep going until you reach **Rand Park**, a large park with serpentine drives
and overlooks of the Mississippi River.

$\mathcal{P}$ea Ridge

In late April in Rand Park, Civil War reenactors gather with muskets, bay-
onets, cannons, and horses to mess up the sod a bit while thousands of spec-
tators watch them fight the **Battle of Pea Ridge**; free. Although the two-day
battle took place in Arkansas, it was won by Union troops led by Keokuk's
hometown hero, General Samuel Curtis (remember the statue of the guy on
the horse earlier in the tour?). Besides putting on quite a show with thunder-
ing cannons, crackling musketry, and clashing sabers, the troops set up camps
that visitors are welcome to visit during this three-day affair. The reenactors
act out their roles so well that the "battle" has been named as Iowa's top
tourism event for several years. With it come period style shows and a military
ball that's quite a hoedown.

From the park's overlook, you can take River Road and head north out of
town on another portion of the Great River Road. Paralleling a railroad track
for about four miles, River Road stays close to the Mississippi then cuts inland
to where a community called Galland used to be. A replica of the **Galland
School** honors the state's oldest school, built here in 1830.

Inside the compound at Old Fort Madison

Farther down the road, you'll enter the small town of Montrose, where you must join Highway 61 if you're going to continue north.

Fort Madison

Rolling into Fort Madison on Highway 61, you pass through the western part of the city before you enter the region where most of the attractions are located. The first place you should stop is the **Old Santa Fe Historic Depot Complex**, Avenue H and 9th Street, (319) 372-7661; admission. It will be easy to spot because of its Santa Fe Railroad sign (which is rare in Iowa), and southwestern mission style architecture (also rare in Iowa). For those interested in railroad history, Civil War displays, and old firefighting equipment including a Silsby steam pumper, this is the place. A display related to Sheaffer fountain pens, which are manufactured at the company's headquarters in Fort Madison, is here too. There's even a room dedicated to how things looked in many places when the floodwaters of 1993 receded. The exhibit looks so real that you'll swear you're in a real house that's still dripping wet with muck; but then you realize that something is missing (mercifully) . . . the stench. It's quite an exhibit.

Nearby is the **Fort Madison Art Center**, 804 10th Street, (319) 372-3996, which has works from more than 40 regional artists, including jewelry, watercolors, oils, and pottery. The center is near downtown and you might want to take a walk to enjoy looking at some of the unusual and historic buildings.

$\mathcal{A}$long the River

Back on Highway 61 again and a bit farther along, you can turn to the right again to enter Riverview Park, which is dominated by two hard-to-miss entities. The first is **Old Fort Madison,** (319) 372-6318; admission, a re-creation of the fort that was built near here in 1808 and abandoned during the War of 1812 after pro-British Winnebago and Sauk Indians attacked it again and again. You enter through the Factory, a trading post that's outside the main walls of the compound. Inside the log walls, you'll find that many of the rooms, such as the enlisted men's barracks and the officers' quarters, look like they're still occupied. Interpretative guides in period dress and uniforms describe life at the fort nearly two centuries ago.

Very close to the old fort is **Catfish Bend Riverboat Casino**, 902 Riverview Drive, (319) 372-2946; (800) 372-2946, which cruises Monday-Friday between May and October (during the rest of the year, it's docked at Burlington). Able to carry 1,300 passengers, the vessel has slots and gaming tables plus a third deck with dining, entertainment, and a dance floor.

On the weekend after Labor Day, Fort Madison hosts the **Tri-State Rodeo**; admission, one of the largest rodeos in Iowa. Located at Rodeo Park (north on either 9th or 15th Streets), it features all you could hope for—broncs, bulls, rodeo clowns, trick riders, barrel racing, and more.

On your way out of town on Highway 61, stay alert because there are a few things to see, and they come up quite quickly.

First, on the right (south) side of the highway and practically right next to its curb is a chimney . . . that's right, a chimney. Called the **Lone Chimney Memorial,** this is where the original Fort Madison was located. Immediately past that on the left is the headquarters of the Sheaffer Pen Company, but there are no tours or any displays for visitors.

If you want to learn more about Fort Madison, the city's **Welcome Center**, 1st and Avenue H, (319) 372-8648, is right here too, at the foot of a huge bridge. Consider picking up the brochure entitled *Driving Tour of Victorian Homes*, which can direct you on a pleasant tour around Fort Madison.

That huge bridge is the **Santa Fe Swing Span Bridge**, the world's longest double-deck swing bridge; it carries vehicles up on top and trains on the lower level and swings open to permit the passage of tows and other large boats on the Mississippi.

Continuing up Highway 61, you will see what looks like a large walled fortress on the right (east). That's the **Iowa State Penitentiary,** opened in 1839 before Iowa was even a state. Its inmates built the wooden buildings at Old Fort Madison within the walls of the state pen. The structures were then disassembled and reassembled by contractors where the reconstruction now stands in Riverview Park.

Burlington

There are two ways to approach Burlington from the south. One is by going up Highway 61 from Fort Madison about 16 miles, and coming into the west side of Burlington, where you turn east on Highway 34 to get to downtown. That's the fast way on four-lane highways.

The other way is to take Highway 61 out of Fort Madison until shortly after you cross the Skunk River, then heading off to the right on Old Highway 61, which will take you directly into the south end of Burlington. The road is known by several other names: Summer Street, Fort Madison Road, and, as it gets into town, Madison Avenue.

Just as you enter Burlington on Madison Avenue, hang a right at the entrance to **Crapo Park**, (pronounced "Kray-poe"). The road winds through the park, which features flower beds, lots of room to play, a fountain, and a log cabin sitting on a beautiful overlook of the Mississippi far below and open for tours on Wednesday and Sunday afternoons, (319) 753-2449; admission. It was near here in 1805 that Lieutenant Zebulon Pike walked up to the top of this bluff and raised the Stars and Stripes for the first time on Iowa soil.

Continuing up the park drive, which becomes Main Street, you'll enter the downtown area. When you reach Washington Street, turn right to go to the riverfront. There you'll find **Memorial Auditorium,** a hard-to-overlook white art deco building but, more importantly, just to its north is what looks like a brick warehouse near the river. That's the **Port of Burlington,** 400 N. Front Street, (319) 752-8731, which houses an **Iowa Welcome Center** with plenty of helpful information, historical displays about Burlington, and audiotapes that serve as guides to historical districts in the city.

Outside on the port's front deck is a great place to look at the **Great River Bridge**, a striking $60 million, cable-stayed bridge spanning the Mississippi. From mid-November to mid-May, the port also serves as the dock for the **Catfish Bend Riverboat Casino** (see Fort Madison in this chapter).

If you're thinking about grabbing the literature and simply leaving the Welcome Center and its gift shop, think again. Take a walk along the river on the **Historic Riverwalk**. As you approach the main fountain near the Veterans Auditorium, you may want to grab a foot massage in the sprays of water shooting up directly from the sidewalk.

Once back in your car, head to Burlington's most popular tourist attraction: **Snake Alley**, between Washington and Columbia Streets at 6th Street, (319) 752-6365; (800) 82-RIVER; free. The best way to reach this undulating thoroughfare in your car is to leave the Welcome Center and go up Columbia Street, which is almost directly inland of the center. Just as you enter a residential area you'll see Snake Alley—one-way going down—off to your left. The street was built with so many turns because, in the old days, the street engi-

A few of the twists and turns on Snake Alley, Burlington

neers knew that no horse-drawn rig could make it down the steep hill without the cart ending up before the horse, if not atop it. So they put in five half-curves and two quarter-curves to make going down a drop of 58 feet a lot easier on the horses, not to mention the mental condition of the drivers. At one time *Ripley's Believe It Or Not* called it the crookedest street in the world. Some might call it the world's best testing ground for brakes.

Once you're at the bottom of Snake Alley, on Washington Street, turn to your right (west) and just a couple buildings away is the **Arts for Living Center**, 7th and Washington Streets, (319) 754-8069; free. A former church, it's now an art center with a gift shop featuring the works of local artists.

Now, go to 8th Street, turn right (north) and in another block turn right (east) again and wind up once more on Columbia. No, this isn't some cruel joke to take you down Snake Alley again (unless you really want to). It's to take you to a place you might have overlooked in going down Snake Alley. Right next to the alley, on its far (east) side is the **Phelps House Museum**, 521 Columbia, (319) 753-2449; admission. Built in 1851 and expanded with an Italianate tower about 20 years later, the Phelps House gives visitors a look at the lives and furnishings of the late-19th-century well-to-do-marble fireplaces, furniture made of walnut and mahogany, oriental rugs, and parquet floors. Displays on the third floor depict the five years the house was used as a hospital, and the gala parties and balls that were held in its grand ballroom.

Just north of the Phelps House is the **Heritage Hill District**, where it's time to turn on one of those audio guide tapes you picked up at the Welcome Center.

If you return to Front Street and continue north, you can park your car and walk on another part of the river walkway that's a bit less urban than the one near the Welcome Center.

To catch some fine baseball action, check the schedule of the Burlington Bees, (319) 754-5705; admission, a Class-A farm team of the Kansas City Royals that plays at the **Community Field**, 2712 Mount Pleasant Road, on the west edge of town. The Bees have been a part of the local scene for more than 110 years.

For the final stop in Burlington, go north of Highway 34 on Highway 61 and in less than two miles after that intersection you'll come upon Sunnyside Avenue, where you'll turn right (east). A few moments later you'll see Irish Ridge Road; turn left to get to **Starr's Cave and Preserve**, 11627 Starr's Cave Road, (319) 753-5808; free. Operated by the Des Moines County Conservation Board, this large mill-like structure houses a nature center and a rock climbing wall, but the real trip here is to walk along the trails that flank Flint Creek. If the water's low, you can wade across the creek to the trails that lead to Starr's Cave itself. Partway up a 100-foot limestone cliff, the cave is reached by walking up a steep set of stairs. It's not a large cave and it quickly gets too narrow for anyone with more than a 36-inch waist, but it's neat to visit. On the way out of the cave, you see what really counts, a very nice view of the Flint Creek valley.

If you're not into wading, you can drive just past the preserve's main entrance to what's called the overlook entrance, park there and hike to the cave.

SIDE TRIPS

To the West

From Burlington, take Highway 34 to the west 25 miles to **Mount Pleasant**. There, follow the signs to the **Midwest Old Threshers Heritage Museum**, 405 E. Threshers Road, (319) 385-8937; admission. Lovers of antique tractors know about this place and think it's heaven on earth. And if you're not interested in such things, you're going to be fascinated anyway by the operating steam engines, old gas-fired tractors, the eight cars of the electric trolley that carries visitors around the grounds, the carousel, and the large, gentle draft horses that pull antique farm equipment.

Another interesting part of the complex is the **Theatre Museum of Repertoire Americana**, (319) 385-9432; (888) 826-6622; admission. Here, early American theater comes back to life in the form of backdrops, fanciful stage curtains full of advertisements, and pastoral scenes, scripts, playbills, and music scores from as far back as the 1850s.

Just past the downtown square on Highway 34 is the **Van Allen House Heritage Center**, 502 W. Washington, (319) 385-2460; (800) 421-4282. A combination welcome center and historic home, the center has helpful information about southeast Iowa and tells the story of James Van Allen. A scientist at the University of Iowa, his experiment on America's first satellite proved that radiation belts encircle the earth.

Drive another 11 miles west to **Lockridge**, the home of the **Johnny Clock Museum**, 711 W. Main, (319) 696-3711, which features the handiwork of modern clock maker John R. McLain. Although similar in a way to the Bily Clocks (see the "Side Trip" for chapter 16), McLain's clocks are more contemporary and whimsical.

To the North

To stand where explorers once did, head north of downtown Burlington on the Great River Road, which is Highway 99 (Main Street in Burlington). After 24 miles you'll reach the **Toolesboro Indian Mounds**, Highway 99, (319) 766-4018; (319) 523-8381; free, where a small visitors center is open noon–4 p.m. daily. It's believed that French explorers Louis Joliet and Jacques Marquette first stepped onto Iowa soil here in 1673, close to where the low-lying burial mounds are. However, recent evidence suggests that the Indians they visited may have lived in a village farther south, near Keokuk and in Missouri. Still, the Toolesboro Mounds are nice to visit and you can learn something about the early inhabitants of this region.

LODGING

Burlington

Best Western PZAZZ!, 3001 Winegard Drive, (319) 753-2223; (800) 373-1223. West end of town. Indoor pool, restaurant, continental breakfast. $$

Holiday Inn Express, 1605 N. Roosevelt. (319) 752-0000; (800) HOLIDAY. West end of town. Near restaurants. Indoor pool, continental breakfast. $$-$$$$

Comfort Inn, 3051 Kirkwood, (319) 753-0000; (800) 228-5150. West end of town. Near restaurants. Outdoor pool, continental breakfast. $-$$

Fort Madison

Days Inn, Highway 61 W, (319) 372-7510; (800) 423-2693. West edge of town. Indoor pool, restaurant, continental breakfast. $$

Keokuk

Holiday Inn Express, 4th and Main Streets, (319) 524-8000; (800) HOLIDAY. Downtown. Indoor pool, complimentary breakfast bar. $-$$

Super 8 Motel, 3511 Main Street, (319) 524-3888; (800) 800-8000. West end of town. Restaurants nearby. Continental breakfast. $-$$

Mount Pleasant

AmeriHost Inn, 1100 N. Grand Avenue, (319) 385-2004; (800) 434-5800. East end of town. Indoor pool, continental breakfast. $$-$$$$

Ramada Ltd., 1200 E. Baker, (319) 385-0571; (800) 272-6232. East end of town. Indoor pool, continental breakfast. $- $$

BED AND BREAKFASTS

Burlington

Mississippi Manor B&B Inn, 809 4th Street, (319) 753-2218. Near downtown and Mississippi River. Four rooms. $$

Schramm House B&B, 616 Columbia Street, (319) 754-0373; (800) 683-7117. In historic district near Snake Alley, downtown, and Mississippi River. Four rooms. $$-$$$

Fort Madison

Coffey House B&B, 1020 Avenue D, (319) 372-1656. Near Santa Fe Depot and Riverview Park. Three rooms. $$

The Ivy Manor, 804 Avenue F, (319) 372-7380. An 1887 Victorian home close to downtown. Outdoor pool. Two rooms. $$

Kingsley Inn, 707 Avenue H, (319) 372-7074; (800) 441-2327. Downtown in historic brick building. Near Riverview Park. Eighteen rooms. $$-$$$$

Kountry Klassics B&B, 2002 295th Avenue, (319) 372-5484; (888) 310-6549. Countryside B&B that caters to children with hay rides. Four rooms. $$

Morrison Manor, 532 Avenue F, (319) 372-5876; (888) 750-1640. An 1881 Victorian Italianate manor near downtown. Four rooms. $$$-$$$$

Keokuk

Grand Anne B&B, 816 Grand Avenue, (319) 524-6310; (800) 524-6310. On historic Grand Avenue on bluff overlooking Mississippi. Five rooms. $$-$$$

River's Edge B&B, 611 Grand Avenue, (319) 524-1700; (888) 581-3343. A 1915 Tudor mansion on Grand Avenue with Mississippi River view. Four rooms. $$-$$$$

DINING

Burlington

Abe's Family Restaurant and Steak House, 2921 Bock Street, (319) 752-7117. North side of city.

Big Muddy's, 710 N. Front Street, (319) 753-1699. A renovated railroad warehouse on the riverfront just north of the bridge. Seafood and steak.

Jefferson Street Café, 300 Jefferson, (319) 754-1036. Downtown. Seafood, steak.

Season to Taste, 218 Jefferson Street, (319) 753-2345. Downtown. Lunch café.

Fort Madison
Alpha's on the Riverfront, 709 Avenue H, (319) 372-1411. Downtown.

Ivy Bake Shoppe and Café, 622 7th Street, (319) 372-9939. Downtown bakery-café.

North Shore Bar and Grill, 318 Riverview Drive, (319) 372-6477. Near the waterfront.

Keokuk
Beef, Bread, and Brew, 2601 Main Street, (319) 524-7476. West edge of town. Fine dining.

Chuck Wagon, 706 Main Street, (319) 524-5916. Downtown. Family-style.

Fourth Street Café, 22 S. 4th Street, (319) 524-9354. Downtown. Family-style.

Fort Worth Barbeque, 526 S. 5th Street, (319) 524-9880. Family-style barbecue.

Tiramisu, 719 Main Street, (319) 524-9723. Downtown. Italian.

Mount Pleasant
Iris' Restaurant and Lounge, Highway 34 W, (319) 385-2241. West end of town. Family-style.

Sirloin Stockade, Highway 218 N, (319) 385-8500. East side of town. Steaks.

INFORMATION

Burlington Convention and Tourism Bureau, 807 Jefferson, PO Box 6, Burlington, IA 52601, (319) 752-6365; (800) 827-4837; www.visit.burlington.ia.us

Fort Madison Area Convention and Visitors Bureau, 933 Avenue H, PO Box 425, Fort Madison, IA 52627, (319) 372-5472; (800) 210-8687; www.tourriverbend.org

Henry County Tourism Association, 502 W. Washington, Mt. Pleasant, IA 52641, (319) 385-2460; (800) 421-4282); www.henrycountytourism.org

Keokuk Area Convention and Tourism Bureau, 329 Main St., Keokuk, IA 52632, (319) 524-5599; (800) 383-1219; www.keokuktourism.com

Chapter 23

Van Buren County: The Essence of Iowa

At one time or another, many people find themselves overwhelmed by the rush of modern life: supersonic travel, super fast highways, and overnight delivery of goods from countries thousands of miles away. They yearn to retreat to a place where the pace is more like three miles an hour—human walking speed—or perhaps the speed of a canoe floating on a gentle current. So it is at the **Villages of Van Buren County**, a cluster of small communities along the Des Moines River in the southeast portion of the state. At one time they were well-known riverside stops; now, they're backwaters in time, almost akin to those sleepy southern towns in Faulkner's novels but with a Midwestern touch.

Keosauqua

Located within a loop of the Des Moines River, the town of Keosauqua is as good a place as any to begin visiting the villages. If you're wondering, the town's name is described as being an Indian word that means either "river of the monks" or "big bend." You choose.

As you enter the town from the north on Highway 1, look for the sign indicating the **Van Buren County Courthouse**, 904 4th Avenue, (319) 293-7111; free. The oldest courthouse in continuous use west of the Mississippi River, this modest-sized, two-story brick building was at one time—believe it or not—also one of the largest buildings west of the Mississippi. The courtroom, which is not broken by pillars or supports, is where Iowa's first death sentence was handed down in 1845. Found guilty of murdering Don Coffman and his child, William McCauley was hung near the courthouse on April 4, 1846, and that area remains known as Hangman's Hollow. When court's not in session, you're welcome to tour the second-floor courtroom that appears much like it was when constructed in 1843.

The historic Hotel Manning in Keosauqua

A few blocks away is another building from about the same era, the **Pearson House**, Dodge and Country Roads, (319) 293-3311; (319) 293-3211; admission, built in 1847. Stone was used for the first floor and brick for the second, giving it a rather distinctive look. Owned now by the Van Buren County Historical Society, the house served as a stop on the Underground Railroad and runaway slaves passed through a trap door to a hideaway below the first floor. The entire second floor had been an open room often used for church services. Now, tours are conducted from 1 to 4 p.m. on Sundays or by appointment.

Another fine old structure is the **Twombley Building** on Main Street. Built in 1875 and used by a Medal of Honor recipient, Voltaire Twombley, to house his grocery and newspaper office, this stone building was later used as the town's post office and telephone exchange. Now, it holds the Twombley Historical Museum.

A few blocks away is the **Hotel Manning**, quite an architectural star from yesteryear that retains its elegance as well as its purpose. Built in 1899 as an inn, this brick structure still serves as a hotel. Even if you don't plan to stay there, step into its lobby with 16-foot ceilings and a large wooden staircase, and feel the gentle warmth of another era slowly overtake you. You'll feel like you could just settle into a chair and lose track of time—and perhaps you should. The guest rooms that line a quiet hall upstairs are not as spacious as those in modern hotels but there's something about them that continues to entice guests again and again. When you walk out through the front door and toward the river, note the white lines painted on the bricks at the far corner of the building. They're the high water marks from when the nearby Des Moines River has flooded in past years.

A small park across the street from the hotel is a nice place to let the kids romp.

Leave town by continuing south on Highway 1 and, after crossing the river, you'll come upon the entrance to **Lacey-Keosauqua State Park**, (319) 293-3502; fee for camping. At 1,653 acres, Lacey-Keosauqua is Iowa's largest state park and its drives and trails lead you to high bluffs and down to the edge of the Des Moines River, which was once a highway of sorts for people traveling to and from the interior of Iowa. A portion of the Pioneer-Mormon Trail crossed the river at Ely Ford, its location now marked by a large stone. There are campsites, cabins, and picnic facilities here as well as a 30-acre lake where you can swim, fish, and canoe.

A hike-bike trail connects the park with Lake Sugema, a 574-acre lake south of the state park with similar amenities including log cabins that visitors can rent from a concessionaire, **Red Fox Lodging Company**, (319) 293-3041; (877) 293-3224. Lake Sugema can also be reached by roads that come up to it from Highway 2 to the south.

If you would like to canoe the Des Moines River, **Hawkeye Canoe Rental, Ltd.**, Highway 1 N, (319) 293-3550; fee, can supply canoes, equipment, and shuttle service to areas upriver and downriver of Keosauqua. With various places to put in and take out, you can arrange any length of trip you want. The farthest upstream landing that's usually used is near the small town of Selma, about 20 miles or four hours away by canoe from Keosauqua. And if you put in at Keosauqua, you can leave the river at Bentonsport, Bonaparte, or Farmington, the latter of which is about 18 miles from Keosauqua, or about three hours of canoeing at an easy pace.

Bentonsport

Less than a mile south of the bridge that crosses the Des Moines River near Keosauqua is County Highway J40, where you should turn to the left (east). This will take you directly to the town of Bentonsport. It's not large so it's easy to find your way down to the small clutch of buildings that form its tiny downtown near the river. The most striking building is **Mason House**, another original inn that served steamboat passengers, including Mark Twain and a tall lawyer from Illinois named Abraham Lincoln; and it's still hosting today's travelers. Built in 1846 in the Federal style of architecture that one might expect in New England more than southeast Iowa, Mason House is supplemented by a former general store next door. Breakfasts are served in the keeping room where, if you're gutsy enough, you can take a bath in a old, copper-lined bathtub that folds down from the wall. If you're going out and about, let the innkeepers know and they'll prepare you a sack lunch for your excursion.

Across the road from the inn is the old bridge that spans the Des Moines River to Vernon, a town that's virtually nonexistent today. Vehicles are prohibited from the bridge now but pedestrians can walk across it.

The Federal-style Mason House, Bentonsport

Also in the area is a short line of old buildings that now house small businesses catering to visitors, selling everything from jewelry to fudge to handcrafted works of art. All are a delight to visit. Across the street from them is a small riverside park with a gazebo and the stony ruins of old mills that the residents have turned into nice flower gardens. It's nice just to walk around the streets here, looking at houses that remain in this once prosperous river town. Up the hill from the little business district is the old **Presbyterian Church**, which, like so many other structures in the villages, reflects the Greek Revival style of architecture. If the doors are open, have a look inside.

Bonaparte

You can leave Bentonsport on County Highway J40 and continue to the east, where in a few minutes you'll roll into another of the villages, Bonaparte. The first building that's going to grab your attention here is the Meek Grist Mill, built in 1848. Now it houses **Bonaparte's Retreat**, (319) 592-3339, a well-known restaurant that draws patrons from many miles away. (Check out the house specialty, canned beef. There's nothing finer.) Next door, **Bonaparte Mill Antiques and Collectibles**, (319) 592-3274, is located in the old Meek Woolen Mill. Across the street and down the block are other buildings from past years that are still in use today. For example, the city library and museum are located in the **Auntie Green Hotel**, the town's first brick building, built in 1844. As at Bentonsport, gardens, including one to attract butterflies, add color alongside part of the river where ruins from an old set of locks can still be seen (the locks were part of a failed program to help boats navigate the river).

Not far to the east, or downriver, from Bonaparte's Retreat is an active archaeological dig. It's on the site of an old pottery factory that stood for 30 years before being covered by a lumberyard until the flood of 1993, which tore away the upper structures, (319) 592-3620; tours by appointment. The University of Iowa is conducting the dig, which you're welcome to watch. Everything from small shards to complete plates is being unearthed as the work continues.

In 2001, Bonaparte was named one of the "Dozen Distinctive Destinations" by the National Trust for Historic Preservation for being one of the best-preserved and unique communities in the nation. A few years earlier, this village of 457 people was the smallest community in the nation to be awarded the trust's Great American Street Award for the preservation work done by its residents.

West of Bonaparte, as you approached it on County Highway J40, is the beginnings of a Renaissance village that's used for three weekends each

Bonaparte's Retreat, a popular restaurant, in Bonaparte

October. Check with the Villages of Van Buren tourism office, (319) 293-7111; (800) TOUR-VBC, for more information.

Farmington

From Bonaparte, take Highway 78 across the Des Moines River to Highway 2, the main east-west road across the southern part of the state. Going straight onto Highway 2 (which is curving at this point) will lead you east to the last of the villages, Farmington. On the way there, you may want to visit **Indian Lake Park**, (319) 878-3706, which offers picnic and camping facilities, brand new cabins, fishing, swimming, and hiking. If you're getting the idea that this is a quiet part of the state, you'd be right. But that's the beauty of this section of Iowa: about all you can do here is relax.

Continue on the highway through Farmington and take it easy on the other side of town as you begin to enter **Shimek State Forest**, (319) 878-3811. Tall pines, oaks, and hickory trees line the road as it curves through the countryside. For a few moments, you wonder if you're still in Iowa as the view of trees everywhere around you certainly doesn't fit the usual image of vast farm fields. As at the other preserves in this area, Shimek has trails, fishing, and sites for both primitive camping and RVs.

So there you go. If you were expecting tons of things to *do*, forget it. Just come here and enjoy life in the slow lane. It's very comfortable.

SIDE TRIP

To the West

At Keosauqua, get on County Highway J40 at Franklin Street (at the northeast edge of town) and go west to Bloomfield, about 12 miles away and actually in Davis County. Here you'll find the quintessential Iowa town square—a collection of businesses set in old but well-kept buildings surrounding a jewel of a courthouse. Built in 1877 in the French Second Empire style with a mansard roof, the Davis County Courthouse sits impressively on an expansive lawn. In the courtroom, original seats and benches are still in use.

For those feeling a touch of "Haven't I been here before?" well, you may not have been but artist P. Buckley Moss features this area so prominently in her works that you may have seen some of these scenes elsewhere. For a relaxing walk, peruse the 40-some businesses that form the courthouse square.

A couple blocks to the east of the square on East Franklin is the **William Findley House**, 302 E. Franklin, (641) 664-1855; 664-1512; open from 1-5 p.m. Saturdays and by appointment. Built in 1844, the structure now houses the **Davis County Historical Museum**. Also on its grounds are a Mormon-built log cabin, country school (complete with a dunce's stool that still fits all ages and sizes), a 1902 country church, and a restored livery barn.

A nice place to orient yourself is the **Davis County Welcome Center**, 301 N. Washington, (641) 664-1104, which is on the main thoroughfare three blocks north of the courthouse square. Set in an original Sears catalog home that was built in 1910, the center has racks of literature about the area and a small gift shop featuring crafts made by locals and residents of the nearby Amish communities. Maps are available of local historic buildings and Amish businesses in the countryside west of Bloomfield.

Among the Amish businesses are buggy manufacturers (in case you're thinking of changing to a slower lifestyle), sawmills, furniture shops, greenhouses, general stores, quilt shops, and harness shops. Considering the Amish make things by hand, you aren't going to get much better service than here. Remember that the Amish don't appreciate being photographed and be careful sharing the roads in the countryside with their slow-moving, horse-drawn buggies.

On the north edge of Bloomfield is the **Weaver House** on Highway 63 just north of the intersection of Washington and North Streets, (641) 664-2802, the former home of General James B. Weaver who twice ran for president after the Civil War—and lost, obviously, which is why his name is unfamiliar. Now a bed and breakfast, the two-story, brick home was a hot spot on the Chautauqua circuit years ago and speakers such as Carrie Nation, Billy Sunday, and William Jennings Bryan gave speeches here.

To return to Keosauqua, go south of Bloomfield to Highway 2 and head east. After you pass Cantril, you should spot a large blue water tower in the countryside and very close to that is one of the largest and most impressive round barns you'll ever see—the **Wickfield Sales Pavilion**. You can drive up to it but, since it's undergoing restoration, if you want to see the interior it's best to contact the tourism office of the Villages of Van Buren to learn when it's open or arrange a tour (donation appreciated). Built in 1917 to show Hampshire hogs, the barn has offices on its second floor and a card room and parlor on the third.

LODGING

Bentonsport
Mason House Inn, (319) 592-3133; (800) 592-3133. Historic 1846 riverfront inn. Eight rooms in the main house and a former general store adjacent to the house. Full breakfast. $$-$$$

Bonaparte
The Little Cottage, (319) 592-3620. Along the Des Moines River just east of Bonaparte's Retreat. A bed-and-make-your-own-breakfast establishment with kitchen. Three rooms. $$-$$$

Bloomfield
Southfork Inn, junction of Highways 2 and 63, (641) 664-1063; (800) 926-2860. Motel on south side of town. Restaurant and lounge. $

Weaver House, on Highway 63 just north of the intersection of Washington and North Streets, (641) 664-2802. B&B in a historic home on north edge of town. Full breakfast. Three rooms. $-$$

Keosauqua
Hotel Manning B&B, 100 Van Buren Street, (319) 293-3232; (800) 728-2718. An 1899 inn that's still hosting guests next to the Des Moines River. Full breakfast in large old hotel dining room. Eighteen rooms. $-$$

The Mansion Inn, 500 Henry Street, (319) 293-2511; (800) 646-0166. Built in the 1880s and located near tennis courts, golf course, and swimming pool. Full breakfast. Five rooms. $$

Riverview Inn, 100 Van Buren Street, (319) 293-3232; (800) 728-2718. A modern motel just behind the Hotel Manning and under the same management. Coffee and doughnuts. Nineteen rooms. $

DINING

Bloomfield

Southfork Inn, junction of Highways 2 and 63, (641) 664-1063; (800) 926-2860. South edge of town.

Stable Inn, Highway 63 N, (641) 664-3364. Weekends only. In the country north of town.

Uncle Bob's, Highway 63 N, (641) 664-2510. On north edge of town.

Bonaparte

Bonaparte's Retreat, (319) 592-3339; (800) 359-2590. In a historic gristmill overlooking the Des Moines River. The specialty is what's called canned beef.

Farmington

Bridge Cafe and Supper Club, (319) 878-3315; (888) 878-3315. Restaurant and piano lounge.

Keosauqua

George's Restaurant, (319) 293-3999. Lunches and suppers.

Old Farmer's Creamery, (319) 293-6255; 293-3521. In an old creamery. Homecooked meals. Live entertainment. Imported beers.

Red Barn Bistro, (319) 293-6154. About 8 miles west of town on County Highway J40. An antique-filled barn with homecooked meals featuring Mexican and Italian some evenings.

INFORMATION

Davis County Welcome Center, 301 N. Washington, Bloomfield, IA 52537, (641) 664-1104.

Eastern Iowa Tourism Region, PO Box 189, Dyersville, IA 52040, (563)875-7269; (800) 891-3482; www.easterniowatourism.org

Villages of Van Buren County, PO Box 9, Keosauqua, IA 52565, (319) 293-7111; (800) TOUR-VBC; www.800-tourvbc.com

Index

More Great Titles from Trails Books and Prairie Oak Press

ACTIVITY GUIDES

Great Cross-Country Ski Trails—Wm. Chad McGrath

Great Wisconsin Walks: 45 Strolls, Rambles, Hikes, and Treks—Wm. Chad McGrath

Great Minnesota Walks: 49 Strolls, Rambles, Hikes, and Treks—Wm. Chad McGrath

Wisconsin's Outdoor Treasures: A Guide to 150 Natural Destinations—Tim Bewer

Acorn Guide to Northwest Wisconsin—Tim Bewer

Paddling Southern Wisconsin: 82 Great Trips by Canoe and Kayak—Mike Svob

Paddling Northern Wisconsin: 82 Great Trips by Canoe and Kayak,—Mike Svob

Wisconsin Golf Getaways: A Guide to More Than 200 Great Courses and Fun Things to Do—Jeff Mayers and Jerry Poling

Wisconsin Underground: A Guide to Caves, Mines, and Tunnels in and around the Badger State—Doris Green

Best Wisconsin Bike Trips—Phil Van Valkenberg

TRAVEL GUIDES

Sacred Sites of Wisconsin—John-Brian Paprock and Teresa Paprock

Great Minnesota Weekend Adventures—Beth Gauper

Tastes of Minnesota: A Food Lover's Tour—Donna Tabbert Long

Great Indiana Weekend Adventures—Sally McKinney

Historical Wisconsin Getaways: Touring the Badger State's Past—Sharyn Alden

The Great Wisconsin Touring Book: 30 Spectacular Auto Tours—Gary Knowles

Wisconsin Family Weekends: 20 Fun Trips for You and the Kids—Susan Lampert Smith

County Parks of Wisconsin, Revised Edition—Jeannette and Chet Bell

Up North Wisconsin: A Region for All Seasons—Sharyn Alden

Great Wisconsin Taverns: 101 Distinctive Badger Bars—Dennis Boyer

Great Weekend Adventures—the Editors of Wisconsin Trails

The Wisconsin Traveler's Companion:
A Guide to Country Sights—Jerry Apps and Julie Sutter-Blair

PHOTO ESSAYS

The Spirit of Door County: A Photographic Essay—Darryl R. Beers

**Wisconsin Lighthouses: A Photographic and
Historical Guide**—Ken and BarbWardius

Wisconsin Waterfalls—Patrick Lisi

NATURE ESSAYS

Wild Wisconsin Notebook—James Buchholz

**Northern Passages: Reflections from
Lake Superior Country**—Michael Van Stappen

To order, phone, write, or e-mail us.

Trails Books
P.O. Box 317, Black Earth, WI 53515
(800) 236-8088 • e-mail: books@wistrails.com
www.trailsbooks.com